The First Offensive, 1942

ROOSEVELT, MARSHALL, AND THE
MAKING OF AMERICAN STRATEGY

RICHARD W. STEELE

THE
FIRST
OFFENSIVE
1942

Roosevelt, Marshall and the
Making of American Strategy

INDIANA UNIVERSITY PRESS
Bloomington and London

Published in Canada by Fitzhenry & Whiteside Limited,
Don Mills, Ontario
Library of Congress catalog card number: 73-75792
ISBN: 0-253-32215-4

MANUFACTURED IN THE UNITED STATES OF AMERICA

Contents

Introduction

On 8 November 1942, American troops came ashore at several points along the coast of North Africa, beginning the first Anglo-American offensive in the European theater during World War Two. The decision to undertake that effort, codenamed TORCH, at that place and at that time was controversial, both then and since. And well it might be, for by directing their initial thrust at North Africa the Allies in effect chose the Mediterranean as the focal point of military activities in the West during the next several months. This in turn almost unavoidably delayed the initial massive confrontation between the Allies and Germany in western Europe—the "Second Front"—until the summer of 1944, thus seriously affecting the duration of the war and stimulating several decades of postwar discussion of the decision and its aftermath.

Anglo-American differences on the first offensive were in part the natural result of differing strategic outlooks; the cautious strategy of attrition espoused by the British triumphed over the aggressive steamroller tactics championed by the Americans. Yet these differences played a smaller role than postwar polemicists have suggested. The policy discussions that culminated in the decision to invade North Africa actually involved little conflict between American and British military strategists. Strategy for the first offensive in fact largely resulted from the efforts of George C. Marshall, Army Chief of Staff, to accommodate his own military judgment to the politico–military demands of President Franklin D. Roosevelt. Both Roosevelt and Marshall, it is true, drew support from "the British"—the President frequently using the arguments of Prime Minister Churchill and Marshall drawing occasionally on the recommendations of the British military; but each was pursuing American interests as he perceived them.

The President's principal objectives for the first American offensive were political—to arouse American public interest in the war against Germany and to indicate to America's allies, particularly the Soviet Union, that the United States was committed to unlimited participation in the European war. The first offensive, from the President's point of view, was thus to be a morale builder designed to create the national attitudes necessary for victory. Looked at in this way the first American offensive had only two requirements: it must be launched at the earliest possible moment and avoid tactical defeat. The strategic advantages accruing from the operation, particularly its level of direct military assistance to the Allies, were significant considerations for the President but not decisive ones. What Roosevelt wanted, and sought for more than a year before the invasion of North Africa, was a token of American military involvement that would boost spirits at home and abroad until the decisive battles of the war could be fought and won. When General Marshall finally realized this in the spring of 1942, his task, as he saw it, was to fit the Army's strategic designs—a compound of doctrine, military expediency, and institutional jealousy—to the President's requirements. The circuitous path this situation forced on him led ultimately to failure. But in the process a doctrine of concentration of force, frequently ignored in 1941–42, hardened into a dogma referred to repeatedly in the controversies which arose after TORCH and after the war. Roosevelt's search for a suitable first offensive and General Marshall's efforts to adapt his quest to the Army's requirements are the themes of this book.

My task thoughout was made easier by the work of others. *The U.S. Army in World War II,* particularly the volume by Mssrs. Maurice Matloff and Edwin Snell was a valuable source of information and guide to the incredibly voluminous records of the war. Considerable help in coping with this problem was given by Edwin A. Thompson whose work as research editor for the

Eisenhower Papers gave him an expertise from which I profited. Also helpful were a number of archivists, particularly Robert Parks and Charyl C. Pollard of the Roosevelt Library, and William H. Cunliffe of the Modern Military Branch of the National Archives. Alfred D. Chandler Jr., Steven Ambrose, and Lawrence D. Stokes supplied me with valuable critiques of my work in its early stages. Above all I am indebted to my wife Elaine for her many contributions, including those of editor, typist, researcher and adviser.

The First Offensive, 1942
ROOSEVELT, MARSHALL, AND THE MAKING OF AMERICAN STRATEGY

ONE

The Early Search for
Offensive Action

I

Although the decision to invade North Africa arose out of the immediate circumstances of America's first months at war, the President's thoughts on the subject, and hence the origins of the operation, may be traced back to the early summer of 1940. The course of events from then until the launching of the North African operation is complex and circuitous but the rationale for Roosevelt's persistent interest in the project is straightforward and consistent.

Roosevelt believed that a German conquest of Britain and France would be both morally wrong and inimical to the security of the United States. As a result, from the outset of the war in September 1939 and with increasing intensity after the fall of France in July 1940 the President applied himself to insuring the survival of Britain and later the Soviet Union as well. This he sought to do by providing them with the maximum aid he deemed possible. His views in this regard were shared by most members of his administration. Both Secretary of War Henry L. Stimson and Secretary of the Navy Frank Knox were strong supporters of increasing aid to Britain, including if necessary a declaration of war. So were Secretary of the Interior Harold Ickes, and Secretary of the Treasury Henry Morgenthau Jr.[1] Secretary of State Cordell Hull, while sharing his colleagues' desire to aid Britain, adopted a more cautious approach. Hull, who was chiefly responsible for justifying administration foreign policy to Congress, was especially sensitive to public and congressional opposition to American involvement. Moreover, he

3

was more aware than his colleagues of the rapidly deteriorating relations with Japan, and concerned lest the United States become so involved in European affairs that it could not back up the rather strong stand it was taking in the Pacific.[2]

The nation's military service heads, Chief of Naval Operations Admiral Harold R. Stark and Army Chief of Staff General George C. Marshall, were divided over what course the United States should follow. Stark, reflecting perhaps the Navy's advanced state of readiness, favored an aggressive policy. Marshall, while equally committed to the support of Britain, was considerably more reluctant to employ America's small, unprepared Army toward that end.

Though determined to assist Britain, Roosevelt apparently shared Hull's caution concerning how fast he might move. Pressure for action from within the Administration could not push him into acting hastily. The only factors significantly affecting the President's policy were Great Britain's needs, the willingness and capacity of the armed services to act, and his perception of the state of American public opinion.

Attitudes toward the war in the year before Pearl Harbor divided the American people into three groups. The "Isolationists" believed that the United States had no stake in the war and that therefore its outcome was of little consequence, especially in consideration of the sacrifices that American involvement would entail. A second group, the "Interventionists," thought that Axis success would mean the eventual destruction of democracy throughout the world and would pose a serious threat to the United States. They supported any measures necessary to prevent an Axis triumph. Between these two comparatively small but extremely vocal groups stood the mass of Americans. Most, while generally preferring an Allied victory, were uncertain about what the United States should do to ensure it.

Gradually during 1941 as the triumph of Hitler in Europe became increasingly likely, suggesting an inevitable confrontation with Germany, opinion swung from a position close to that of the isolationists to one approaching that of the interventionists. There was, however, little diminution of the desire to avoid costly direct involvement. Thus, while the public increasingly

4

approved of belligerent actions, most Americans, according to the polls, held back from approving full scale intervention.[3]

The President was aware that the public as a whole was less than enthusiastic about making great sacrifices in support of Britain, and saw this as a major obstacle to his pursuit of a policy which would ensure British survival. As a result, he was anxious to move the public to an appreciation of the gravity of the German threat, and an acceptance of a bolder American policy —including possibly eventual cobelligerancy. His need to educate the public led him, under great pressure from interventionist friends and advisors, to establish a national propaganda agency, first as part of the Office of Civilian Defense (May 1941), and later as an independent agency called the Office of Facts and Figures. Its jobs were to organize community participation in civilian defense, thus giving the public a sense of involvement in the war, and to provide facts and figures concerning, mostly, American mobilization in order to make people aware of the nation's growing military strength. However, the President was afraid of possible adverse reaction to overt propaganda and consequently kept the activities of the morale agencies at a low key. Nevertheless, these efforts suggest the President's concept of executive responsibility in the mounting crisis. His policies were guided by the belief that effective foreign and military policy rested on his ability to narrow the public's psychological distance from the war. Roosevelt realized that though polls might show a shift toward public support of a more belligerent policy, only a national feeling of the immediacy and reality of war would provide an adequate psychological basis for actual American involvement. This belief was chief among those factors which led him to consider the early offensive employment of American troops, an interest that drew him to French Africa.

Roosevelt first became interested in Africa because French West Africa was the most obvious jumping off point for an Axis attack on the Americas. As a continental power with a comparatively small surface Navy, Germany threatened the Western Hemisphere only at those points within flying range of Axis bases. A glance at the map reveals two such vulnerable areas: Northeastern Canada, which could be approached along a route from Norway through Iceland and Greenland and on to the

5

North American continent; and Northeastern Brazil, which was vulnerable to air attack across the Atlantic Narrows—the 1,700 mile wide stretch of ocean separating the New World from Dakar, French West Africa.

Although the northern route was to receive important consideration by the Administration, attention concentrated for the most part on the southern crossing. It is easy to see why. The distance is shorter, and preparations for operations simpler. To begin the conquest of South America the Germans needed only to acquire Dakar from the sympathetic Vichy French government. Establishment of the northern route was far more demanding, requiring the capture of Iceland and Greenland, both occupied by British forces. Also important, at least in the President's view, was Axis influence in Brazil and other South American countries.[4]

The supposed importance of "fifth columnists" in the defeat of the Spanish Republic, Norway, and other nations gave credence to the belief that a relatively small (airborne) Axis force could successfully secure a base in the Americas with the aid of organized support from within. The President may also have been influenced by the imaginative claims of the proponents of air warfare, especially airborne operations, whose views enjoyed widespread popularity during the early forties.[5] The President's interest in French Africa went beyond a simple concern for the defense of the Western Hemisphere. Had this been his only or even his primary concern, an expanded defense of the Northeastern tip of Brazil offered a more direct means. Such was in fact the recommendation of the American military.

Although the Army and the Navy had drawn up joint plans for American action to forestall a possible German expedition to Brazil,[6] these did not satisfy the President, who sought to project American power, not just to protect American territory. Even if plans and preparations for securing Brazil could be perfected before a German attack, and Brazilian opposition made this difficult, the President was not disposed to sit back and wait for a Nazi assault on the Western Hemisphere. A defensive posture would tend to reinforce American feelings of insularity—the very opposite of the public attitudes he hoped to foster. Moreover the fate of the French and the Maginot Line were evidence fresh in Roosevelt's mind of the futility of relying excessively on defense. As he explained to Harry Hopkins in the late summer of 1940, existing American coastal defenses could guard less than 1.5 percent of the East Coast of the United States, and could not prevent an enemy expeditionary force from landing "at any one of innumerable points on our shores." Therefore, Roosevelt reasoned, if the United States was involved in war "it would be highly desirable for us to land on the enemy shores first—as for instance, the northwest coast of Africa."[7]

The French possessions were a particularly inviting target for the first offensive. Under the terms of the armistice signed by France and Germany in mid-June 1940, the Germans were to occupy three-fifths of France including all of its northern and western coastline. This left the French government, now seated at Vichy, in control of the area encompassed by an arc extending approximately 300 miles inland from Marseilles. In addition, Axis forces were not to occupy France's overseas possessions. In Africa these included Tunisia, Algeria, Morocco and West Africa, territories that take in most of the northern and western coasts of Africa from the Libyan border around to and just past the port city of Dakar at the westernmost point of the continent. Under the very lenient terms imposed by Hitler the French were also permitted to retain their fleet, a 100,000 man army in unoccupied France, and an equal force in her African territories. The possibilities of this situation almost immediately caught Roosevelt's attention.

In September 1940, the President set in motion a complex program of diplomacy and espionage designed to keep French Africa out of German control and prepare the way for a friendly French reception of some future American invasion force. Within a few months, with the national elections out of the way, the President began the gradual education of the American public to the threat of a German invasion of the New World by way of Africa and the Atlantic Narrows.

On 29 December 1940, on the eve of the great public debate over an Administration measure to supply munitions to Britain without payment,[8] the President addressed the nation over radio on the subject of national security. Declaring that the Nazi quest for world domination created an unprecedented threat to America, Roosevelt supported his thesis by referring to the vulnerability of the Americas to a cross-Atlantic assault. Initiating a theme he would repeat in subsequent speeches, the President illustrated the proximity of the German threat by observing that the distance between Africa and Brazil was less than that between Washington and Denver and could be traversed by plane in five hours. He warned that this made a hostile occupation of South America an immediate possibility and a clear and present menace to the United States. Only British control of the sea now prevented invasion, and, he warned, if Britain should go down "all of us in the Americas would be living at the point of a gun." Since Britain was America's first line of defense the President asked Americans to apply themselves to the job of meeting Britain's needs "with the same sense of urgency, the same spirit of patriotism and sacrifice as we should show were we at war."[9] The creation of a great American "Arsenal of Democracy" was the surest way for the United States to avoid war.

The President's January State of the Union address took much the same line. Once again he pointed out the vulnerability of the United States to a Nazi attack based in West Africa. Enlarging on the theme, he declared that the first phase of an invasion of this hemisphere would be the occupation of strategic points in the Americas "by secret agents and their dupes," a great number of whom he claimed were already in position. Once again the first line of defense lay in increased production, which, he observed, was currently falling short of his expectations. Again the President urged the need for sacrifice while at the same time emphasizing that he intended to go on with attempts to solve the nation's economic and social problems.[10]

The possibility of an Axis airborne attack, although perhaps not realistically the best reason for the United States to oppose Germany, was easily the most demonstrable. It was a threat that could be shown to the people on a map, it played the responsive chords of preserving the Monroe Doctrine, and it was the argument that could best conjure up thoughts of Nazi soldiers marching through American territory en route to challenge not only the ideals of Americans, but their personal interests as well. The potential threat from Africa lent itself naturally to the President's efforts to illustrate America's stake in the war, and prepared the way for possible employment of American troops overseas.

II

Following a lull in the European war during the winter of 1940–41, Germany had resumed its active and successful prosecution of the conflict. In the spring of 1941 the doubling of British shipping losses, coupled with significant defeats in the Middle East, seemed to set the stage for a German occupation of French African territory, and an invasion of England itself. Those Americans worried by the prospect of a German victory now pressed the Administration for more direct and effective American intervention in the war. With the rising pressure for action came considerable discussion of immediate American occupation of French Africa or the Atlantic Islands. Though General Marshall shared the general concern over a possible British defeat, he was ill-disposed to respond with the half-way measures suggested by occupation of French, Portuguese, or Spanish colonial territories. In Marshall's view, the question before the Administration was whether the President should seek the immediate declaration of war that he apparently felt necessary to maximize American assistance to Britain.[11]

In mid-April Marshall asked the senior members of his planning staff for an appraisal of the current military situation so that he might be prepared to present the President with the Army's recommendations.[12] In response the War Plans Division indicated that Army unpreparedness made it unwise for the United States to become directly involved in the war unless a British capitulation appeared imminent. They pointed out that only one United States Army division was currently ready, and that an additional two which would be ready by the end of the month were ear-marked for hemisphere defense.[13] Though convinced that Britain should not be permitted to collapse, they were apparently unwilling to recommend immediate intervention.[14]

That afternoon, 16 April, General Marshall, accompanied by

9

his close friend and advisor General Stanley Embick, went to the White House to advise the President on future military action. As it turned out the President kept the interview very general. He questioned Marshall and Embick on the prospects of the British in the Eastern Mediterranean and, significantly, also discussed the strategic importance of the west coast of Africa and Dakar "at considerable length."[15] There is no evidence, however, that Roosevelt specifically sought General Marshall's advice, and so the General was spared the embarrassment of telling him that the Army could offer no positive alternative to the current policy of inaction. Moreover, a series of briefings that Marshall hoped to initiate to inform the President about the realities of the military situation failed to materialize. In fact, according to the President's appointment book, Marshall did not reappear at the White House for more than two weeks following the meeting of the 16th, during which time the British crisis subsided. Thus while General Marshall joined Hopkins, Stimson, and others in lamenting the President's indecision, he was apparently not prepared to suggest bold action. The President was thus left to his own strategic devices.

Indeed during the latter half of April the President seemed to be overcoming some of his indecisiveness as he sought ways of meeting the serious U-boat problem facing the British in the Atlantic. On the 24th he hesitantly approved a system of naval patrols to assist the British in detecting Axis submarines. The President's action was welcomed by the interventionists in the Administration, and it appears that the President was at least considering a bolder policy of aid to Great Britain. Public statements by Secretary of the Navy Frank Knox, Secretary Hull, Vice President Henry Wallace, and the President on the 24th and 25th suggest that Roosevelt was sounding out the public in this regard.[16]

The President seems to have been considering sending American expeditions to either French Africa or the Atlantic islands. During the last week in April the President received reports from London and Vichy of increasing signs that Germany intended to move into French Africa in the near future.[17] And in May the continued pressure of events finally led him to risk a possible hostile public reaction and undertake armed intervention in the European war. Repeated German victories, the latest in Greece and on Crete, and the threat of an imminent German invasion of French Africa or the Atlantic islands, suggested that measures would have to be taken immediately or the opportunity for action lost forever. Moreover, the President became aware during May that Churchill's spirit was flagging under the impact of continuous and seemingly unending defeats, and that without some sign of American military commitment his will to persevere might collapse.

On May 8th Stimson and Marshall learned that the President was thinking of delivering a speech the following week in which he would declare that the Azores and Dakar must not be allowed to fall into German hands.[18] On the 9th, in approving a buildup of Marine Corps strength to 75,000 men, the President told Knox that he wanted the units of the Corps concentrated and that he expected the Marine Corps Commandant to make the creation of an expeditionary force his first priority: "As you and I know [an overseas expedition] actually may be the next step we take."[19] A few days later the President ordered the shift of United States naval forces from the base at Pearl Harbor to stations in the Atlantic.

On the 19th the President met with Congressional leaders, who later reported to the press that Roosevelt had discussed "the situation that would confront this hemisphere" should Vichy permit Germany to occupy French possessions including Dakar. The President "indicated strongly," according to a *New York Times* report, "that this government would not allow such a situation to arise if there were any way to avoid it." The *Times* speculated that there were indications the Administration was about to "step out in dynamic fashion after a period of comparative inactivity."[20]

Indeed this seems to have been the President's intent, for that same day he requested Under Secretary of State Sumner Welles to draft a message outlining the dangerous implications of recent indications of French collaboration with Germany. The draft, which Welles forwarded to the President on 20 May, warned that Axis control of ports in Western Africa or the islands of the Atlantic, some of which were "barely 1600 miles distant from the coast of South America," would menace the freedom of the Atlantic Ocean and "constitute so immediate a threat to the peace and safety of the Western Hemisphere that the situation arising therefrom could not be regarded passively by the United States."[21] After conferring with Hull, however, the President, possibly chastened by the Secretary, decided to drop the idea of a message to Congress for the time.[22]

The movement toward military action reflected in these developments was brought directly to General Marshall's attention on the 24th when the publisher of the *Minneapolis Star Journal,* John Cowles, came to the War Department seeking information on the possibility of an American expedition to West Africa. Cowles gave the impression that he "had been urged by certain administration circles" to use his paper to advocate "the attack on and securing of Dakar."[23]

The apparent imminence of American military action was of course a matter of the utmost concern to General Marshall and his staff. The Army refused to be stampeded. On 20 May Army Intelligence (G-2) had completely rejected the evaluation of the situation in French Africa which the President had received from various other sources. G-2 reported to the War Plans Division (WPD) that reports emanating from North Africa that a German intervention was in the offing were false. Moreover, according to Army Intelligence, estimates given by French agents to the State Department regarding the amount of aid required to resist Axis invasion were too low and their estimates of pro-Allied sympathy too high.[24]

On the 22nd the WPD completed a long memorandum on the alternative methods of meeting the Axis threat to South America inherent in a German seizure of Dakar. In analyzing the feasibility of a preventive occupation of West Africa the planners noted that since a sympathetic attitude on the part of the French in the colony was not certain, any expedition to Dakar would have to comprise sufficient forces to overcome possible opposition. An adequate force was estimated at 115,000 men. An expedition of that size, together with the necessary shipping and naval units, could not be assembled before 15 November 1941, and in any event, the extreme heat and high incidence of disease in West Africa would make operations in the area before November costly and risky.

Quite apart from these practical objections the War Planners were fundamentally opposed to the operation on strategic grounds. Adopting a position it was to reiterate with increasing frequency over the next few months, the WPD observed that "the diversion of forces to this expedition would seriously delay BLUE [American] efforts in the decisive European Theater. . . . Highly involved, with large forces in a theater requiring a line of communications extending over 3700 miles of vulnerable ocean, BLUE would be expending a major effort to gain a minor objective." The best defense against the expected German move, they declared, was the occupation of critical bases in Brazil rather than an expedition to Dakar.[25]

Apparently neither Marshall nor Stimson conveyed the Army planners' position to the President, and American action seemed imminent. French Africa and the Atlantic Islands appeared earmarked for seizure by Germany. This would be another serious setback to the British at a time when their situation was already none too secure. Moreover, should Germany act, she would be in a position to threaten the Western Hemisphere and would indefinitely close Africa and the Islands to future Anglo-American use as a base of operations against Europe. A military move in the North Atlantic was overwhelmingly supported by the President's advisors with the significant exception of General Marshall, who apparently did not make his thinking on the matter available to the President.[26]

It also seems likely that the President felt that even token military action in the Atlantic would produce the change of public attitudes necessary for the continuously expanding involvement in the war which the Administration felt was necessary. Since the Lend Lease debate at the beginning of the year the President had exercised little public leadership, except to use various Administration spokesmen to emphasize the importance of West Africa and the Atlantic Islands to American security. Roosevelt was apparently convinced that the needed revolution in American public attitudes toward the war could not be accomplished by "leadership" in the form of speeches, but could only be effected by action. A sense of involvement would not come from reasoned statements, or impassioned pleas, but only from actual involvement. A warlike spirit and a singleminded commitment to Hitler's defeat could only come from a warlike situation. The dispatch of American troops to some overseas destination where they might be engaged in combat, or would at least be exposed to danger, was a long step in that direction. Here would be a reality to give substance to presidential exhortation.

Taking cognizance of the apparent approach of action, the Chief of Naval Operations on 22 May wrote to General Marshall that "pressure is being put on [the] U.S. to capture [the] Azores, Cape Verde Islands and French West Africa" and that the President "may demand [an] operation on short notice." As a result, Stark recommended that the Army cut down on its overseas garrisons so that an expeditionary force of 100,000 men plus air units, along with the required shipping, might be concentrated for offensive use.[27]

Indeed, a decision for action was imminent. Late that same afternoon (22 May), the President met with his senior military advisors and directed them to complete at once plans for a joint Army–Marine Corps occupation of the Azores. The President pointed out that the operation would probably be "merely a take-over from the Portuguese or the British," but Marshall responded that regardless of the probability, the expeditionary force should go prepared to fight. He therefore asked for time to assemble adequate forces and shipping. Admiral Stark supported the Chief of Staff, declaring that it would take at least three months to prepare for the expedition. The President, unconvinced, gave Marshall and Stark "30 days in which to have ready an expedition of 25,000 men to sail for, and to take the Azores."[28]

Several factors seem to have influenced the President's decision to choose the Azores rather than French Africa as the site of United States intervention. Possession of the Azores was of crucial importance to the Battle of the Atlantic, which was currently at a peak of ferocity, and Churchill had indicated to the President that Britain was more interested at this time in the Atlantic islands than in Dakar. Moreover, Robert Murphy, in French Africa to survey the situation for the President, reported that the danger of a German occupation of West Africa had subsided, for the moment at least, and had cast doubt on the likelihood of the French in Africa assisting an American expeditionary force.[29] Also contributing to the decision were various tactical problems involved in an attack on Dakar that made the Azores operation much the safer of the two.

On 27 May with the Azores decision out of the way the President finally made his expected address to the nation. Having decided to take a significant step toward increased American involvement in the war, Roosevelt sought to use the speech both to justify the move and to prepare the public for further Administration efforts in the same direction. "Unless the advance of Hitlerism is forcibly checked now," he warned, "the Western Hemisphere will be within range of Nazi weapons of destruction." The President noted that Germany threatened to occupy "the Atlantic fortress of Dakar," and the "island outposts of the New World—the Azores and Cape Verde Islands." The latter, he observed, were only a seven hour flight from Brazil and along with the Azores were vital to the defense of the sea lanes to Great Britain. It was United States policy, the President declared, first to "resist wherever necessary, and with all our resources, every attempt by Hitler to extend his Nazi domination to the Western Hemisphere, or to threaten it," and second, to give all possible aid to Britain and to take all measures required to see to it that American goods intended for Britain were delivered. Roosevelt took the opportunity to stress again the need for unity and sustained civilian morale and to assure the public that dedication to the war effort would not mean the loss of social advances brought by the New Deal. He concluded by declaring a state of unlimited national emergency, thus lending a sense of urgency and drama to his remarks.[30]

The President, by this speech and his orders of the 22nd of May to Marshall and Stark, was in effect clearing the decks for action. He wanted the military prepared to act and had even specified an object for their first offensive operation. But the final decision had yet to be made, and whether or not it would be depended on the course of events in the next month.

The deliberations leading to the decision to occupy the Azores are significant in that they reveal an aspect of relations between the President and the Chief of Staff which was to play a central role in the evolution of American policy in regard to the first offensive. For a variety of political reasons, the President had decided that immediate military action was required. Marshall, conscious of the weakness of his forces in relation to the various missions they might be called upon to perform, was reluctant to provide the troops necessary for the Azores operation or similar projects. His skepticism concerning the plan and his attempts to delay its execution, however, were both overruled by Roosevelt. Thus in the first consideration of a major utilization of Army forces, the Chief of Staff failed to appreciably influence the final decision. In succeeding months, indeed through the spring of 1942, relations between Roosevelt and Marshall followed this precedent, and gave every indication that the site and timing of the first offensive would be determined in the White House, not at the War Department.

A short time after Roosevelt ordered the Azores expedition, political developments dictated its abandonment, and before the summer was out, Dakar was to regain its position as the primary objective for the first offensive.

In the weeks following his May 22nd meeting with his military chiefs, Roosevelt learned that the British were now more interested in an American relief of the British garrison on Iceland than they were in an American occupation of the Azores.[31] Also, the Portuguese had reacted very strongly to rumors of the impending occupation of their possessions, indicating that they intended to defend the islands against any attempted Allied landing.[32]

These difficulties coincided with increasing evidence that Hitler was about to strike at the Soviet Union. A campaign in Russia would of course appreciably lessen the likelihood of immediate German action elsewhere, and would thus diminish the need for American military action in the Atlantic Islands.[33] Although the President continued to entertain the idea of an expedition to the Azores on invitation, planning for the operation was soon suspended and priority accorded the occupation of Iceland.[34] Thus, except for a brief revival of interest in August, Salazar's opposition and the Iceland operation ended serious consideration of the Azores as a target for United States intervention, much to the relief of the War Department.[35]

The demise of the Azores project coincided with reports of

increasing German pressure on the French, and of German espionage and Fifth Column activities in Africa. These led the President to renewed concern about a possible German occupation of North and West Africa either before or after the expected campaign in Russia. This is turn provided General Marshall and Secretary Stimson with an opportunity to press for the military bases in Brazil which the Army had long sought.

Arguing that German penetration of West Africa might well be the prelude to an attack directed against South America, the Army leaders sought to impress the President with the gravity of the German threat to Brazil and to obtain his support for the steps they deemed necessary to deal with it. The planners felt that establishing American bases in Northeastern Brazil was the best method of insuring hemisphere security, since it was a safe and simple way of dissuading the Axis from attempting to cross to the New World. With these thoughts in mind, General Marshall in June 1941 began to press for Roosevelt's cooperation in securing American bases there.

On 27 May the War Plans Division recommended that since the seizure of Dakar and the Atlantic Islands were beyond American capacity, the Chief of Staff should seek a Joint Board[36] recommendation urging the President to approve the occupation of bases in Brazil.[37] On 19 June General Marshall and Secretary Stimson went to the White House to brief the President on the failure of their efforts to secure Brazilian cooperation with Army plans for the defense of that nation. They pointed out that the continuing crisis in Africa made this a matter of grave and immediate concern. The President, according to Stimson, said he appreciated the gravity of the situation and thought the only question was whether the Brazilians could be persuaded to invite United States forces into their country. He indicated that he would take the matter up with Under Secretary of State Welles at once.

Despite the President's apparently sympathetic attitude, the interview must have left the Army leaders with some doubts about his intentions. In the first place, Marshall had reason to believe that Welles and Ambassador Jefferson Caffery in Rio did not agree with the Army's assessment of the Brazilian situation. More significantly, during the meeting the President had once again mentioned the desirability of organizing a 75,000 man expeditionary force for possible use in areas *outside* the Hemisphere. The renewal of this proposition seemed to suggest that regardless of the outcome of Army efforts to occupy bases in Brazil, the President had not been distracted from the idea of committing American forces overseas.[38] Following the meeting the Chief of Staff conveyed his misgivings about the President's attitude to his deputy and chief planner General Leonard T. Gerow. Marshall was worried about Roosevelt's continued willingness to expose undertrained and ill-equipped American troops to possible combat. Feeling that such units would meet disaster at the hands of the Germans, Marshall said he was determined not to give his consent to the use of any but fully prepared units. Gerow went further, urging the Chief of Staff to persuade the President to call off even the Iceland expedition, which he termed a political rather than a military move.[39]

As Marshall may have anticipated, his interview with the President failed to produce the results he had hoped for. Roosevelt refused to intercede personally with Brazilian President Getulio Vargas, and while the Army continued to demand action in Brazil[40] its efforts, lacking Presidential support, got nowhere.

III

Events during July and August 1941 pointed to West Africa as the scene of the President's next effort to involve American ground forces in the war. On 22 June 1941 German forces invaded the Soviet Union, beginning a campaign which to all appearances would end in a speedy Russian defeat. While few in Washington expected the Soviets to hold out for more than a few months, it was nevertheless recognized that during this time the Germans would probably be thoroughly occupied, and that therefore a German move into Africa was unlikely for the moment. However, there was no agreement on the larger implications of this development.

The Army planners, and probably General Marshall as well, felt that the attack on Russia made Britain secure for the time being, removing the pressure for immediate American involvement in the war.[41] On the other hand Stimson and Hopkins, and probably others among the President's advisors, thought that the German preoccupation with Russia presented a good opportunity for safely expanding American support of Great Britain.[42] This position gained support from the continued decline of Britain's fortunes despite the German campaign in Russia. Although her military situation at the beginning of June 1941 was not as desperate as it had been a year before, it nonetheless remained grave and unrelieved by signs of possible improvement. Moreover, the British anticipated that when the Germans had disposed of Russia, which was expected sometime between 1 August and the end of October, the Axis would be able to concentrate all its efforts on driving them from the Middle East.[43] Even if the Germans ignored North Africa to concentrate on the campaign in the western desert the results could diminish the possibility of American intervention in French Africa. For if Germany succeeded in driving the British from Egypt, the French in Africa would very likely be unable to resist German demands for bases and other concessions in the colonies.[44]

It appeared that American intervention, if it were to occur at all, would have to be initiated immediately. This conclusion was reinforced by additional information received by the President in July. On the 10th Murphy reported that General Weygand had unexpectedly been summoned to Vichy.[45] Washington interpreted this to mean that Germany was "putting extreme pressure to bear upon France in order to secure arrangements whereunder, directly or indirectly, Germany would secure entire control of such ports as Casablanca and Dakar. . . . "[46]

Shortly after learning of Weygand's recall, the President received a *Fortune* survey[47] which indicated that although the public identified the defense of the Western Hemisphere and England most closely with American security, 42 percent of those polled expressed a willingness to see the United States take steps to prevent the Germans from occupying the West African port. Russell Davenport, the editor of *Fortune,* in a note accompanying the poll, thought it significant that though the importance of Dakar and the Azores was not yet well understood by the public, approval of intervention there just failed to obtain majority support.[48]

The First Offensive

On 11 and 12 August the Prime Minister, Roosevelt, and the British and American military staffs met aboard H.M.S. *Prince of Wales* and U.S.S. *Augusta* in Placentia Bay, Newfoundland, for a series of discussions which came to be known as the Atlantic Conference. A large part of the strategy talks at the meeting revolved about the German threat to North Africa and the Atlantic islands and what might be undertaken jointly to meet it. Two weeks before the conference, Churchill had raised the same question with Harry Hopkins and suggested French Africa as a particularly suitable area for American military operations should the United States become involved in the war.[49]

Once the conference began, Churchill himself took up the issue with the President, telling him of his concern about a possible German occupation of North Africa. Roosevelt, however, despite continued Portuguese opposition, reverted instead to the Azores project declaring that he intended to occupy those islands if the German threat became more immediate and if the British found themselves unable to intervene. Churchill now in effect gave this operation his blessing, noting that since the British were readying forces for the seizure of the Canary Islands in about a month's time, they would not have enough troops available for an effective occupation of the Azores should the need arise. Discussions among the military were less harmonious. The British Chiefs pressed for American agreement to an expedition to Africa in the event of United States involvement, but General Marshall stubbornly refused to commit American ground forces to any operation outside the Hemisphere.[50]

Despite the Americans' refusal to accept British plans for African operations, the Atlantic meeting probably increased the likelihood of eventual United States involvement in Africa. For the meeting gave the Prime Minister an opportunity to make known to the President personally and in his own dramatic fashion his thoughts on America's first offensive, thus adding his own influence to the tide of events and advice directing Roosevelt to the opportunities in France's African possessions.

At the same time it is not unlikely that the Atlantic meeting increased General Marshall's fear of British influence on the President's military outlook. In June he had learned that there were "definite indications" in London of a political effort to have the United States commit troops to a West African expedition.[51] It was now clear that the British were indeed pushing for United States involvement in a peripheral strategy starting in West Africa, which General Marshall was increasingly determined to avoid.

The face-to-face meeting between the President and the Prime Minister, on this as on subsequent occasions, almost certainly weakened Marshall's influence. The Prime Minister at these conferences supplied the President with an alternate body of professional knowledge and intelligence which he might weigh against the expertise supplied by his own military advisors. Marshall was unable to retain the near monopoly on military advice upon which much of his influence was bound to rest. Further, from the Atlantic meeting until the spring of 1942 Churchill and his advisors retained the initiative in proposing aggressive operations in which the United States might participate. The Chief of Staff might frown on these, as he did, but until April 1942 he failed to offer an attractive and politically acceptable alternative. In assessing the competition between Churchill and Marshall for the direction of the President's strategic thinking, we must bear in mind that the Prime Minister's bold aggressiveness, along with his wit and fluency, gave him a great advantage in presenting his case over the rather aloof and conservative American Chief of Staff.

By the end of the summer of 1941 it was clear that President Roosevelt was keenly aware of and interested in the possibility of sending an American expeditionary force to Africa or the Atlantic islands (especially the Azores). Yet despite apparent opportunities and pressures the President held back—circumstances, except for a brief time in late March, never seemed just right. During the fall, however, the President's inclination for an African expedition developed rapidly until by the time the Japanese struck at Pearl Harbor the project seemed certain to become the United States' first full scale offensive operation.[52]

General Marshall's response to the possibility of imminent overseas involvement had been generally hostile but not unequivocally so. General Staff thought on when and how American forces should be used was somewhat confused by the impossibility of predicting the exact military situation and the state of American preparedness at the commencement of hostilities. The result was that Army planners were torn between the desire to provide the British and Russians with immediate military assistance, and the principle that the accumulation of a force capable of decisive action should not be interfered with or the lives of American troops jeopardized by their piecemeal premature commitment to the struggle.

Immediate prewar planning for possible war with Germany and Japan dates from November 1940, when Chief of Naval Operations Admiral Harold R. Stark sought in a memorandum to predict the general outline of future American strategy. Stark postulated four courses of action should the United States, either before or after a British defeat, enter the war against Germany, Italy, and Japan. The principal United States effort might be directed toward one of the following:

A. Hemisphere defense.
B. Full offensive against Japan.
C. Maximum possible effort in both the Atlantic and the Pacific.
D. An eventual concentrated offensive in the Atlantic, while assuming the defensive in the Pacific.

Stark chose from these alternatives plan "D" (Dog), arguing that it offered the best chances for victory over America's potential enemies, adding significantly "particularly if we insist on equality [with the British] in the political and military direction of the war."[53] Stark's recommendation that in the event of war with Japan, Germany, and Italy, the United States concentrate on Germany first, was accepted by the Army and submitted to the White House in mid-November. The President, while not officially approving what was now a joint Army–Navy plan, did let it be known that he accepted it.

The Army planners had an opportunity to expand on this basic proposition at the high level Anglo-American military conference held in Washington in late January 1941.[54] Both sides at these meetings agreed that for some time after American involvement, major Allied offensive operations would have to be confined to economic pressure and extensive bombing. The

British, conscious of their weakness and recalling the slaughter of 1914–1918, hoped to put off direct confrontation with the Wehrmacht on the Continent until Germany was severely weakened. They intended to use the initial stage of the war to create a ring of bases around Europe from which the assault against a weakened Germany could be launched. Under this "closing the ring" or peripheral strategy, operations in the Middle East and North Africa were important both to prevent the further expansion of German power and to provide bases for the final assault on the Continent.

American strategic thought, reflecting a sense of the nation's potential strength in men and material, as well as a disposition to strike decisively and avoid protracted conflict, emphasized the concentration of Allied force for a single blow. The Americans saw the first months of their participation as a period in which men and material would be accumulated in Great Britain, or possibly in the Atlantic islands, to prepare for an early major attack.[55] Adherence to this concept made the Americans generally unsympathetic to becoming involved at the periphery of German power—including naturally Africa or the Middle East. While there was a significant body of thought within the War Department which did not totally reject the peripheral strategy,[56] General Marshall and his staff held to the single thrust, opposing the indecisive operations they thought implicit in the British approach.

Following the American–British conference, the Joint Board recommended that American planners draft a basic plan for possible war with Germany, Italy, and Japan. The resultant plan, RAINBOW 5, was completed in April 1941. Possibly as a result of extensive Anglo-American contacts since the Washington meeting (ABC) in January, RAINBOW 5 showed the influence of the peripheral approach. Thus the scheme called for the application of economic pressure, a sustained air offensive, and the conduct of raids and minor offensives against the Axis at every opportunity. It also recommended military action aimed at the early elimination of Italy from the Axis partnership, and support of the resistance movements within the Axis-occupied territories. Finally the plan recommended the capture of positions around the periphery of Europe from which an offensive against Germany could eventually be launched. Since the war planners felt that planning for the ultimate major offensive could not proceed without precise information on the military situation at the time of its launching, no plan for the final thrust was drawn up.

Though RAINBOW 5 thus supported in every respect the peripheral strategy recommended by the British, it also reaffirmed the fundamental American commitment to the single thrust approach, declaring that "the primary immediate effort" of the American Army, in addition to cooperating with the British in the tasks enumerated above and defending the Western Hemisphere and the British Isles, was "the building up of a large land and air force for major offensive operations against the Axis Powers."[57] At this stage General Marshall and his staff apparently could not foresee that the peripheral scheme would be incompatible with their desire to build up American strength for the single thrust.

The difficulties in maintaining an alliance between what proved to be conflicting concepts were suggested to General Marshall during the military discussions at the Atlantic Conference in August.[58] The British took the initiative by offering for discussion a paper setting forth their general strategic concepts and their recommendations for Anglo-American strategy in the event of United States involvement. The British concept was the by now familiar one of defeating Germany primarily by wearing her down through strategic bombing, economic blockade, and the promotion of subversion and eventual revolt among the captive peoples of Europe. Land campaigns would initially be confined to the periphery of Europe with the object both of containing the Germans and of providing bases from which the primary tasks indicated above might be better carried out. Invasion of the Continent was not contemplated by the British until the final stage in the war when German strength had been severely weakened.

The Americans were skeptical. Marshall was especially dubious about the British attachment to maintaining their position in the Middle East, and rebuffed their efforts to interest him in operations at Dakar. Marshall noted that the occupation of Dakar would entail a continuing commitment of shipping and sup-

ply that would interfere with other more important operations.[59]

These differences, later to assume great significance, had little
practical importance in August 1941 since the United States was
not yet at war. Even so the British were disappointed by the
American military's display of caution. General Marshall was
clearly reluctant to commit the United States to much beyond
the creation of a powerful American force to be employed
against Germany sometime after the United States entered the
war. For the immediate future he appeared committed to an
"America first" program. General Marshall surprised his future
Allies by his concern over what seemed to them the remote
possibility of a Nazi coup in Brazil, and his suggestion that the
United States might have to occupy parts of Colombia and
Venezuela, as well as Brazil, to forestall German actions in South
America that would threaten the Panama Canal.[60] Notwithstanding his general acceptance of peripheral operations as outlined in RAINBOW 5, at the Atlantic Conference General Marshall
refused to approve American participation in the occupation of
Dakar. Indeed the Chief of Staff seemed reluctant to entertain
the possibility of any immediate American military operations
other than in Latin America, Iceland, or possibly the Azores.

The discussions of Plan Dog, ABC-1, RAINBOW 5 and those at
the Atlantic Conference indicate that until the fall of 1941 at
least, General Marshall and his planning staff supported, albeit
somewhat ambiguously, the need for, if not the desirability of,
operations on the periphery of German power. They apparently
viewed these, however, as little more than time-fillers that
should not be allowed to interfere with the eventual full scale
confrontation with German power on the Continent. The question left open in all these discussions was what operations,
where and on what scale, the American military would countenance until the single thrust could be launched. The fate of the
African project rested with the answer.

Within a month of the Atlantic Conference, Marshall would
discover, if he did not already know, that the President neither
accepted the Army approach to strategy nor shared his misgivings concerning an African expedition. Roosevelt favored the

peripheral strategy (as well as the African operation), and flatly rejected the idea that the United States should raise a large European expeditionary force.

IV

The President's hostility to the idea of creating the large ground force favored by Marshall probably reflected in part his fear that an invasion of the Continent before Germany had been severely weakened would bring a repetition of the bloodletting of 1914–1918. Moreover, he had reason to believe that the public in the early fall of 1941 still did not support the antifascist cause with the passion and dedication necessary to sustain the sacrifices entailed in unlimited war. Evidence of that had most recently come to light during the debate over an Administration sponsored revision of the draft law.

In July, the Administration introduced a bill to extend the service of draftees currently on duty for the duration of the national emergency and to eliminate the provision of the existing law which limited the service of drafted men to the Western Hemisphere. Polls conducted during the debate revealed that only a bare majority of the public supported extension, while a clear majority opposed eliminating the geographical restrictions. Congressional attitudes reflected this hostility. The Administration, and particularly President Roosevelt, was accused of bad faith in seeking to keep the men in service. Opposition in fact was so strong, emotional, and politically explosive that the President felt obliged to avoid direct intervention in the controversy, fearing that he might do the measure more harm than good. He delegated the task of mobilizing congressional support for revision to General Marshall. The ploy was successful. Congressmen who mistrusted Roosevelt or were afraid to associate themselves with the Administration were willing to accept the arguments of the Chief of Staff. Even so, the vote was close. On August 12 extension of duty passed by the narrowest of margins. The term, however, was set at eighteen months instead of being left open ended as the Administration and Marshall had hoped. Moreover, the restriction of service to the

Hemisphere that the President had sought to remove, remained in the new Act.[61]

The less than satisfactory resolution of the draft extension controversy reflected the public's lack of enthusiasm for the government's defense preparations and its failure to believe that the international crisis warranted personal sacrifice. The President was painfully conscious of this attitude and the limits it imposed on military policy. On 19 August 1941, in off-the-record remarks to the press, he aptly compared the current situation to that at the beginning of the Civil War. Quoting from Lincoln's remarks in 1861, Roosevelt told the assembled reporters that they made a "rather interesting parallel" with the present situation:

> the fact is the people have not yet made up their minds that we are at war with the South. They have not backed down to the determination to fight this war through; for they have got the idea into their heads that we are going to get out of this fix somehow by strategy. . . . They have no idea that the war is to be carried on and put through by hard, tough fighting, that it will hurt somebody; and no headway is going to be made while this delusion lasts.

The President noted that, as in 1861, there were "a lot of people who haven't waked up to the . . . danger."[62] These "off-the-record" and indirect remarks, however, presaged neither a change in public attitudes nor bolder efforts by the President to "educate" public opinion.

At the end of August Secretary Stimson, reporting to a Cabinet meeting on the defense effort, noted that public apathy was contributing to a lag in munitions output. The Secretary declared that the Administration was faced with two alternatives: "to go to war at once and change the set-up of production so as to get a war psychosis; or else to have the program so delayed that the war would probably be over before we got through with it." The President, without commenting on Stimson's conclusion, agreed that the defense program had not yet involved "the little man of America" and that production was suffering as a consequence.[63]

The First Offensive

In early September another aspect of the public's response to defense policy was brought to the President's attention by General Marshall. On the 6th the Chief of Staff advised the President that parents were so confused by the international situation and so influenced by Administration critics that they were bringing "an unfortunate influence to bear on their sons in the Army," with the result that "fighting efficiency was being impaired." General Marshall insisted that "something" should be done to make people understand "the national emergency and . . . the necessity for a highly trained Army." Two weeks later the President replied: "In effect you say . . . do something about this weakness on the part of the civilian population. Got any ideas?"[64] Actually Marshall had recommended in his letter that the Administration's "morale agency," the Office of Civilian Defense (OCD), do its job. In October the President acknowledged the failure of OCD and established a new agency, the Office of Facts and Figures (OFF), to make information on the defense program and policies available to the general public.[65] Unable to effect any quick change in public attitude, the President remained its captive, and now in the fall of 1941 it made him loath to accept the Army's idea of building a large ground force for use in an eventual massive confrontation with German forces. He was aware that many of those Americans who accepted the likelihood of eventual American involvement in the war believed that the nation's participation might be limited to providing Great Britain and the Soviet Union with war materials and perhaps, if necessary, with naval and air support as well. The Russians and British would supply the manpower and do most of the fighting. American ground forces would be limited to numbers sufficient to guard the Western Hemisphere, and almost all American munitions production could be made available to Britain and the Soviet Union.

These views were given significant expression on 20 September when Walter Lippmann, writing in his nationally syndicated column, challenged Army plans for expansion on the grounds that a large American force was not warranted by the current world situation. The influential journalist noted that when Army expansion began in the summer of 1940 it was expected that the defeat of Great Britain would soon leave the United States isolated in the face of the Axis threat. Now, however, with the Russians in the war (Lippmann apparently thought they would survive) the conditions which called for a mass army no longer prevailed and therefore the efforts to expand military manpower were both unnecessary and undesirable. Great Britain's survival, he said, meant that America's major role was in the factory, not on the battlefields of Europe or Asia. Lippmann concluded by demanding that "all popular doubts, all political confusion, all ambiguities should be removed by a clear decision to shrink the Army and concentrate our major effort on the Navy, the air force and lend-lease."[66]

The Lippmann article appeared just at the time Army planners were completing a detailed examination of the nation's future military manpower and production needs. In July the President, anxious to get an accurate picture of the scale of American production required to ensure an Allied victory, had asked the Army and Navy to prepare such a report. Obviously, accurate estimates would have to be based in part on American and Allied strategy, and on the extent of American participation in the war. If the United States was to deploy a large ground force, the type of munitions produced and especially the priority of production and distribution would be quite different than if America's contribution were to be limited principally to naval and air forces. As a result the Army planners were obliged to include in their response an outline of American strategy in the event of United States involvement. The total scheme came to be known as the Victory Program.[67]

In light of the Lippmann article and the discussion of a limited size and role for the Army, General Marshall may well have concluded that his idea of creating a large Army, designed to execute the single decisive blow, would not be accepted as national policy. Marshall thought that the threat to these concepts was encouraged by American naval and air officers who, together with the British, were attempting to make certain that their organizations continued to receive most of America's munitions. Believing that Roosevelt was strongly influenced by these elements, especially the Navy, the Chief of Staff was moved to fight to save the large Army concept.[68]

On the day Lippmann's column appeared, General Marshall

held a staff conference at which he called attention to the article and noted that he was going to the White House on the 22nd to discuss with the President "a proposal [by Lippmann?] to reduce the strength of the Army in order to make more material available for other purposes." Marshall pointed out that this idea was incompatible with the President's "indicated desire" to occupy various Atlantic bases including Dakar, and directed the WPD to assemble data concerning the forces needed for the several military expeditions that Roosevelt had from time to time mentioned. Obviously Marshall felt that Roosevelt's attraction to "side-shows" constituted a strong argument in favor of building a large American ground force.[69]

The President had expected to receive the Army–Navy "Victory Program" on 22 September. On that day, although the final report was not yet finished, Marshall and Stimson, armed with a large packet of supporting documents, went to the White House. Judging by the documents they carried, the Army leaders probably supported their case for a large army at least in part by referring to the large number of overseas operations which the United States might eventually be obliged to undertake.[70] This conclusion is sustained by the contents of the Victory Program that Stimson and Knox delivered to the White House three days later. Along with its production estimates the program contained the first detailed consideration of United States strategy and its relationship to requirements for men and material. Significantly this strategic "survey" implicitly supported the British concept of a peripheral strategy and acknowledged the desirability of eventual American operations against the Atlantic Islands or French Africa.

The Army–Navy strategic estimate began by repeating the basic assumption of American military thinking: the defeat of Germany was the first priority in a war against Germany, Italy, and Japan. The Joint Board noted, however, that the small number of American troops then sufficiently equipped and trained for offensive operations made it "out of the question to expect the United States and its associates to undertake in the near future a sustained and successful offensive against the center of the German power." The alternatives offered were a continuation and strengthening of the existing British economic blockade; air and sea offensives against German economic resources; support of subversive activities in the conquered territories; and finally "the prosecution of land offensives in distant regions where German troops can exert only a fraction of their total strength." In this connection the report noted the importance of continued British control of the Red Sea, Iraq, and Iran and urged the maintenance of an active front in Russia and the "prevention of Axis penetration into Northwest Africa and the Atlantic Islands." The latter consideration was declared "very important, not only as a contribution to the defense of the Western Hemisphere, but also as security to British sea communications and as a potential base for a future land offensive." The report called special attention to the opportunities available in French Africa, noting that the French troops in North and West Africa constituted "potential enemies of Germany, provided they are re-equipped and satisfactory political conditions are established by the United States."[71] Thus America's military leaders, while not recommending immediate action in Africa, did indicate that in the event of United States involvement offensive operations should commence at the periphery of German power, specifically in French Africa. The Army's only stated reservation was that a peripheral strategy based largely on air and naval forces might not be sufficient to accomplish the defeat of Germany and "that it *may* be necessary to come to grips with the German armies on the Continent of Europe" (italics added). Further, the plan asserted that the equipment of land armies "necessary to meet this contingency should be provided as part of the overall production requirement."[72]

The Chief of Staff, in conditionally approving the principal tenets of the peripheral strategy and the desirability of operations against Africa, encouraged Roosevelt to accept a large army by suggesting relatively bloodless tasks for its employment. Possibly that was not Marshall's motive. Nevertheless, whatever the rationale, Army endorsement of the "Victory Program" indicated the flexibility of its strategic outlook—a flexibility that at this time did not discourage the President from pursuing his own plans in regard to America's first offensive.

When Stimson brought the "Victory Program" to the White House on 25 September he had the opportunity to discuss with

31

The First Offensive

Roosevelt the whole question of American military policy. Once again he urged the President to get the country "into the frank position of war" so that planning and preparations for action could go ahead on a firm basis and production benefit from the resulting boost to public morale. According to Stimson, the President fully agreed with him but was afraid of "any assumption of the position that we must invade Germany and crush Germany. He thought that would make a very bad reaction." Stimson replied that involvement in the war need not mean immediate head-on confrontation with the Germans,[73] thus again suggesting that the Army might favor participation limited to relatively safe operations such as an expedition to French Africa. When the Secretary left the White House he carried away with him a request by the President that the Army draw up a study for American military action in West Africa.[74]

This request, along with Roosevelt's expressed reluctance to come to grips at once with the bulk of German forces, indicates that he was very much attracted to the prospects of American action at the periphery of German power and looking for a likely opportunity. This conclusion is also indicated by an article Roosevelt wrote for *Colliers* (October 1), in which he said that, in his view, the United States could consider itself attacked as soon as any base from which American security could be threatened was occupied by a hostile power. He emphasized that the base might be thousands of miles from United States shores and specifically mentioned Africa, the Azores, and the Cape Verde Islands.[75] The President apparently thought the need (or opportunity) for American action would come if the Germans attempted to occupy French Africa or the Atlantic Islands, as they were fully expected to do once winter weather halted their offensive in Russia, probably sometime in November.[76]

In early October, General Marshall presented the President with his formal response to the Lippmann thesis, and he again linked his request for a large army to an endorsement of the peripheral strategy. Rejecting the idea of limiting the United States' contribution to supplying munitions to the armies of the other nations, the Chief of Staff declared that the nation needed a force of 215 divisions which would *eventually* be used to "come to grips with and annihilate" the Germany army. However, before that decisive stage arrived Marshall recommended what he called "our broad concept of encircling Germany and closing in on her step by step" to wear her down. Africa, along with Brazil, England, and the Middle East were mentioned as possible areas where an American Task Force of 154,000 men might be required during the initial stage.[77]

On 7 October Roosevelt received the War Planners' analysis of possible United States operations against West Africa that he had requested from Stimson on September 25. According to the planners, any force seeking to occupy West Africa would have to be prepared to meet French resistance and should therefore number 160,000 men with 50,000 additional in reserve. Since a force of that size would take some time to assemble and since the West African climate ruled out a summer expedition, the operation, in their opinion, could not take place before November 1, 1942.[78] Thus, while the Army endorsed an African expedition in principle, it made clear that the possibility of opposition ruled out any such operation for at least a year. Marshall did not, however, say the operation was strategically undesirable, and he left the way open for its use if the President could guarantee no French opposition.

TWO

GYMNAST: The British Challenge

I

In spite of the Army's efforts to turn the President away from any immediate move on French Africa, the project, albeit in somewhat altered form, was gathering increased support within the Administration. On the morning of October 7th Secretary of the Navy Frank Knox came to Secretary Stimson "full of a brand new idea which he had gotten from Bullitt," a recent Ambassador to France. The idea was the dispatch of an American expeditionary force to Casablanca in Northwest Africa.

The project was not new but rather the revival of a proposal which had been suggested more than once since the fall of France. This time, however, it enjoyed rather more important and enthusiastic support than it had in the past. Stimson, in recounting his interview with Knox, noted the Secretary of the Navy had the plan "all spelled out."

> The brilliant mind of Bullitt had taken him captive. He thought that it would draw off the attention of the Germans from the British Isles and would help save Britain. In fact it was such a brilliant idea that he was quite chippered up with it.

Stimson hastened to call in Generals Marshall and Embick to help him "straighten out a good friend who had gone wrong." Together they attacked the proposal on a variety of grounds: it was simply another diversion from the true line of action, it would require more men than were available, it would immobilize shipping that might be needed elsewhere, the Germans could reinforce the area quicker than the United States could and, finally, Weygand would be of no help because his forces had been stripped of their weapons on German orders. In short, Knox was informed, the plan was "perfectly hopeless."[1] Nevertheless, since Stimson believed that Bullitt had a "great deal of influence with the President and also with others in the Administration," he thought it wise to set him straight too. With this in mind he met with the former Ambassador on the 10th. At the close of this meeting he was convinced that he had completely changed Bullitt's views on the subject of North Africa.[2] He was, as we shall see, quite mistaken.

In mid-October Lord Louis Mountbatten, who was in the United States on a special mission, accepted the President's invitation to stay at the White House. During his visit Mountbatten had occasion to speak to the President at some length[3] and he took the opportunity to outline British plans and preparations for the coming months, very likely including a scheme for a descent on French North Africa.[4] At the end of the visit Roosevelt asked Mountbatten to tell the Prime Minister that he was interested in the possibility of a United States occupation of North Africa in the event that "Petain goes and Weygand plays with us."[5] Mountbatten was to inform Churchill that the President regarded French North Africa, Dakar, and the Atlantic islands with "special interest not only from an American but from his personal ways of thought."[6] North Africa held a special interest for the Prime Minister too, and from this time until the final decision to invade north Africa some nine months later, the Prime Minister conducted an effective campaign to keep the President's interest in the project alive.

The campaign began on October 27th when Roosevelt received a long letter from Churchill outlining his plans for North Africa. The Prime Minister noted that British forces in Cyrenaica would shortly begin an offensive which he hoped would bring them to Tripoli. If the offensive was successful, he reasoned, Weygand might voluntarily rejoin the war or be forced to do so by German demands resulting from the pressures of the British advance. Churchill went on to say that he was holding a force ready for use about mid-November to take advantage of a possible favorable change in Weygand's position.[7]

The First Offensive

Although the Prime Minister received no reply to his message he learned from Lord Halifax of Bullitt's scheme for landing 150,000 men in Morocco, and of the interest of Knox and others in the idea. Though Churchill "had the feeling that the President was thinking very much along the same lines as I was about acting in French Northwest Africa," he decided not to press the issue with Roosevelt until the success of the coming British desert offensive was assured. In the meantime he ordered a force of three divisions to stand ready to move into French North Africa if the occasion arose. On 28 October the British gave the plan for the invasion of French North Africa the code-name GYMNAST.[8]

While Roosevelt heard no more from Churchill during November on the subject of an African expedition, events in France and the progress of General Claude Auchinleck's offensive in Libya continued to draw the President's attention to French Africa. He was aware that the French might capitulate to German demands for bases in North Africa even before the British succeeded in reaching Tripoli. That of course would destroy the possibility of an unopposed American landing. On 1 November he wrote the recently appointed Ambassador to France, Admiral William D. Leahy, expressing his concern that "should the Germans change the direction of their main activities from Russia to the Mediterranean . . . [the] French will not be able to hold out much longer against increasing German demands. . . ."[9] The Ambassador in turn reported rumors that the Germans not only intended to increase their pressure on Vichy, but that they would also seek to force the removal of General Weygand.[10] In the light of such rumors the State Department, which had been considering ordering Murphy back to the United States to discuss a clandestine program of military assistance for North Africa (the French had approached the Department on the subject again in mid-October),[11] decided instead to have him remain in touch with the situation.[12]

On 18 November Weygand was removed, raising the possibility that his successor might not only curtail American subversive activities in Africa, but might also collaborate with the Germans in resisting Anglo-American efforts to occupy North Africa. However Washington's anxiety was probably somewhat relieved by reports from Murphy to the effect that "reliable official sources" insisted that Weygand's replacement would "cause no immediate change in the French African situation nor an immediate Axis intrusion."[13] Thus for the time being at least, plans for military action in North Africa continued to hinge on the success or failure of Auchinleck's army.

The President, aware that the British desert offensive (CRUSADER) was to begin at dawn on the 18th,[14] arranged a luncheon meeting with Bullitt at the White House on that day.[15] Although there is no record of what was said, it is almost certain that the President told Bullitt of CRUSADER and its objectives and of his hopes for an American occupation of North Africa in conjunction with a successful British drive toward Tripoli. It was probably also at this meeting that the President suggested that Bullitt go to Egypt to act as his personal observer and informant in the area.

The President had become anxious over the situation in the Middle East. Reports that the British military establishment in Egypt was disorganized and inefficient were reaching Washington. The American Ambassador in Cairo, Alexander Kirk, had noted on several occasions since June that the absence of unified command in the Middle East and the resulting lack of coordination of effort were restricting the effectiveness of the war effort in that theater. As a result, Kirk declared, the United States was "presently wasting the precious material we are sending to this area. . . ." This information was known to Hopkins and, therefore, no doubt to the President as well.[16] He probably hoped that Bullitt's trip to the Middle East, "by way of Africa," would give him additional information on the problems jeopardizing the success of CRUSADER.[17]

Roosevelt's selection of Bullitt for this task (confirmed by a formal authorization dated 22 November)[18] was probably prompted at least in part by his desire to give the former Ambassador something to do. Since returning from France in July 1940, Bullitt, a man of great energy, enterprise, and ambition, had been impatient to assume some responsible task related to the defense effort or to international affairs. He had approached the President on several occasions, and had most recently come away from a mid-September meeting at the White House "terribly hurt" at Roosevelt's apparent unwillingness to use him in the preparedness setup.[19] Roosevelt had some serious objections to bringing Bullitt into the Administration, probably based on the latter's excessive ambition and unpredictable political behavior. Anxious to oblige but reluctant to give him a major post, the President probably felt that his need for information about the situation in Africa and his desire to find an assignment for an old friend made Bullitt's selection an obvious solution to two problems.

The President's growing interest in Africa and the Middle East gave General Marshall and Secretary Stimson further cause for alarm over the lack of Army influence at the White House. At the end of October the Chief of Staff told Stimson "he was worried that there was a movement at the White House to get in a new circle of advisors on war strategy around the President who should act between him and his regular advisors." Marshall seemed especially concerned about the role of Harry Hopkins.[20] Two weeks later Stimson confided to his diary his own unhappiness over the situation in the White House. He felt that the President had delegated a great deal of authority to personal agents such as Hopkins, Harriman, and Donovan, who frequently went directly to the President "about some matter that infringes on our jurisdiction," and that as a result the President was forming opinions and prejudices without the benefit of professional military opinion. This "topsy-turvy, upside down system of poor administration," Stimson complained, was the source of most of his problems at the War Department.[21] Marshall and Stimson were clearly concerned by what they considered to be the decline of Army influence. The whole discussion of an American expedition to North Africa, insofar as they were aware of it, probably impressed the Army leaders as an unfortunate expression of the President's unorthodox approach to strategy and decision-making. The Bullitt mission obviously fit the same pattern. His discussion of his trip with War Department representatives did nothing to alter the impression.

On 27 November Bullitt went to the War Department to ascertain the Army's views on operations in Africa and to brief the Department on the scope and objectives of his mission. Meeting with Colonel Charles Bundy, Chief of the Plans group of the

War Plans Division, and Assistant Secretary of War for Air Robert Lovett, Bullitt told them that he had been asked to go to the Middle East "so that the President could feel almost as though he had seen it with his own eyes." The President felt that the information he was currently receiving from military and naval observers was "sometimes contradictory and unsatisfactory from an overall viewpoint," so that he was not getting a true picture of the situation. Bullitt proceeded to make the War Department representatives even more unhappy by holding forth on the virtues and prospects of United States intervention in North Africa. Bundy and Lovett tried as diplomatically as possible to point out the fallacies in such thinking, citing in particular the fact that the current scale of lend-lease commitments severely limited the Army's capacity to take offensive action,[22] but their efforts were wasted.

Three days later Bullitt, still convinced of the wisdom of a North African operation, left for the Middle East. Within the week the Japanese attack on Pearl Harbor put the United States into the war, thereby greatly increasing the chances that the hopes and plans of Churchill, Roosevelt, Bullitt, and others concerning America's first offensive would soon be realized.

II

Immediately upon hearing the news of the Japanese attack on Pearl Harbor, Churchill decided to meet the President as soon as possible to discuss the future conduct of the war. Roosevelt welcomed the idea and on December 12, the Prime Minister and his senior military advisors set out for the United States and the first Anglo-American wartime conference, codenamed ARCADIA.

Anticipation of this meeting naturally led the War Department to reappraise America's role in the war against the Axis. Though they remained firmly attached to the "Hitler first" concept set forth in RAINBOW 5,[23] limitations of supplies and trained men tended to direct the Chief of Staff's attention to immediate problems of self-defense. For while America's armed strength had not been increased by the events of early December, its military commitments had. As a result, General Marshall felt no more able to countenance immediate offensive action against Germany now than he had before the Japanese attack.

Problems of hemisphere defense were the Chief of Staff's most immediate concern, since the German and Italian declarations of war on 11 December increased the immediate possibility of an Axis descent on Brazil. But a new problem in connection with the security of the Brazilian bulge arose early in December 1941 when the United States completed an air supply route to the Middle East and the Pacific. The string of air bases making up the route ran through Northern Brazil across the Atlantic Narrows to British West Africa, with one branch going from there on to Egypt and another continuing east to India and Australia. The threat to existing sea communications posed by Japanese advances in the South Pacific made this route appear vital to the American position in the Pacific.

According to War Department thinking, the route was vulnerable at two points; in Brazil, where Axis inspired and supported Brazilians might seize air fields in the nation's remote and isolated northeastern tip, and across the Atlantic, where a German occupation of Dakar would put the Axis in a position to interrupt the route as it passed through British West Africa. General Marshall appears to have been primarily interested in protecting the Brazilian airfields with an American security force. Stimson and the Air Force Chief of Staff, General Arnold, were equally concerned about West Africa and hoped to counter the threat to the air route at both points by an Allied occupation of Dakar.

Efforts were first directed at the Brazilian problem, and Marshall and Stimson approached the President twice during the first weeks after the Pearl Harbor attack to have him pressure the Brazilian government into permitting the stationing of American armed forces there. Roosevelt, however, again refused to intercede personally and directed the Army leaders to the State Department instead.[24] On the 29th, at a meeting of the State–Army–Navy Standing Liaison Committee, General Marshall broached the problem of the Nazi threat to Brazil, pointing out that "the life-line to General MacArthur" (in the Philippines) passed through that area. Undersecretary Welles replied that he did not think Axis influence in Brazil was as great as General Marshall thought, noting that "Brazilian opinion has swung toward the United States in the past ten days," and that hopes for an amicable settlement of the issue were looking up.[25] Welles refused to press the Army request and there the Brazilian problem rested for the time.

The Army leadership, under pressure from the Air Corps, now came for a short but critical period to support operations against Dakar as a way of securing the air route on both sides of the Atlantic Narrows. On the 18th Undersecretary of War for Air Robert Lovett and Deputy Chief of Staff for Air General Henry H. Arnold, in a memorandum which Stimson sent to the White House, noted that increasing evidence of German designs on North Africa suggested a threat to the west coast of Africa, and therefore the possibility of Axis interdiction of the air route to the Far East. Under these circumstances, Lovett and Arnold recommended that "the protection of the Western bulge of Africa and this essential air route be moved up to the highest priority classification" in the ranking of possible American military actions.[26]

On the same day that the State Department in effect turned down the Chief of Staff's latest plea for intervention in the Brazilian situation (20 December), Stimson prepared a memorandum for the President concerning the subjects to be treated at the forthcoming meeting with the British. Stimson's paper, which was endorsed by Marshall, the chief of war planning General Gerow, and General Arnold, stressed the importance of Dakar to Allied communications and placed West Africa second in priority only to the Southwestern Pacific in a list of problem areas requiring immediate American military attention.[27]

The War Department's flirtation with the West Africa project was short-lived, however, as it was soon apparent that military unpreparedness made the operation impractical. On the day before the ARCADIA Conference began, the War Plans Division prepared a set of notes on the general agenda which the British had suggested.[28] The position adopted by the Army planners, while emphasizing the danger to Brazil and the need for direct action to forestall possible German action there, seemed to rule out an African expedition as a way of countering the threat. "Essential air and naval bases in Brazil are in serious danger of Axis sponsored attack. Until the security of the Western Hemisphere has been assured the United States cannot assume the strategic offensive." The only operations currently within the military capabilities of the United States, according to the Army planners, were the defense of Hawaii and the Western Hemisphere, the relief of the British forces in Iceland and reinforcement of the Philippines or the Dutch East Indies, and the possible occupation of "some other base not seriously defended." While acknowledging that the Army's immediate task was to contain Japan, Europe was still considered the principal theater of war and an offensive with the main effort in Western Europe was envisaged when the means to carry it out became available. In the meantime the planners repeated the position adopted in the Victory Program, again recommending a program very much like the "closing the ring" strategy. This included the employment of economic pressure and a sustained air offensive against Germany, raids and minor offensives against Axis controlled areas, propaganda and subversion in the occupied countries (Vichy France and its territories included), the assembly of the necessary forces for an eventual major assault on the Continent, and the capture of positions from which the operation could be launched. The exact nature or approximate time of the offensive or of the operations which would preceed it were not set forth.[29]

In short, the position of the Army planners at the outset of the ARCADIA Conference was as follows: Europe remained the major theater of operations and an offensive against Germany after various preliminary steps had been taken was foreseen. Among such steps might eventually be operations in Africa as part of an effort to secure bases around the periphery of Axis occupied territory. For the present, however, efforts would have to be confined to defending the Western Hemisphere and America's foothold in the western Pacific. Significantly it was conceded that nothing could be done immediately to prevent the Axis "from operating in adequate strength this winter to gain possession of Northwest Africa from Tripoli to Dakar."[30]

There is no evidence that this WPD paper was passed on to the White House. As a result the War Planners' opposition to an African expedition was probably not known to the President. On the contrary it is likely that Roosevelt, aware only of General

Marshall's endorsement of the Victory Program in September (which accepted the desirability of African operations while leaving the timing vague), of the Lovett-Arnold memo of December 18th, and of the Stimson memo of the 20th, concluded that the War Department did not oppose American action in French Africa. As a result, on the eve of the meeting with the British, the Chief of Staff and the Secretary of War, whatever their true feelings, may have left the President with the impression that an African expedition was not beyond the strategic pale. The Army's tacit acceptance of the project left the field clear for the reinforcement of Roosevelt's inclination to take military action in French Africa. During December information and advice from other than Army sources, much of it from Africa itself, was to do just that.

Notwithstanding the removal of the supposedly pro-Allied General Weygand in November, relations between Vichy and Germany remained poor during December 1941.[31] At the same time a small group of American undercover agents was busy in French Africa promoting the Allied cause, undermining Axis collaboration, and in general hopefully preparing the way for a bloodless American occupation. These efforts gave every appearance of being successful.[32]

Directing the cloak and dagger operation in Africa was William (Wild Bill) Donovan. In addition to his espionage activities, Donovan was the collector and correlator of intelligence information derived from his own agency (Office of Coordinator of Information) and other sources. This made him in effect the President's chief advisor on the political situation in Africa, and this, combined with the President's high regard for his ability and judgment, gave him a key role in the development of Roosevelt's attitude toward intervention.[33] During December, information and advice coming to the President from Donovan, while not definitely recommending American intervention, did confirm the long-standing and widespread belief that Germany would act in Africa soon and that the time remaining for American intervention was short. In mid-December Donovan reported that a German seizure of North Africa was a certainty. While not specifying when, he indicated that it would be designed to forestall British or American occupation of the French colonies.[34]

Immediately before the ARCADIA Conference opened in Washington (22 December), Donovan sent the President another report on Africa indicating that the Germans were probably already preparing to move against northwest Africa in a two-pronged assault from Spain and Italy.[35]

On the 21st the President met with Stimson, Navy Secretary Knox, Chief of Naval Operations Admiral Stark, Marshall, Arnold, and Hopkins at the White House for a final briefing. His thoughts were by now firmly fixed on Africa and the opportunity it offered to bring United States forces into the fight against Germany. His understanding of the situation made the President feel that a fully prepared combat force might not be required for the African scheme. Given a British victory in Libya, he believed it quite possible that the French, softened by their supposed good will toward the United States and by the activities of American agents in Africa, might welcome Americans as their liberators, or at least offer no more than token resistance. Once established, the British and Americans could proceed with the gradual buildup of forces and, with the aid of the sympathetic French, ward off any German counterattack.

Marshall, apparently concerned by the cautious WPD report of the 21st,[36] now reminded the President that only enough American troops were currently available to carry out the relief of British forces in Iceland and Northern Ireland and to establish a base in Australia, all of which he thought took precedence over the African expedition. Roosevelt accepted that assessment for the present, and it was agreed that operations against West Africa were to have first priority after forces had been allocated to the other areas. Landings on the Cape Verdes and the Northwestern coast of Africa were also to be given further study while consideration of the Azores would be dropped for the time.[37] It is important to note that General Marshall apparently voiced no opposition to the African expedition other than mentioning the current shortages of men. He thus gave the President the impression that the operation was warranted should the requisite forces become available.

The Conference at the White House on December 21st completed American preparations for the series of meetings with the British scheduled to begin the following day. The President, his interest in Africa long in the making, was now anxious for action. Political preparations both overt and covert were well underway, while the military prerequisite—a British victory in the desert— seemed close at hand. Moreover the American military discussions before ARCADIA left the President with the general impression that operations in Africa were strategically desirable and feasible if current shortages of men and equipment could be overcome.

THREE

ARCADIA: A Crisis for Army Leadership

I

Following his initial shock at the extensive losses inflicted on the fleet, the President was probably gratified that the Japanese attack on Pearl Harbor had at least taken the politically sensitive and perplexing problem of war or peace out of his hands. The issue of how and when the United States might become an active participant in the fight for what the President conceived to be the nation's own security was answered. However, the problem was not entirely solved since the Japanese action and the gratuitous German declaration of war on December 11th failed to arouse the militant warlike spirit that Roosevelt felt necessary for an effective war effort. In the President's view the morale problem remained and even after the United States was officially at war the desire to stimulate public enthusiasm remained a central element in his outlook on military policy.

Before December 7th the President felt constrained in his efforts to aid Great Britain by the reluctance of a great many Americans to see the United States become involved in the European war. Although once the nation was in fact involved few doubted that the country should defend itself, personal commitment to total war was far from complete. Roosevelt recognized that if the war was to be pursued with the vigor and determination required to achieve a speedy absolute victory, more was needed than passive public acceptance of the situation thrust upon it. What was necessary was an attitude which would lead Americans to put forth a maximum effort and enable them to sustain the personal sacrifices they would have to make. Except for a short period following the Japanese attack, such a unified, dedicated, positive attitude toward the war did not exist.

President Roosevelt was extraordinarily interested in public attitudes and was very likely as well informed about them as any political leader. The New Deal encompassed a wide variety and large number of new and controversial measures. Most did not enjoy established interest-group backing, and success for many rested on the support of the general public. To a greater degree than before or since, the New Deal was dependent on sympathetic public attitudes. Roosevelt knew it, and his efforts at shaping them—the famous fireside chats, for example—testify to his concern. Somewhat less is known of his efforts at gauging what attitudes were.

In fact Roosevelt devoted considerable time and energy to assessing public opinion. During his early years and through the election of 1940, he relied on a variety of informal sources from which he derived more or less accurate impressions of public thinking. Information on the public mind and mood came to him in his correspondence and from the impressions he and his close associates, including Mrs. Roosevelt, gathered from their public contacts. During election years these were supplemented by straw votes—ad hoc samplings of public opinion conducted by the Democratic National Committee.

Roosevelt was also keenly interested in the attitudes of the nation's editors and news commentators, and though he complained that the nation's press was hostile toward him, he never succumbed to the temptation to ignore it. Besides his own daily sampling of a number of papers, he received weekly digests of the editorial opinion and news content of several hundred papers, compiled first in the Office of Emergency Management and later in the Office of Government Reports.

Although Roosevelt continued to utilize such techniques to the end of his public service, during the 1940s his methods of gauging public opinion became more scientific and probably more accurate. Basically the shift was a response to the President's growing need to know what the public was thinking and the increased availability of more convenient and reliable methods of discovering it.

By 1941 the overriding national concern was the extent of

The First Offensive

American involvement in the European war, and how Americans felt on that issue determined to a large extent the limits and direction of national policy. The critical importance of the great isolationist–interventionist debate intensified government interest in public attitudes, an interest that coincided with the coming of age of scientific opinion polling techniques. In 1936 a straw poll conducted by the *Literary Digest* predicted that Alfred M. Landon would thwart Roosevelt's bid for reelection. The election results were a stunning defeat for Landon, the *Literary Digest,* and straw polls, but in the process of destroying the credibility of the haphazard questioning of the "man in the street" the election provided a great boost for the recently developed technique of scientific polling. For while *Literary Digest* was misreading Roosevelt's popularity by a grand margin, polls conducted by Gallup, Roper, Crossley, and others using carefully chosen questions and representative samples of the population, correctly predicted the outcome with estimates that missed the actual popular vote by a very few percentage points.[1] During the late 1930s polling techniques were refined and systematized as academics joined public relations experts in developing a sophisticated and increasingly respected professional discipline. As polling results on public issues became an increasingly popular feature in newspapers and magazines, polling intensified. By 1941 politicians and the public had ample resources for judging public opinion.

The availability of poll results came at a propitious time for the President. From 1941 on, the time and energy Roosevelt could devote to informal methods of gauging public attitudes diminished. Increasingly he was obliged to meet and deal with soldiers, diplomats, foreign leaders, and others who could tell him little of what the public was thinking. As his traditional sources dried up, the President found himself deluged by reports and analyses of opinion based on scientific polling. Some he solicited himself. Many were provided directly by pollsters interested in helping to shape national policy. Most came from zealous White House assistants or other Administration figures seeking to keep the President up to date on public responses to policy. The most systematic and regular source of information came from the several information agencies established by the

Administration to help shape public attitudes. The large number of polls in the President's files make it apparent that he was both interested in public attitudes and extraordinarily well informed.[2]

The picture of public opinion drawn by the polls and passed on to the President was a disquieting one. The Japanese attack, it is true, abruptly silenced criticism of the Administration's prewar foreign and military policies and created a patina of unity that contrasted sharply with the bitter divisiveness that had characterized American politics since 1933. However, the dramatic abatement of public criticism reflected no deep-seated alteration of attitudes, and within a short time after December 7th it was clear that the nation was far from unified on the objectives of the war or how it should be fought. Though the majority of Americans supported the war effort, many did so with an attitude of rational resignation rather than with the emotional dedication associated with the militant spirit. The situation was much as it had been before the war when people had supported aid for Britain without identifying with the struggle.

Perhaps even more disturbing to the Administration was the indifference of a large minority to the struggle against Germany. In the weeks following the Japanese attack and the Axis declaration of war, polls found that a "peace bloc" of about 25 percent of the population favored an immediate end to the war with Germany through negotiation, or (for 10 percent) on any terms.[3] Not even the war in the Pacific evinced universal enthusiasm. A poll taken immediately after Pearl Harbor showed that only 59 percent of those polled were willing to fight an all-out war against Japan that included the bombing of Japanese cities.[4] This figure dropped slightly during January and did not rise until after the fall of Singapore in mid-February. Apparently a substantial minority hoped that if the United States limited its war effort its enemies would do the same. A related characteristic of public opinion was a widespread ignorance of American war aims brought to light early in December when more than 45 percent of a polling sample admitted they had no clear idea of what the United States was fighting for.[5]

The likely results of the attitudes indicated by such polls was suggested to the President by at least two members of the Administration during the first month of the war. In mid-December intelligence chief William Donovan wrote the President recommending a surprise attack on units of the French Fleet, which had been immobilized in various French ports, suggesting that such action was desirable not only because it would deprive the Germans of possible future use of the ships, but also "because there will be few opportunities in the coming months for offensive action by us, and such offensive action is necessary both from a morale and strategic standpoint."[6]

Donovan was concerned that strong public support of the war effort would not survive a period of protracted military inactivity. This same point occurred to the deputy director of the Office of Facts and Figures (OFF), Robert Kintner. On the 24th Kintner recommended to his Chief, Archibald MacLeish, that priority be given to consideration of the country's "need for an offensive concept of the war rather than a defensive one."[7] On December 27th, MacLeish, apparently also impressed by the problems implicit in a defensive psychology, recommended that the President initiate a comprehensive propaganda program designed in part to combat the danger. The OFF director suggested that the President utilize his State of the Union address to make the following points: that Hitler was the leader of the united Axis attempt to dominate the world, and Japan and Italy merely carried out his orders; that the world-wide Axis threat had to be met by a global strategy involving hitting the Axis wherever it would hurt most; and finally that the public "must guard against complacency, defeatism, and the enemies' efforts to divide us."[8]

In line with Kintner's recommendation, the Committee on War Information, the coordinating body for Administration propaganda,[9] took up the problem of the nation's defensive attitude at a December 29th meeting. The OFF representative warned the Committee members that their major task was to persuade "the country that it cannot fight an America First war —that it must fight a full-out offensive war" hitting the enemy wherever he is most vulnerable "even at the cost of injury to its own cities and its own citizens." The major and peculiar difficulty involved in undertaking this task, according to OFF, was that "it is not easy to create a risk-taking, daring, offensive spirit without offensive *action.*" The Agency's representative warned that the emotional upsurge produced by Pearl Harbor was wearing thin and that national unity would be threatened unless something was done quickly. Speed was especially important since February was ordinarily a low morale month. He noted that American forces were not in a position to take the offensive action needed and that a propaganda campaign would have to be substituted to "convince the American people that the United States cannot *win* a defensive war . . . [but] that it *can* win an offensive war if we throw into it everything we have." OFF warned that in the absence of offensive action or such a program, war production would suffer and national unity would be sorely tested.

The proposal received the Committee's approval[10] and the White House permitted MacLeish to go ahead with his plans. However, Roosevelt never gave him the direct support and cooperation upon which the prestige and hence the effectiveness of his efforts depended. The President apparently preferred to pursue the goal of a unified, European oriented, offensive-minded public opinion in his own way, apart from the efforts the propaganda agencies might make. Ultimately his own way would involve action, not just "public relations."

Another aspect of public opinion which concerned the President was that what public enthusiasm for the war did exist was focused on Japan—not on Germany. This situation was of special importance since Roosevelt and his military advisors had decided that in the event of war against Japan and Germany, the Allies should first concentrate on the defeat of Germany. The Germans were far stronger than the Japanese and any delay in ending the European war, it was felt, might mean the elimination of Russia or Britain or both, leaving the United States the almost impossible task of defeating the European Axis alone. Finally, it was believed that the Japanese could be held at bay with a relatively small commitment of men and material and then disposed of at leisure after Italy and Germany had been dealt with.

Immediately following the Japanese attack the President concluded that the public "would insist that we make the war in the Pacific at least equally important with the war against Hitler."[11]

The First Offensive

As a result he decided to make the "Hitler first" idea the theme of his first wartime broadcast to the public. In a "fireside chat" delivered on 9 December, two days before the German declaration of war, Roosevelt declared:

> Germany and Japan are conducting their military and naval operations in accordance with a joint plan. We must realize for example that Japanese successes against the United States in the Pacific are helpful to German operations in Libya; that any German success against the Caucasus is inevitably an assistance to Japanese [in] . . . the Dutch East Indies; *that a German attack against Algiers or Morocco opens the way to a German attack against South America, and the Canal* [italics added].
> Remember always that Germany and Italy, regardless of any formal declaration of war, considered themselves at war with the United States at the moment [of the Japanese attack]. . . .[12]

Despite the President's effort the Pacific-first attitude continued to enjoy great popularity. The disposition of many people to disregard the Administration's view and concentrate their hate on Japan was reflected in the polls. Opinion sampling conducted in late December revealed that almost one third of the American people felt that Japan, not Germany, was the nation's number one enemy.[13] As Secretary of War Stimson later remarked (to Churchill a year after United States involvement): "The enemy whom the American people really hated, if they hated anyone, was Japan which had dealt them a foul blow."[14] This natural inclination to focus on Japan was intensified during the first months after Pearl Harbor by news media coverage of the war. Press and radio war reporting were dominated during this period by Japanese exploits and by exaggerated stories of the heroic American struggle in the Philippines. The war in Europe naturally assumed secondary importance, with coverage centering almost exclusively on the Russian front. The fact was, of course, that the American military contribution to the war against Germany was, until November 1942, hardly greater than it had been before the Japanese attack. Before ARCADIA and increasingly thereafter, sufficient evidence was at hand for Roosevelt to conclude that a potentially serious deficiency in the public's attitude toward the war was developing. It was to become an important factor in the position he adopted at the first wartime strategy conference and indeed in all his thinking on military policy during the first year of the war.

II

Fifteen days after the Pearl Harbor attack, with the first flush of public militancy already fading, the ARCADIA meetings began in Washington. The President, aware of the unsatisfactory direction of American war thinking, was probably especially keen that the conference produce a scheme for immediate American action in the European theater. This disposition lent itself perfectly to the Prime Minister's objectives because a major reason that Churchill sought the meeting was his hope of securing an American commitment to an immediate expedition to North Africa. On 11 December the Prime Minister had cabled the President that he was "anxious to discuss offering Vichy a cursing or a blessing following a British victory in Libya"; and during his passage to America he wrote to South African Prime Minister Jan Smuts telling him of his hopes of obtaining Roosevelt's "assistance in a forward policy in French North Africa and in West Africa." Although Churchill thought that American participation in an African expedition had the President's support, he was afraid that Roosevelt might be diverted from the operation by his naval advisors and the American public, both of which he felt could be expected to exert pressure for a Pacific-first strategy.[15] Churchill apparently intended to counter such influences by stimulating the President's interest in an African expedition. The Prime Minister also hoped to head off a possible American decision to commit munitions production to the rapid creation of a "vast United States Army of 10 millions" which, for at least two years while it was training, would deprive Britain of needed supplies and "stand idle defending the American continent." The best way to insure the proper use of both forces and munitions as they became available, he thought, was to enable the Americans to regain their naval power in the Pacific "and not . . . discourage them from the precise secondary overseas operations which they may perhaps contemplate."[16]

53

The First Offensive

The Prime Minister reasoned that a piecemeal commitment of United States resources would avoid the unwanted massive American buildup. Operations in French Africa clearly suited Churchill's purposes.

The Prime Minister and his party arrived in Washington on December 22nd. That night they would meet their new allies for the first of a series of conferences which were to continue through mid-January. The British position at ARCADIA was based on a set of documents produced by the Prime Minister during the eight day voyage to the United States. In them, he outlined the future course of the war as he thought "it should be steered." The final defeat of Hitler would quickly follow Allied landings at several points on the European continent, assisted by revolts among the "captive peoples." The invasion, Churchill felt, could be undertaken in 1943, by which time he expected Germany to be reduced to a state of near collapse by blockade and air attack. Germany's weakened condition would mean her final overthrow could be accomplished by relatively small numbers of Allied troops. The war should end, he thought, by late 1943 or early 1944.

North Africa bulked large in Churchill's plans for the immediate future. In preparing for the final assault on Europe, the Prime Minister hoped the Allies would direct their efforts toward completing the ring of bases around the periphery of German-dominated Europe by filling in the remaining gaps—Turkey and Northwest Africa. The Turks presented a political problem which Churchill expected would be readily resolved through diplomacy once there were distinct indications of eventual Allied victory. Filling the North African "gap" would be accomplished by an Anglo-American expedition (for a time called Super-GYMNAST, later just GYMNAST), which would be the main offensive effort in the West in 1942. Churchill hoped the operation would benefit from the aid, or at least the passivity, of the French in Africa: "The German setback in Russia,[17] the British successes in Libya[18] . . . above all the declarations of war exchanged between Germany and the United States, must strongly affect the mind of France and the French Empire. Now is the time to offer to Vichy and to French North Africa a blessing or a cursing."

Britain, Churchill declared, should hold forces in readiness to take advantage of anticipated favorable developments in French Africa. In addition he intended to ask the United States to contribute a force of at least 150,000 men which could be brought into North Africa through Casablanca and other Atlantic ports. However, before undertaking the North African operation, Churchill also wanted the United States to send the equivalent of three inexperienced infantry and one armored division to Northern Ireland. Their presence there, he felt, would deter the Germans from any future attempt to invade the British Isles, enabling the British to increase the size of the combat-ready forces participating in the African expedition.

The object of GYMNAST 5, according to Churchill, was to secure the whole of the North African shore, including the Atlantic ports of Morocco, before the Germans were able to move. Once established the Anglo-American forces, properly supported in the air and with the aid of the French, would make it difficult and costly for the Germans to seize the area. Favoring the operation, Churchill thought, was the vulnerability of the enemy's communications across the Mediterranean which could be more easily interdicted than the Allied supply lines across the Atlantic. Although Churchill expected that the French could be persuaded to throw in their lot with the Allies, his plans did not depend on French cooperation and he did not rule out "the possibility of a half-hearted association of the defeatist elements in France and North Africa with Germany." Although such a development would make the task more difficult, he believed the operation could still be successful. The capture of Dakar, he thought, might be undertaken in a second stage of the operation, but in any event the seizure of all of French Africa was to be accomplished before the end of 1942. The Prime Minister was optimistic. The only prerequisite to his plan was the successful completion of General Auchinleck's offensive across Libya, and that seemed assured.[19]

While the Prime Minister was composing his outline, the British Chiefs drew up their own strategic appraisal. More conservative than Churchill, the Chiefs produced what the official British historian has called a "sombre list of defensive commitments, actual or prospective . . . which did not leave much margin for offensive operations, apart from those, such as the occupation of the Canary Islands or Madagascar, which were directly dependent on expected moves by the enemy."[20]

After considerable discussion a compromise paper for AR-CADIA was finally worked out between Churchill and the Chiefs which, reflecting the caution of the military, removed the North African operation from the important position it had in the Prime Minister's appraisal. The essential features of grand strategy reflected in the final paper were: the realization of armaments production goals; the maintenance of essential communications; closing and tightening the ring around Germany; wearing down and undermining German resistance by bombardment, blockade, subversion and propaganda; the development of plans and preparations for eventual offensive action against Germany; and the defense of vital interests in the Pacific. The capture of Northwest Africa was viewed as part of the effort to "close the ring," but the special emphasis on that operation found in Churchill's proposal was absent. Large scale land offensives against Germany, except on the Russian front, were declared unlikely during 1942, although the possibility of a return to the Continent in 1943 as a prelude to the final assault on Germany itself was mentioned. The British professionals apparently failed to attach as much significance to committing the United States to immediate military action in the European theater as did the Prime Minister.[21]

Notwithstanding the British military's attitude toward the African project, the Prime Minister on meeting Roosevelt on the evening of December 22nd gave the President his own strong views on the opportunities offered there. Thus from the outset the meetings were dominated by Churchill, who overshadowed his own military representatives[22] and quickly established a direct and close rapport with the President. According to Churchill's account, the conferees, who significantly did not include military representatives of either side, agreed that although Hitler would probably not act immediately, a German move into North Africa through the Iberian peninsula was still quite likely in the near future, and that something should be done to forestall it.

Since the attitude of the French was held to be an important factor, a variety of suggestions as to how they could be induced to cooperate were broached. It was agreed, however, that in any event the Allies should be prepared to go into North Africa even without an invitation. The President, according to Churchill, "was anxious that American land forces should give their support as quickly as possible" and favored the idea of planning for an invasion "with or without invitation."[23] The two men agreed that the United States should proceed with the relief of British troops in Northern Ireland; neither thought that the operation need interfere with the African expedition. Finally, they acknowledged that the availability of adequate shipping, along with the success of the Libyan campaign, were the major prerequisites of the project. The possibility and desirability of a combined Anglo-American attack having thus been decided at the top political level, GYMNAST was turned over for study and recommendations to the Combined Chiefs of Staff[24] (the name applied to the American and British Chiefs of Staff when acting as a single body).

At the first full scale meeting of the ARCADIA conference the following day (23 December), the Prime Minister once again expressed his anxious interest in the GYMNAST scheme and, despite his preconference agreement with his military chiefs, succeeded in focussing the discussion on the operation. He noted that matters in North Africa were quickly coming to a head since, as the British pressed toward the Tunisian border, the Germans were increasingly likely to demand that the French give them the use of the port of Tunis to bring in reinforcements for their retreating army. In the face of such a demand it was possible that the French might ask for Allied military intervention. Churchill said he thought that would be the moment for American and British troops to land on the coast of Northwest Africa to join the French in resisting German designs. He therefore suggested that the subject be given serious study by the military. The Prime Minister now spoke, however, of an *invited* occupation and did not mention the desirability of carrying out the operation without assurances of French cooperation, as he had suggested to the President the day before. His omission may be

57

accounted for by the presence of the military, a factor which seems to have made both Churchill and Roosevelt cautious in their statements.

The presence of the military at this meeting probably also accounted for Roosevelt's now appearing more interested in West Africa than in North Africa. Cognizant of the importance which Stimson and Marshall attached to the security of the trans-African supply line to the Far East and probably anxious to gain their support, Roosevelt spoke of the threat which a German seizure of Dakar would pose to that important route.[25] Nevertheless, in response to Churchill's observations concerning Northwest Africa, the President agreed that planning for GYMNAST should be pursued, adding that once the North African landings had been accomplished Dakar might be taken from the rear using French colonial troops.[26]

The President had no difficulty in accommodating his position on African operations to the interests of the military, since the exact site of American action mattered less to him than the action itself. Obviously concerned by signs of a developing "phony war" atmosphere in the United States, Roosevelt hoped to stop the trend by providing military activity to stimulate public interest and enthusiasm. Thus he explained his attraction to the African expedition by telling the meeting that he felt it "very important to morale to give this country a feeling that they [sic] are in the war, to give the Germans the reverse effect, to have American troops somewhere in active fighting across the Atlantic."[27] Roosevelt thus expressed for the first time a requirement he was to stress repeatedly in the months ahead, one that was to have an important effect on Allied strategy making. The President followed up his declaration by suggesting that the Army should ready an expeditionary force for use in "Africa or elsewhere"; the "elsewhere" emphasizing that action, not Africa, was his principal concern.

The contrast between the views of Roosevelt and Churchill at this meeting provides insight into the President's thinking on African operations and on strategy in general. For important military reasons, the Prime Minister was interested more in North and Northwest Africa—the area encompassing Morocco, Algeria, and Tunisia—than he was in West Africa. Operations in the north could be undertaken in direct concert with the British offensive in Libya which was already underway. If successful, they would clear the Axis from the southern coast of the Mediterranean, thus securing British communications to the Middle and Far East, setting the stage for bringing Turkey in and knocking Italy out of the war, thus closing a large gap in the ring around German-occupied territory. The occupation of Dakar (over 1,200 miles south of Casablanca) was a distinctly separate undertaking which would have little effect on operations in North Africa. Moreover, the seizure of the northern coast of Africa would seriously interfere with a German move against West Africa. Thus for Churchill the capture of Dakar, despite its advantages, was clearly of secondary significance.

Roosevelt's approach to the African issue was quite different. The President had no grand design for the war and his outlook was more political than strategic. For him the operation itself was the objective. If it resulted in strategic gains so much the better, but the President's primary consideration appears to have been successful action to demonstrate to the American public, to the nation's allies and enemies, and to the neutral states that the United States was fully committed to the war against Germany. French Africa was available; it presented a comparatively safe opportunity—so far the only one—for engaging the Germans. Given the President's optimistic temper it is likely that he anticipated a bloodless occupation followed by French cooperation against the Axis reaction. The result would be American action against Germany in circumstances favorable to an Allied victory.

To Roosevelt, the very different strategic considerations involved in operations in North Africa as opposed to an expedition to West Africa (Dakar and environs) were of little significance. What was important was obtaining a maximum basis for agreement on immediate offensive operations between the British and his own military advisors. The President's efforts to link GYMNAST with operations against Dakar probably reflected this desire. He apparently hoped that by picturing the occupation of North Africa as a prelude to the capture of Dakar he could demonstrate to General Marshall GYMNAST's contribution to the security of the trans-African air route and thus secure his support for Churchill's project. Given the President's approach, the meeting of the 22nd understandably witnessed no consideration of the relative military merits of the Northwest versus the West African operations. Roosevelt and Churchill simply made clear their desire for American action and the meeting concluded with an agreement that the various African proposals would be studied.

Neither GYMNAST nor the operations against West Africa generated much enthusiasm among the military planners. The negative attitude of the British military so clearly demonstrated on the voyage to America was probably expressed by Chief of the Imperial General Staff (CIGS), General Alan Brooke, who had remained in London during the conference. Brooke was worried by the Prime Minister's interest in Africa, coming as it did at a time when the Japanese were making unexpected progress in Southeast Asia. The CIGS felt that the defense of Singapore, Burma, and communications through the Indian Ocean were second in priority only to the security of the British Isles themselves, and that the "shipping available does not admit of both occupying North Africa at [the] request of [the] French, and reinforcing [the] Far East."[28]

The American General Staff, including in all probability General Marshall, had even greater objections to the scheme. Opposition had been expressed within the War Plans Division for some time and seemed to increase with the growing strength of American forces. The planners opposed operations in North Africa on almost every conceivable ground. According to their pessimistic picture, supplies for an American expedition would have to be brought by ship across the submarine infested Atlantic and landed at the small port of Casablanca. From there they would have to travel by inadequate facilities eastward over a route through Morocco and Algeria exposed to enemy attack (especially from the air) based, in all probability, in Spanish Morocco. The planners also felt that the inadequacy of the Moroccan ports put the Allies at a disadvantage in the race with Germany for a buildup of forces in North Africa. They also agreed with General Brooke that the shipping needed to carry troops and supplies to Africa would seriously curtail the reinforcement of Allied forces in the Far East and eliminate all other major operations in the Atlantic for the three months following a positive decision on GYMNAST. Other objections were that even if successful the operation would not be a decisive blow against Germany; that French collaboration was uncertain and regardless of any assurances received could not be relied upon; and that the maximum number of men the Allies would be able to use in the operation was hardly a minimum to insure success.[29]

Opposition to the African operation among the Army planners was most forcefully articulated by Major General Stanley Embick. A member of the Supreme War Council during World War I, Embick had been called back to Army service from retirement in February 1941. Since that time he had been a strategy advisor to General Marshall, a longtime friend. Possibly because of his experiences in dealing with the politics of coalition warfare in the First World War, Embick (representing a substantial faction within the War Department) was jealous of the Army's prerogatives and suspicious of and hostile to the supposed influence which the British exerted on the formation of American military policy.[30] On 16 December, writing of the current military situation, Embick declared that it was essential for the Allies to "avoid any and all commitments that will dissipate our present limited resources without assurances of adequate return; that each [Ally] accept as the first essential the security of the home citadel, and . . . proceed at maximum speed to the development of the war machine which the potential of the nation permits."[31]

GYMNAST was the kind of dispersion of strength which Embick wanted the United States to avoid. He thought that the British proposals were "motivated more largely by political than by sound strategic purposes," and he rejected the idea that control of North Africa would restore Allied communications through the Mediterranean or that it would provide an advantageous area from which to invade the Continent. Embick pointed out that once involved in Africa the Allies would be hard pressed to sustain their forces across long and exposed lines of communication. Moreover, the expedition would be greatly jeopardized should the Germans decide to make a major effort to dislodge it. Embick discounted the value of the British offensive in Libya and declared that a "commitment in North West Africa at this time would prove to be a mistake of the first magnitude." He therefore recommended that all offensive plans for Africa be abandoned and that the British revert to the strategic defensive in the Middle East with the object of denying the Germans access to the Indian Ocean and a junction with the Japanese.[32] Although General Marshall in all probability shared Embick's views, he did not say as much directly to the President. He apparently relied instead on the anticipated difficulties in carrying out the operation to convince the President of GYMNAST's impracticality, some of which was quickly apparent as a result of the Anglo-American staff work.

A major part of the study of GYMNAST undertaken by the Anglo-American Joint Planning Staff as a result of the decision of the 23rd involved determining the logistical requirements of the proposed operation. The Joint Planning Staff concluded that the shipping required to transport an initial force of three American divisions together with air and service units would preclude any other major troop movement in the Atlantic for at least three months and would seriously curtail troop movements from Great Britain to the Far East.[33] Plans for replacing British forces in Northern Ireland and Iceland with American troops would also be a casualty of the GYMNAST shipping squeeze.

These conclusions had the gravest consequences for Allied strategic planning. The relief of British forces had been agreed upon at the ABC and was the major American military commitment in the Atlantic theater. Indeed, the Iceland operation was already underway. As for Northern Ireland, the British thought that stationing American troops there would contribute greatly to the defense of Great Britain and therefore gave the undertaking the highest priority.[34] Moreover, Churchill in his pre-ARCADIA strategy paper (which he gave to Roosevelt on the 23rd) had assumed that some of the British troops released by the American occupation of Northern Ireland could be used in North Africa. As a result he had warmly welcomed the President's confirmation of the American commitment on the opening day of the conference, especially since he thought that it would not conflict with the dispatch of an American force for North Africa.[35]

On the 26th the Combined Chiefs briefed Roosevelt and

Churchill on the results of their studies. Their reports indicated that although they had reached agreement on a general plan of operation, the details had yet to be worked out. General Marshall pointed out that a major obstacle to the completion of planning was uncertainty over how large an expedition would be necessary to convince the French that they were confronted by an irresistible force and hence that discretion dictated a speedy capitulation. This, Marshall declared, was a political problem which would have to be solved by the President and the Prime Minister.

Roosevelt apparently believed that current American espionage activities in French Africa would permit the virtually unopposed landing of a small Allied force. He anticipated that arrangements for an unopposed landing might be completed at any time within the next three months. He therefore wanted troop movements to Northern Ireland and Iceland to go ahead as previously scheduled, with the proviso that their shipping allotment might be diverted for use in GYMNAST as soon as an expedition appeared opportune. Although the President wanted forces available to exploit any break in the political situation in French Africa immediately, he did not at the meeting of the 26th insist that they be kept from other operations for the purpose.

Churchill for his part wished the movements to Northern Ireland, Iceland, and Africa to go ahead simultaneously, declaring that "he would be frightfully unhappy if he had to adjust" between GYMNAST and other projects. The Prime Minister found it difficult to accept the pessimistic predictions of the Combined Planners as to the shipping required for the African expedition, observing that if two million American men could be transported to Europe in five months during 1918 there should be no difficulty in shipping 250,000 men to Africa in a three month period in 1942. The President agreed.[36]

Despite discussions of the critical situation in the Far East at the meetings, both men apparently overlooked the huge numbers of ships required to form an effective defensive perimeter in the Western Pacific. While a round trip between the eastern United States and England took about two months, because of the greater distances and poorer port facilities in the Far East shipments to that region tied up cargo vessels for about twice that time. The situation was made worse by the additional shipping required to transport the construction material required to expand the ports of Australia and the Pacific Islands.[37]

Failing to recognize the serious shipping drain, Roosevelt rejected the limitations on Allied strategy contained in the planners' report. While he agreed that the reinforcement of Northern Ireland and Iceland was more urgent than the African expedition, the prospect of seizing the initiative against Germany through GYMNAST made him reluctant to abandon the African project. Encouraged by the Prime Minister, the President seems to have felt that the logistical objections posited by the Combined Chiefs were in large part a product of the military's natural conservatism. The President agreed with Churchill that a determined effort could meet the material requirements of both the African project and of the Allies' other commitments. His experiences in meeting the Depression crisis and as Assistant Secretary of the Navy in World War I convinced him that professional subordinates often underestimated what might be accomplished in a given situation.

In a sense the President may have been correct in concluding that a powerful will to proceed with GYMNAST would mitigate the material objections raised by the military. The estimate of GYMNAST shipping requirements was based on moving a force large enough to make the success of the operation virtually certain. The force strength in turn reflected a reluctance to accept a high risk to carry out an operation that Army planners considered to be of dubious merit anyway.[38] Given the Chief of Staff's lack of commitment and the widespread and strong opposition to GYMNAST within the War Department, it is safe to conclude that Marshall and his planners made no determined effort to overcome the difficulties involved in seeing the African project through to fruition.[39]

The President, besides minimizing the difficulties which General Marshall emphasized, was willing to undertake the risk of the African operation because it offered the opportunity of confronting the German forces on relatively favorable terms. During the crucial stage of the operation, the landings, only French forces could resist since no German troops were currently in

French Africa. Moreover, even that resistance, which was expected to be light, might be avoided if political arrangements worked out as planned. The result would be that the Germans would be engaged only after the Allies were established in Africa, and, it was hoped, had obtained French assistance. Once so established they would confront the Germans with a two front war, the Afrika Korps sandwiched between the Allies based in Egypt and at Dakar or Casablanca. Whatever the weakness of the Allied position under these circumstances, the likelihood of the American force suffering a total disaster was remote. French Africa offered the opportunity to initiate the American military action against Germany that Roosevelt hoped would keep enthusiasm for the war high and direct it, as far as possible, against Germany rather than Japan.

His concern for public opinion was in itself a powerful stimulus to the President's desire for military action. But other influences pointed in the same direction. By far the strongest of these was the Prime Minister, who took advantage of his prolonged stay in America and his personal, daily contact with Roosevelt to press the case for American participation in GYMNAST. According to his personal physician, Lord Moran, Churchill was "possessed with one idea to the exclusion of all others. He feels he must bring the President into the war with his heart set on victory."[40] The Prime Minister felt that American involvement in GYMNAST would firmly attach the President to a forward-looking policy in Europe, much as the President felt the same operation would arouse and rally American public opinion in favor of an aggressive all-out war against Hitler. As a consequence, the Prime Minister in his talks with Roosevelt conducted himself, according to Moran, with uncharacteristic "restraint" and self-discipline, apparently content to listen as Roosevelt spoke. Moreover, when the Prime Minister did speak it was "always something likely to fall pleasantly on the President's ear."[41]

A week of this assiduous cultivation by the Prime Minister had helped make the President so anxious to seize the opportunity for action in Africa that he seriously considered launching the operation without prior assurance of French neutrality. On December 27th he received a memo from William Donovan indicating that immediate American action would be required to forestall an imminent German move on North Africa.[42] On the following day Roosevelt asked Marshall if it would be feasible for American forces to land at Casablanca under fire, that is, without the certainty of French passivity. The Chief of Staff, obviously disturbed by the proposal, responded by calling it "extremely hazardous," pointing out that a reversal would be especially bad because of its "very detrimental effect on the morale of the American people."[43] Marshall's response was singularly appropriate given the President's preoccupation with morale, but the task of overcoming the latter's disposition to take immediate action in French Africa was by now formidable.

Though this exchange between the President and the Chief of Staff produced no direct result, it must have been obvious to Marshall and his associates that the President was moving rapidly toward a decision in favor of GYMNAST—probably without reference to his professional military advisors. Nevertheless, in spite of strong opposition to African operations within the War Department and his own misgivings, Marshall made no effort to resist the President's growing interest in the project, except (as above) to indicate that an opposed landing would be "extremely hazardous." In fact at his next meeting with the President, the Chief of Staff seems to have given the scheme his outright endorsement, at least in principle.

In the late afternoon of New Year's Day 1942, the President met with Marshall, Stark, and Arnold to discuss a message he had recently received from William Bullitt in the Middle East. Bullitt and Oliver Lyttleton, British Minister of State in the Middle East, had induced General Georges Catroux, the Commander of the Free French Forces there, to draw up a plan for an Allied occupation of North Africa.[44] The Bullitt-Lyttleton telegram recommended the reinforcement of the British forces in the Middle East and the immediate initiation of preparations, including propaganda and subversion, looking toward Allied landings at Casablanca and in Tunisia. The President, after reading the message to the military chiefs, suggested they consider the proposal immediately, before the British were scheduled to return home. At the close of the meeting at Marshall's instance the chiefs agreed to begin planning at once for operations and troop movements both to North Africa and Iceland.[45]

Marshall's apparent acquiescence in Roosevelt's rush toward action in Africa probably reflected his inability to decide finally on the merits of the operation, and his reluctance to oppose the President's wishes without an alternative to offer. In any event his neutral stance on the issue did not reflect the attitude of his principal War Department subordinates. Discussions on the 2nd and 3rd among Marshall and several top Army planners, including General Joseph Stilwell, who was responsible for African planning, found them unanimous in their opposition and unhappy at their inability to redirect the President's thinking. Their frustration was apparent when the Army planners and Marshall approached Secretary of War Stimson only to find that while agreeing with their opposition to GYMNAST, he felt unable to take the issue up with the President because he found it "very hard to always say 'no,' " suggesting that it would be easier if "there were only some alternative."[46]

Whatever the objections to GYMNAST within the Department, General Marshall was apparently still not totally opposed to the project. This was evident at a meeting he held on January 4th with Arnold, Gerow, Stimson, Knox, and Stark. Even though the obstacles to the success of GYMNAST were discussed in great detail, "everyone" (Stimson's description) conceded the strategic soundness of the operation and the discussion therefore centered on overcoming the anticipated difficulties. The conferees seemed to assume, perhaps just for the sake of discussion, that the question of shipping would be solved. The major problem discussed, therefore, was maintaining Allied air supremacy over and off the coast of Morocco, at least during the initial stages of the operation. General Arnold was confident that it could be done, and General Marshall reported that British Air Chief Marshal Sir Charles Portal, the head of the Royal Air Forces, shared his optimism. Moreover, Admiral Ernest King, Commander in Chief United States Fleet, had reluctantly agreed to supply the expedition with aircraft carriers to provide the early air cover. Marshall, arguing at this meeting for the first time in favor of GYMNAST, declared that if the Allies did not act, the Germans might seize North Africa and that dislodging them once they were established would be much more difficult than forestalling their move. He thought that some risk should be accepted so that the United States might get into North Africa first.

Summarizing the results of the GYMNAST discussions, General Marshall declared that no firm conclusions could be reached as to the feasibility of the operation because figures on the shipping required and on hand were not yet available. Shipping needs, of course, depended upon the size of the force committed, which in turn was at least partially determined by the unknown factor of the amount of resistance likely to be encountered. Moreover, the Chief of Staff felt that more information was needed on the terrain, landing fields, ports and communications in North Africa before proper planning could be completed. Marshall hoped that Donovan's intelligence operation would be able to supply the answers. Until then, however, he found it hard to predict the project's chances of success.[47] Thus, while Marshall seems to have accepted the desirability of GYMNAST, he withheld his full approval until convinced that circumstances made a successful outcome virtually certain.

At the end of the meeting the American military leaders went to the White House for discussions with the President, the Prime Minister, and the British Chiefs. There Secretary Stimson was asked to brief the meeting on the American military's attitude toward GYMNAST. Reflecting some of the hostility to the plan in the War Department,[48] the Secretary fretted over the political situation in French Africa and stressed the difficulties involved in establishing air supremacy and in assembling adequate shipping for the operation. In response the President acknowledged that the attitude of the French and Spanish was still in doubt. However, he challenged the asserted lack of shipping, refusing in particular to accept an estimate of two weeks to unload ships at Casablanca. He suggested that an order to accomplish the task in half the time would have the desired effect. Although the chief Navy planner, Admiral Richmond Kelly Turner, stuck to his estimate, the President appeared unconvinced.

In spite of his stubborn optimism the President was not prepared to make a final decision in favor of GYMNAST at the January 4th meeting. He preferred instead to keep the operation under study, apparently hoping that events would clarify the risks involved: "We must be ready . . . we have to be prepared for any eventuality—things may remain quiet for the next couple of months or the theatre of operations may turn in our direction at any time." Roosevelt was not inclined to gamble on "our first major expedition being a failure," declaring that "if the risk looks great, we must think twice before we go ahead." In the meantime the President wanted the relief of the British garrisons in Iceland and Northern Ireland to proceed as quickly as possible. General Marshall summarized the inconclusive results of the meeting by observing that while everyone agreed on the strategic importance of the expedition, a number of points involving its feasibility still required study and clarification.[49]

Even as the President discussed the uncertain elements in the GYMNAST puzzle, an entirely new and unexpected threat to the operation was developing. The success of CRUSADER, General Auchinleck's offensive in the western desert, had from the first been considered a necessary preliminary to the landings in Morocco. The original GYMNAST proposal assumed that the approach of British forces to French African territory would encourage a friendly French reception of the Anglo-American expedition and moreover that unless the British were able to take Tripoli and Tunis, the Axis would be able to use those ports for resupply and reinforcements, thus seriously threatening the success of any Allied expedition.

Little had been said about CRUSADER at early ARCADIA meetings because during December the British campaign seemed to be progressing well. By the first week of the new year, however, there were indications that Auchinleck's offensive was in difficulty. For even though the British continued to advance, they seemed unable to come to grips with and destroy Rommel's forces. Therefore, as the Axis units fell back along their supply lines, their strength relative to that of their pursuers increased and their resistance stiffened. The situation was reported to Washington on the first of January by the American Ambassador in Cairo, Alexander Kirk. The Ambassador recommended that American air and tank units be sent to assist the British.[50] Kirk's warning was confirmed on the 9th and 10th of January when Churchill received telegrams from General Auchinleck indicating that the bulk of seven-and-a-half Axis divisions had eluded a British trap. The Prime Minister also learned that an enemy convoy had managed to get past the British blockade and reach Tripoli with supplies for Rommel's army. As a result prospects for a speedy conclusion of the campaign were greatly diminished, and indeed even eventual victory seemed in doubt.[51]

Even while these disappointing events were taking place in the desert, news from another quarter contributed further to the destruction of the President's hopes for GYMNAST. Allied strategy agreed upon midway in the ARCADIA meetings had called for the maintenance of a defensive line running through Malaya, Sumatra, Java and North Australia, with operations as far forward of this line as possible to oppose the Japanese southward advance. The United States was also to continue its efforts to defend the Philippines.[52]

Substantial numbers of men and large amounts of equipment were required if these tasks were to be accomplished. The long Pacific distances, however, made providing reinforcements difficult and slow, and the effort absorbed large amounts of shipping for long periods of time. Nevertheless, the situation was critical and if the forces already committed to the area were to be saved and the bases for the eventual offensive against Japan retained, shipping would have to be found.

The diversion of ships assigned to other projects appeared to be the only answer, and during ARCADIA the need for reinforcing the Far Eastern garrisons loomed as a threat not only to GYMNAST but to the higher priority MAGNET (American replacement of British troops in Northern Ireland). On January 11th General Eisenhower noted that responsible officials in Washington had suddenly realized that the situation in the Far East was critical. "Now we've all got to find some way to rush troops there—but [the] political situation won't let us give up MAGNET!!!"[53] That same day the Chief of Naval Operations, Admiral Stark, raised the question of shipping for the Far East with the Combined Chiefs, who referred the problem to Allied shipping experts. They in turn found that by delaying the scheduled movement of troops to Iceland and Ireland, and the sailing date of the African expedition, the needed shipping for the southwest Pacific could be found.[54]

Thus by mid-January GYMNAST was seriously threatened by Allied military problems in both the Middle East and the Pacific.

CRUSADER seemed to be losing momentum and the requisite decisive British victory in Libya was uncertain. In the Pacific the swift and widespread success of the Japanese pointed toward the need for a maximum Allied effort to preserve a foothold in the area, an effort possible only at the expense of the various Atlantic enterprises and especially of GYMNAST. This was the gloomy picture as ARCADIA drew to a close.

On January 12th the President and the Prime Minister met again with the Combined Chiefs. Churchill opened the conference by announcing that Auchinleck's arrival in Tripoli would apparently be long delayed. This news, while disappointing for all, made it somewhat easier for the American Chiefs to press their request for a reallocation of shipping from the Atlantic to the Pacific. However, the Combined Planners also noted that the Pacific move would force a reduction of the shipping available for Iceland, Ireland, and the supply of the Soviet Union.

The President felt obliged to accept the adjustment as it applied to the GYMNAST, MAGNET, and Iceland operations, but he resisted cutting back on shipments to Russia, indicating that there might be "unfortunate repercussions in Russia if at the very time they are pinched we let them down." Continued Russian resistance was central to Allied prospects for victory. Moreover, Roosevelt hoped that Stalin could eventually be persuaded to participate in the war against Japan.[55] In these circumstances the President felt that the supply commitment to the Soviets had to be fulfilled, and so assigned Harry Hopkins and Britain's Minister of Supply, Lord Beaverbrook, the task of turning up the additional six ships needed for the purpose. Despite the new shipping demands of the war in the Pacific and the maintenance of aid to Russia, the President still hoped that the African expedition might yet be realized. The Pacific reinforcements and the ships for Russia, he learned, would delay the loading date for GYMNAST only until mid-April, and on that basis he approved the plans for the reallocation of shipping.[56]

The timetable for GYMNAST was settled at a final top-level conference held on January 14th. It was agreed that if the North African political situation remained unchanged the operation would be carried out in May. The President noted, however, that if the Germans should attempt to move against the French colonies before then, the Allies would have to repond with whatever forces were then available. The Prime Minister agreed. They also acknowledged that the political softening up of the area remained an important preliminary to an Allied invasion attempt,[57] and Roosevelt assured the meeting that efforts to encourage and organize opposition to a possible German occupation of French Africa and to obtain the cooperation of the French and the Moroccan natives were well underway.

The agreement of the 14th was almost immediately made meaningless by the course of events. For in mid-January, after a short pause in the war in the Middle East while both sides prepared for the next round, the Germans had taken the offensive. By January 25th Rommel had captured Msus and with it the supplies the British had been accumulating for their push, destroying British chances of an early victory and with it one of the prerequisites to GYMNAST.

Almost simultaneously, Allied plans suffered another serious setback. At the end of December the President had decided to sound out General Weygand on his willingness to secretly return to North Africa to prepare for and assist an Allied invasion. H. Freeman Matthews, a career diplomat attached to the Embassy in Vichy, was designated to carry out the mission and on 28 December the President briefed Matthews on his assignment and gave him a personal note to deliver to Weygand. The President's scheme was to be conveyed to the General verbally.[58] On January 20th Roosevelt supplemented these messages, which had not yet been delivered, by asking Ambassador Leahy to tell Marshal Petain that the United States would regard French assistance to Germany in Africa as hostile and that conversely any resistance to Axis demands would be looked upon favorably and would have "the physical support of the United States by every possible military and naval assistance we could bring to bear." Leahy was also to point out that the President was France's "best friend" and that his friendship would be of great value in her postwar efforts to recover her colonial empire.[59] On the day that this "cursing or blessing" was cabled to Vichy, the American Embassy finally succeeded in delivering the President's December 27th message to Weygand.[60]

On 25 January the President learned that the approach to

Weygand and Petain had fallen flat. Weygand had refused to associate himself with the proposal that he assume command of the pro-Allied French in Africa.[61] Moreover, the General had told his American contact he felt obliged to inform Petain of the American overture.[62] Two days later Leahy reported he found Petain unimpressed by the bribe implicit in Roosevelt's message of the 20th. The French head of state assured the Ambassador there was no chance that the French Fleet would be surrendered or that the Germans would be granted bases in North Africa. Nor was it likely, he said, that the Germans intended to invade Africa in the near future. However, the Marshal made it clear that his Government would "resist invasion by British, Gaullists, Germans or Americans" and would accept military aid from the United States only if he asked for it. As a result of this interview Leahy concluded that "America cannot expect any cooperation whatever by Vichy in an effort to exclude the Axis from French Africa when and if Germany were to move in that direction."[63] Taken together, the defeat in the desert and the uncooperative French attitude made it certain that it would be some time before an Anglo-American expedition would be in a position to go to North Africa.[64]

III

The forced abandonment of GYMNAST meant that ARCADIA produced no firm plans for future operations. The principle of "Hitler first" was affirmed, unity of Allied command established through a formal Combined Chiefs of Staff organization, and primary strategic responsibilities for the various theaters and defense arrangements for the Far East were agreed upon. However, a number of factors prevented the meeting from producing a decision on the site and timing of the first Anglo-American offensive. Allied offensive capacity was severely limited by inadequacies in shipping, trained manpower, and material. The Allies were further hampered by a number of defensive obligations which had to be met before they could undertake offensive operations.

Nevertheless the meeting was a triumph for Churchill. He had

73

lived at the White House on terms of the greatest intimacy with the President, lunching with him every day usually alone or with only Hopkins present. He had attended a meeting of the Cabinet and addressed a joint session of Congress. He had found America resolved to settle finally with Japan. But, as he told his War Cabinet on returning to England, he believed any thoughts there might have been of an all-out war in the Pacific were now gone. Gone too was the possibility that the Americans might leave large numbers of troops standing idle in the United States or that equipment might be hoarded for some eventual massive expedition. The President was convinced of the benefits of the peripheral strategy and of the importance of North Africa. Even though Roosevelt's advisors had expressed some misgivings, their attitude at this stage was not one to provoke British concern; and any discordant notes that may have reached Churchill's ears during his Washington sojourn were certainly erased by the President's last words to him: "Trust me to the bitter end."[65]

General Marshall and the Army leadership's view of the Conference was considerably less sanguine. In a sense Marshall had reason to be pleased with the results of the meetings since general command arrangements had been settled satisfactorily with the British, and he had avoided commitment to any immediate offensive undertakings. Nevertheless, the meetings left Marshall and his staff with a good deal to be unhappy about. For though circumstances had ruled GYMNAST out for the time being, Marshall's ambivalent and confused stance during the discussions had resulted in ratification of the peripheral strategy sponsored by the British, and the likelihood that the African expedition would be revived.

This is apparent in the Anglo-American memorandum summarizing the strategy decisions reached at the Conference. As outlined there, the essential features of Allied grand strategy were: a) the realization of Allied munitions production goals, b) the maintenance of essential communications, c) closing and tightening the ring around Germany—defined as running along the line: Archangel, Black Sea, Anatolia, the northern seaboard to the Mediterranean and the western seaboard of Europe, d) wearing down and undermining German resistance by air bombardment, blockade, subversive activities, and propaganda, e) the development of offensive action against Germany, and finally f) the maintenance of "only" those positions in the Pacific theater of vital strategic importance. The memo clearly indicates that the only offensive actions contemplated by the Allies during the next several months were those aimed at "gaining possession of the whole North African coast." As for action on the Continent, the memorandum declared: "It does not seem likely that in 1942 any large scale land offensive against Germany except on the Russian front will be possible" barring some severe erosion of German ability to resist. Perhaps the most startling aspect of the document, given the heated opposition later expressed by Americans to the "British Mediterranean strategy," is the Combined Chiefs' assertion that "in 1943 the way may be clear for a return to the Continent, across the Mediterranean, from Turkey into the Balkans, or by landings in Western Europe."[66] Thus the memorandum summarizing Allied strategy at the end of ARCADIA is very little different from the position paper adopted by the British at the outset.

The meetings, coming so soon after Pearl Harbor, found Marshall somewhat unprepared for America's new status as a full partner in the war. His thoughts tended to focus on the defensive aspects of the American position. Obviously the Japanese advance had to be contained and South America made secure. But apart from those preoccupations and the general proposition that the defeat of Germany must eventually be given priority over the war in the Pacific, Marshall at ARCADIA seems to have had no precise idea of how to conduct the war. Although he favored amassing a huge well-trained and equipped expeditionary force capable of a massive invasion of the European continent in 1943, he felt obliged to support immediate action to protect vital Allied positions and to secure bases from which the final assault might be launched. He apparently had not considered either the exact nature of such interim operations nor the political effect of relative military inactivity. Marshall's caution and confusion led him to accept the British proposals in spite of serious misgivings within the War Department which he probably shared.

Marshall's acquiescence to the British lead at ARCADIA came at a time when there was already considerable opposition among

Army planners to the peripheral strategy in general and to GYM-NAST in particular. The opposition made rapid progress during the meetings so that by the end of January it encompassed Marshall, pushing him off his neutral perch and firmly into the anti-GYMNAST camp. Churchill's plan and his obvious influence on the President alarmed and irritated American Army leaders. Marshall, Stimson, and the planners were generally suspicious and hostile toward Churchill's military views. They found them in turn excessively bold, attributing this to his childish enthusiasm, or overly cautious, reflecting British military weakness and lack of success. Moreover, some aspects of Churchill's recommendations (his apparent preoccupation with Singapore and Suez, for examples) seemed to suggest that British imperial designs lay behind his strategic thinking.

The Army leaders' shift from ambivalence to dogmatic opposition to GYMNAST was largely a manifestation of their reaction to Churchill's domination of the ARCADIA meetings. His supposed strong and insidious influence on the President, and the apparent further reduction of Marshall's already diminished power to affect the direction of United States and Allied strategy, made it obvious, first to members of his staff and then to Marshall himself, that the Army's future role in making military policy depended on offering the President a clear cut alternative to the British proposals.

The fact that the Prime Minister was able to influence the President on military policy challenged the competence of the Staff and was a blow to the pride and position of the Army command. It was recognized that a continuation of the current trend in high level strategy making was likely to lead to unsound military operations and would undermine the morale of the Staff and jeopardize Marshall's effectiveness both as Army leader and as chief military advisor to the President. General Marshall was conscious of the threat to his leadership and made some effort even during the meetings to minimize British influence at the White House. Thus on the issue of establishing the administrative machinery for the combined Anglo-American direction of the war, Marshall, although personally well disposed toward British Field Marshal Sir John Dill, strongly rejected a British proposal that Dill become permanent military representative of the Prime Minister in Washington with direct access to the President.[67]

The impact of ARCADIA on War Department thinking is also reflected in the contemporary comments of some of the officers involved in GYMNAST planning. General Joseph Stilwell, called to Washington in January to take charge of African planning, had quickly found himself switched back and forth between a West African operation (BLACK) and the Northwest African proposal (GYMNAST). Stilwell, who was privy to most of the high level deliberations although not in attendance at all the conferences, was impressed by the confusion and ineffectiveness which characterized the American role at ARCADIA. In explaining the situation in his diary (20 December), Stilwell placed the blame in large part on the President, calling him a "rank amateur in all military matters . . . apt to act on sudden impulses." Stilwell recalled the spring 1941 episode when the President ordered the Army to prepare for an invasion of the Azores in a month's time and then abruptly changed his mind. "The same thing is happening now," he lamented. "We'll do this, we'll do the other, blow hot, blow cold. And the Limeys have his [Roosevelt's] ear, while we have the hind tit. Events are crowding us into ill-advised and ill-considered projects." The Army's problem, according to "Vinegar Joe," was that it had no basic strategic study in existence with which to meet the pressure for immediate action:

> . . . shall we now go to work and prepare seriously for war, and not undertake any offensive till we can do it properly, or shall we attempt to take the offensive? We should prepare till we can pour it on irresistibly, but that does not appear to be the answer. There is tremendous pressure to do something. The Limeys want us in with both feet. So the answer is, we must do something now, with our hastily made plans and our half trained and half equipped troops.[68]

General Eisenhower, deputy to the Chief of WPD, was also displeased with the situation he found in Washington. Having been ordered to devise plans for the reinforcement of American forces in the Southwest Pacific, his views tended at this stage at least to focus on the effects of the planning confusion on the situation in that area: "I've been insisting that the Far East is critical—and no other side shows should be undertaken until air and ground are in [a] satisfactory state. Instead we're taking on MAGNET, GYMNAST, etc."[69]

In mid-January the dangers involved in the confused plans emanating from the high level ARCADIA conferences prompted the officer assigned to the preparation of American combat forces, Lt. General Lesley J. McNair (Chief of Staff, General Headquarters),[70] to seek an American alternative to GYMNAST in order to eliminate what he conceived to be the ineffectual bleeding away of Army strength in pursuit of British sponsored projects. On the 13th McNair asked Stilwell to draft a paper giving "65 reasons why we should not do GYMNAST," and another outlining "an alternative that we can do, within a reasonable time, [or] at least start on."[71] Two days later McNair forwarded Stilwell's reply to General Marshall and urged the Chief of Staff to "abandon GYMNAST completely, and to embark on the substitute plan [for the occupation of Dakar] at the earliest possible date entirely independently of Great Britain." All other activity in the European theater, including North Africa, McNair said, should be abandoned. This included the occupations of Iceland and Northern Ireland and the reinforcement of the British in the Middle East. McNair's all-American landing at Dakar was apparently designed to take the planning initiative away from Britain by undertaking an offensive "in our own way, our own theater, with the greatest possible forces and at the earliest practicable time."[72]

Although McNair and Stilwell may have been extreme in their hostility toward the British, their concern for American independence of British direction and their plea for an assertion of American military policy manifested a growing belief within the General Staff that the Army must take the initiative in formulating strategy. Unless it was done soon Army leaders risked a serious loss of influence in making coalition policy, and an Allied strategy which they opposed.

The end of the ARCADIA conference left many General Staff members restive and frustrated. Though the battle for strategic direction of the war had not been decided, the Army's prospects looked bleak. General Eisenhower, confessing his own battle fatigue, was coming to the realization that the solution lay in an Army sponsored plan for an offensive against Germany which could be initiated in the near future.

> The struggle to secure the adoption by all concerned of a common concept of strategical objectives is wearing me down. Everybody is too much engaged with small things of his own—or with some vague idea of large political activity to realize what we are doing —rather *not* doing.

Realizing that recent Japanese gains made offensive operations in the Pacific impossible for some time to come, Eisenhower now abandoned the all-out aid to that theater he had previously espoused.

> We've got to go to Europe and fight—and we've got to quit wasting resources all over the world and still worse—wasting time. If we're to keep Russia in, save the Middle East, India and Burma, we've got to begin slugging with air at West Europe, to be followed by a land attack as soon *as possible.*[73]

A few days later Eisenhower, after noting that his position on a European invasion had support within the War Plans Division, declared that although the project was going to be "one hell of a job" it was still to be preferred to "sitting on our fannies giving out stuff in driblets all over the world—with no theater getting enough."[74] Lt. Colonel Willard Wyman of the General Staff carried these views a step further when, after discussing the problem with Eisenhower, he wrote him that "the most critical battle of the war will be fought in Washington" over who will achieve leadership of the war effort. Wyman thought that the conflict was between American and British leadership, with the latter apparently at present enjoying the President's support.[75]

The negative reaction of General Marshall and the Army planners to the President's tendency to follow the Prime Minister's lead in military questions was natural enough. Conditioned by education and experience to pride, self-confidence, and patriotism, they were understandably disturbed at being denied the exercise of their professional competence by foreigners. Moreover, the American military leaders felt that Presidential support of British strategy would waste Allied resources and unnecessarily prolong the war, while (in some instances) serving what they conceived to be narrowly British rather than Allied objectives.

Churchill's influence at the White House derived, as Marshall eventually came to realize, from the fact that the Prime Minister offered the kind of military policy that Roosevelt sought but which the Army seemed unable to supply. Roosevelt wanted American troops engaged in the European theater immediately to provide tangible evidence that the United States intended to carry the fight to its enemies. But the advice he received from the Chief of Staff up through ARCADIA was cautious, defensive, and oriented toward action in the indefinite future rather than here and now.

The need was for the General Staff to produce a plan for immediate offensive operations which could compete with Churchill's scheme and win over the President. In the weeks after ARCADIA such a plan was devised, and in the process the ambiguities in Army thinking were resolved. Concentration of force for the attack, much discussed and used in the small scale field exercises of the lean interwar years, was soon applied by Marshall and his staff for the first time to the problems of Grand Strategy.

FOUR

Mounting Pressure for Action:
The Problem of Morale
and Unity, January–March 1942

I

The postponement of GYMNAST left the United States without a plan for immediate offensive operations against Germany. It was a serious problem for the President since in the weeks after ARCADIA the need for such action, at least in his view, substantially increased. There were unmistakable indications that, as he suspected, the American public did not overwhelmingly or wholeheartedly support the vigorous prosecution of the war against Germany. Apathy was not the only problem in regard to public opinion facing the President in the late winter of 1941–42, for by the end of February public dissatisfaction over continuous defeats in the Pacific and the apparent inability of the United States to retaliate had also provoked serious criticism of the Administration, of Roosevelt's direction of the war, and of the principle of Hitler first.

Both morale and criticism were closely related to the course of the war. The picture was mixed. The war against Germany during February was relatively quiescent and hopeful. It was true that the British drive in the Libyan desert had been halted and Rommel was again on the offensive, but in Russia the Red Army had come back from the edge of defeat to gain significant victories in front of Moscow. In the Battle of the Atlantic, although the Allies continued to lose substantial tonnage to German U-boats, the rate of loss was somewhat less than in the previous June and well under what it would soon become.

In the Pacific the story was quite different.[1] There action continued furiously and the outlook for the Allies was grim and becoming increasingly desperate. At the beginning of January the Allies had resolved to attempt to defend the Malay Barrier, a geographic expression defined as the line: Malay Peninsula, Sumatra, Java, and North Australia.[2] Since the Philippines lay to the north of the proposed Allied defensive line, their loss was not expected to seriously undermine efforts to stem the Japanese advance. However, while accepting the probability of eventual defeat in the Philippines, the American military chiefs with Presidential approval had decided to make every effort to assist General MacArthur's forces in the islands.

Events in the Pacific, however, did not conform to Allied expectations. Though American forces in the Philippines were able to prolong their losing battle, the Malay Barrier was rapidly breached. On 27 January, after a totally unsuccessful campaign, British forces in Malaya retreated into Singapore. By 10 February the Japanese had secured control of the Macassar Straits and the northern shore of the Java Sea. On the 15th Singapore fell and within the week General Wavell, now in command of United Nations forces in the Southwest Pacific, informed the Combined Chiefs that there was no longer any chance of holding Java. An unbroken succession of Japanese victories followed, completing the destruction of the Allied position. The loss was formally acknowledged with the dissolution of General Wavell's command on 25 February. It had lasted less than eight weeks.

The one exception to the general debacle was the defense of the Philippines. Although efforts to reinforce its garrison were almost totally in vain General MacArthur and his successor, General Jonathan Wainwright, continued to resist the Japanese advance and the islands' defenders did not finally capitulate until early May.

The uninterrupted series of Allied defeats in the Pacific, the clearly hopeless protracted defense of the Philippines, and the relative inactivity in the European theater helped widen the split between the public and the Administration concerning the conduct of the war. Especially important was the swelling ranks of "Asia-firsters," who formed the core of Roosevelt's critics.[3]

As the American public watched the Japanese advance in the Far East, its frustration and anxiety mounted. Beginning early in January the nation's editors expressed concern over the deteriorating military situation in the Far East, but continued to support the "indivisible war—Hitler first" strategic outlook. By the end of the month, however, their commitment to the Administration position had weakened badly. Strongly internationalist supporters of the President's leadership now joined the anti-Roosevelt Hearst–Patterson–McCormick syndicates in demanding immediate action in the Pacific.[4]

The growth of "Pacific first" sentiment was demonstrated by the strong public reaction to press conference remarks by Navy Secretary Frank Knox. Responding to what he thought was inadequate public enthusiasm for the war against Hitler, the outspoken former publisher addressed the theme that Germany, not Japan, was the major enemy and must therefore be defeated first. The conquest of Germany, Knox said, would mean the end of the Axis.[5] The Administration had done little to prepare the public for the idea and the speech backfired. Instead of arousing support for the European war it provided the occasion for an attack on the President's military policies. The nature of much of the public's response is suggested by a *Time* magazine article which linked the Secretary's remarks to the declaration by Roosevelt and Churchill at the close of the ARCADIA Conference that they had reached complete understanding on the policy needed to win the war. What was this understanding, *Time* wanted to know—"Was this some kind of private war, Winston Churchill and Franklin Roosevelt against Adolph Hitler? Was such a decision indicated by Navy Secretary Knox's sounding off that Hitler was the No. 1 enemy?" "That," *Time* declared, "would be a shock to U.S. civilians who had picked the Japanese as their enemy. . . ."[6] The Office of Facts and Figures (OFF) noted that almost all the newspaper comments on Knox's statement had been unfavorable; the nation's press declaring in effect that the rapid defeat of Japan was at least as important as the effort against Germany. A number of papers went so far as to assert that Germany's defeat would not necessarily mean the collapse of Japan, and to call for the concentration of United States military effort in the Pacific.[7]

At the end of January, OFF reported that continued Japanese advances, Chinese and Australian demands for aid, and the continued resistance of General MacArthur in the Philippines had produced "almost complete agreement in the press that the Far East was at least the most urgent, if not the most important sector of the war today," and widespread support for the view that the United States should devote its efforts and resources to retrieving the situation in the Pacific.[8] A sizeable minority of the American public had long been Pacific-firsters, but by the beginning of April those Americans who expressed an opinion favored concentrating on Japan rather than Germany by a margin of three to one. Sixty-two percent believed that regardless of which enemy posed the greater ultimate threat, Japan had to be dealt with before the European Axis.[9] The public's preoccupation with the Pacific almost inevitably led to some signs of dissatisfaction with the Administration's handling of the war.

By the end of January the superficial unity produced by Pearl Harbor was lost in an increasing barrage of press attacks on the Administration's handling of the war in the Pacific. An OFF survey of news media found that the frequent praise for General MacArthur voiced in the press was coupled with a "growing tendency to blame unspecified authorities in Washington for his plight."[10] In succeeding weeks the nation's editors, "depressed by the military outlook" and "frustrated because we are unable to come to decisive grips with the enemy," lashed out at "Government as usual," i.e. " 'social reforms, boondoggles and bureaucracy. . . .' "[11] OFF also noted a loss of confidence in national leadership and demands for "new and younger blood in posts of authority."[12] Strong criticism was directed against the Administration's information and civilian defense efforts, its management of production, and its handling of organized labor. Though the most vehement attacks came from the sizeable "divisionist" press, "a good deal of impatience and irritation toward the Administration" was apparent among commentators who were fundamentally friendly to Roosevelt.[13]

Although defeat in the Pacific had provoked considerable controversy, Americans seemed slow to respond appropriately to the war in general and "complacency" became a major press topic. Publicists generally agreed that Americans were not sufficiently concerned and consequently were not wholeheartedly supporting the war effort. Many blamed government. By February public apathy toward the war, interrupted only briefly by

Pearl Harbor, had become a national issue.[14]

Various public figures commented on the situation. Senator Francis Maloney (Democrat, Connecticut) felt that in too many instances Americans had apparently concluded that the war was won and that no danger or difficulty lay ahead. Senator David I. Walsh (Democrat, Massachusetts) characterized America's attitude as "smug." Hugh Johnson, onetime head of the National Recovery Administration, remarked that the public did not seem "to give a tinker's dam" about the war. The Executive Director of the Office of Civilian Defense declared that his organization's major problem was that "people have not awakened to the fact that the United States is at war." Radio reporter Edward R. Murrow and columnist Walter Lippmann were also disturbed by popular apathy, agreeing that it probably stemmed from the individual citizen's feeling of remoteness from the actual fighting.[15] Arthur Krock, in assessing the reasons for the lack of a spirit of urgency among the population, attributed it to the distance of the war from American shores. In addition he blamed unwarranted confidence in ultimate victory fostered by MacArthur's protracted resistance, by recent Russian advances, and by over-optimistic statements on the part of some government officials. Krock also cited "continued coddling of labor and industry," which together with the continuation of some New Deal projects suggested to people that the war situation could not be very serious.[16] The discussion of complacency was sufficiently widespread that Elmo Roper, the prominent public opinion analyst, wrote to MacLeish suggesting that the "publicity" might well contribute to a further lowering of morale. Roper thought it time for someone in authority to say that morale was not as bad as it had been made out, lest more Americans become so discouraged by what they heard and read that they too join the ranks of the apathetic.[17] The President himself finally commented on the situation. Asked for his views on the widespread talk of public complacency at a press conference on February 10th, Roosevelt agreed that the charge was largely true, but noted that he thought the problem was diminishing as the public gradually achieved a better understanding of grand strategy.[18]

On 15 February the garrison at Singapore surrendered, beginning what *Time* called the "worst week of the century"[19] for the United States. In response, the President on the 22nd broadcast a "fireside chat" to the nation. Rejecting the possibility of a cautious, defensive or "painless" war, and castigating those who under the illusion of isolationism "wanted the American eagle to imitate the tactics of the ostrich," Roosevelt reaffirmed the nation's determination to "keep on striking our enemies wherever and whenever we can meet them." The President made it clear that although retreats had been made, the ground lost would be regained: "We are daily increasing our strength. Soon, we and not our enemies will have the offensive; we, not they, will win the final battles; and we, not they, will make the final peace."[20]

This speech marked a significant new trend in public opinion. From mid-February through the summer of 1942 public apathy, while not wholly disappearing, seems to have given way in large part to the hope and expectation that an all-out American military effort would bring a quick and decisive victory. The OFF Intelligence Bureau noted that the President's fireside talk had "miraculously restored calm confidence to jangled editorial nerves." Significantly, it was his assurance that the United States would soon seize the initiative which "produced the greatest interest and hopefulness."[21]

Roosevelt's promise of immediate military action quickly gained widespread and intense public support. It was as if a strategy for easy victory had suddenly been revealed. "Offensive action now" had an obvious appeal to a nation stunned and discouraged by nearly three months of continuous retreat, and angered by the seeming inability of the United States to hit back. The idea gained increasing public expression from a variety of sources until by the end of March it dominated popular thinking on the war.

Russian pressure for an immediate "second front" contributed significantly to the growing offensive-mindedness. Five days after Roosevelt's radio address Ambassador Maxim Litvinov, addressing the Overseas Press Club, spoke of the need for each member of the anti-Hitler coalition to bear his fair share of the fighting. The Ambassador declared that merely a material and defensive contribution by the western powers might not be sufficient to defeat the Axis: "It may be of little value to have large, well equipped armies, say, somewhere in the West, if they are not in action while decisive battles are raging in the East. [Only] simultaneous offensive operations on two or more fronts separated by long distances," Litvinov emphasized, could bring about the destruction of Hitler's forces. The initiation of a "second or third front," he concluded, could result in the defeat of Germany in 1942.[22]

America's military chiefs soon added their public support to the demand for offensive action. On March 2nd, Senator Warren Austin, Republican of Vermont, read the Senate a letter sent him by General Marshall warning of the danger of responding to enemy victories by adopting a defensive spirit. "The time has now come," General Marshall wrote, "when we must proceed with the business of carrying the war to the enemy. . . ."[23] Ten days later, Admiral King, at a press conference marking his appointment as Chief of Naval Operations, echoed Marshall's sentiments. King made it clear that he would soon have an answer to the frequent query about the inactivity of the Fleet.[24]

The depressing news from the various battle fronts ever since Pearl Harbor almost guaranteed an enthusiastic press response to indications that an offensive might be in the offing. In mid-March OFF reported that the nation's news media now conveyed an awareness of the gravity of the military situation; accompanying it was "a strident demand for action. . . . The commentators know only that they want desperately to hit back at the enemy." Everyone, it seemed, wanted to tell the Administration where the armed forces should be deployed, but the only real consensus that emerged from the discussion was that the time for action was "this minute."[25] The *New York Times*, for example, welcomed indications of the Administration's intention to take the war to the enemy, declaring that "defense doesn't end wars any more than appeasement prevents them. Attack is not only suited to our temperament, it is also the lifesparing road to a vigorous peace."[26]

While the press's preoccupation with offensive action might eventually shape public opinion, for the time it appeared not to have reflected any important change in popular attitudes toward the war. Offensive-mindedness was more emotional than rational, and much of the growing aggressiveness was directed primarily against Japan. Moreover, notwithstanding the considerable support for offensive action voiced by the press and official spokesmen, there were indications that a defensive psychology was still strongly rooted in public attitudes. Thus a poll conducted in mid-March revealed that only 56 percent of the sampling favored sending American armed forces abroad.[27]

The President attributed the failure of the public to rally solidly behind him largely to the divisive views spread by consistent opponents of his administration. At the beginning of March 1942 an old friend, Russell Leffingwell, wrote Roosevelt urging him to do something to rouse the public from its apathy and passivity. The President replied with an unusual long personal exposition of his views on morale. He admitted that the public did seem apathetic, but added optimistically that there were signs the condition was diminishing. He went on to say that behind the nation's "morale problems" were the prewar isolationists, who were continuing their efforts to confuse the public and harass the Administration. Some members of that group, Roosevelt declared, were:

> publishers like Bertie McCormick and the Pattersons and the Roy Howard papers. The hearts of these people are not in unity and some of them still want a negotiated peace. Some of them are columnists or radio commentators who are actuated by the same motives. Some are politically minded and seek election gains. Some of them are anti-racial and anti-religious like the K.K.K. crowd and some are extreme nationalists like some of the wild Irish.

> The best comment I have heard was by Elmver Davis . . . [who] said 'some people want the United States to win so long as England loses. Some want the United States to win so long as Russia loses, and some people want the United States to win so long as Roosevelt loses.

In response to Leffingwell's plea for presidential initiative in redirecting public opinion, Roosevelt answered that he wished to avoid too much personal leadership. Support of Administration military policy, he thought, should grow slowly; the "nation has only been at war a short time" and time and possibly events would ultimately provide the remedy.[28]

The day after Roosevelt wrote to Leffingwell, he again had occasion to comment on the public's response to the war. At a press conference on the 17th, he was asked about the possible need for legislation to curb strikes in defense industries. Still reluctant to ask sacrifices of labor, Roosevelt replied that production could best be maintained and increased through improved morale. A law could hold a man on the job but could not make him work; what was really needed was greater enthusiasm for war work, which Roosevelt thought might be stimulated by "more bands . . . [and] parades."[29] This observation reveals the President's continuing belief that voluntary public support was the necessary basis of an effective war program.

The potential significance of "divisionist" sentiment was suggested in a mid-April report by Alan Barth of OFF. Barth noted that if a movement for an immediate negotiated settlement really got going, it could count on the firm support of about eight million people, and the sympathy of eight or nine million more.[30] Other "divisionist" attitudes, according to OFF, were 1) a desire to abandon Great Britain and Russia and limit the war effort to continental defense against Japan, 2) indictments of the President for "communist-oriented" New Deal Administration and philosophy, 3) the hope that the war might be converted into a crusade against Communism, 4) hostility toward organized labor, and 5) anti-Semitism. OFF noted that many holding such views were "underprivileged, uneducated, and youthful," and derived their negative attitudes from despair and discontent. The immediate problem, the report concluded, was to prevent "the Divisionist core from infecting other portions of the population."[31]

Roosevelt was aware of the public attitudes reflected in the polls and public discussion of the first three months of 1942. A single course of action readily suggested itself as an omnibus solution to the problems they indicated—American troops in combat against Germany as soon as possible, certainly before the end of 1942.

Before turning from the domestic political factors militating in favor of an immediate offensive it is necessary to mention briefly one further element of this sort—criticism of the President's ability to direct the war effort effectively. In large measure it was directed at the Administration's efforts on the home front.[32] More serious was the dissatisfaction with current strategy and military leadership. Many editors were critical of the military's failure to answer Axis aggressiveness with counter-offensive action. The result was, according to a report provided Roosevelt in late March, that ". . . the President is in danger of losing an essential part of the warm confidence with which most American newspapers have supported his conduct of the war. For there is an uneasy belief that he is fumbling." This attitude, the report emphasized, was not confined to his enemies.[33] While not attacking the President directly, some critics suggested that the job of Commander-in-Chief required a professional military man responsible to the President but with authority to direct and coordinate all United States military planning and operations. At the end of January Democratic Representative John J. Cochran of Missouri wrote the President sounding him out on a move underway in Congress to reform the General Staff.[34] Roosevelt interpreted this as an attempt to create an overall military Commander-in-Chief and, citing the experience of the Civil War, flatly rejected the idea.[35] In mid-February Wendell Willkie, Roosevelt's rival for the Presidency in 1940, commenting on the complexity of modern war, issued a public statement suggesting that General MacArthur be brought home and given "supreme command of our armed forces under the President." *Time* enthusiastically endorsed the scheme, claiming that Willkie's plea was echoed "in the press, in Congress and on the street."[36] In mid-March the President took note of such criticism when he wrote Churchill to commiserate with the Prime Minister over the latter's own political problems. Isolationist elements of the American press, he said, were persistently sniping at the Administration, emphasizing in particular that "I am dreadfully overburdened, or that I am my own strategist, operating without the benefit of military or naval advice."[37]

Demands for a change of some sort in the military command structure, while most vocal outside the Administration, also had support from within. The President's behavior at the ARCADIA Conference, especially his susceptibility to British influence, and the general confusion in the organization of the American high command, led Marshall to support a major alteration in the relationship between the President and the military chiefs. At the end of February, he raised the matter with the President, suggesting that an overall military Commander-in-Chief be appointed with the power to issue orders at once without reference to the President except in matters of broad policy. Marshall recommended former Chief of Naval Operations and current Ambassador to France, William D. Leahy, for the post.[38]

Though the motives of the criticism were questionable in some instances, the manner in which Roosevelt exercised the tremendous powers of Commander-in-Chief were a legitimate source of concern. Authority to decide on every phase of the war effort, from the smallest details of arms design to the grandest issues of strategy, rested entirely with the President. He could exercise the power personally or delegate it to others. All of his subordinates, civilian and military, were responsible only to the President. He in turn was responsible only to the people (at election time). Congress played almost no role in the conduct of the war. Exclusive authority for coordinating the varied tasks of wartime leadership—production, diplomacy, strategy, and the like—rested with the President, and Roosevelt was in fact the only person in the nation who had a complete picture of the mighty endeavor. Yet the application of such massive power depended on an almost haphazard executive structure. Churchill, after witnessing the White House at work, noted, "The President had no adequate link between his will and executive action."[39]

Churchill's wonderment at the American "system" may well be appreciated, for the contrast with the British War Cabinet arrangement is striking. Although Churchill had enormous influence which he exercised in all manner of things, final decisions on major issues rested with the War Cabinet. There, Ministers responsible to Parliament and military chiefs discussed and determined policy and assigned responsibility for its implementation. Moreover, the Government's Ministers, including Churchill, could and on several occasions were obliged to defend their conduct of the war in Parliamentary debate. The shared authority and formal lines of responsibility of their system would seem to have considerable advantage over the more personal administration of Franklin Roosevelt, and it is quite likely that the structure of American wartime leadership laid Roosevelt open to public criticism. Roosevelt was clearly sensitive to the criticism,[40] but he had no intention of giving up any of the duties and prerogatives encompassed under the broadest interpretation of his constitutional role as Commander-in-Chief. In July 1942 continued pressure did lead him to make a gesture toward his critics by appointing Admiral Leahy "Chief of Staff to the Commander-in-Chief." Leahy's assignment, however, was to act as liaison between the President and the Joint Chiefs and not, as Roosevelt made explicit, as the supreme commander of all American forces suggested by Marshall and others.[41]

The lack of unified public support for the Administration's conduct of the war during the first three months of 1942 probably strengthened the President's determination to act quickly against Germany. A successful large-scale engagement with German forces would stimulate enthusiasm for the war and direct public interest toward Europe. That in turn would assure effective and sustained public support for a lengthy conflict. At the same time, successful action would go far toward quieting criticism of the war effort and would also head off any move to diminish the President's role in directing it. The political benefits of these objectives both to Roosevelt and the Democratic Party are too obvious to require elaboration.

These, however, were not the only factors which arose after ARCADIA to contribute to Roosevelt's desire to put American troops into action in Europe in 1942. Relations with and between Britain and Russia also played their part. The President was aware that the perseverance of Churchill and Stalin[42] in the face of military defeat was indispensable to the United Nations' cause. Although his capacity to boost their spirits and stiffen their will was limited, he made the most of every opportunity to do so. The President's task as he saw it was to demonstrate that the United States intended to assume a full share in the active prosecution of the war,[43] and that coalition efforts would eventually be rewarded with total victory. Though the problems affecting American and Allied "morale" were distinct, the solution to both seemed the same—successful offensive action in the West in 1942.

II

The difficulty in maintaining the fighting will of the British and Russians revolved about two related Soviet demands: a "Second Front" and British recognition of the Soviet frontiers of 1941. In early December 1941, British Foreign Secretary Anthony Eden had gone to Moscow in hopes of improving Anglo-Soviet relations. Never good, relations had deteriorated between conclusion of the Russo–German treaty in August 1939 and the German attack on the Soviet Union in June 1941. Even after Hitler's actions had given the two nations a common cause, relations remained strained largely because the Russians believed their new ally was not prosecuting the war with sufficient vigor. Actually the British government, while keenly conscious of the disparity of the military burden the nations bore, was unable to redress the imbalance. The second front, a lodgement of between fifteen and twenty divisions somewhere in the Balkans or France for which Stalin continually pressed, was well beyond British capacity. Moreover, the best British estimates of the strength of German forces on the Continent suggested that even if they could land a considerable force, the Germans could contain and destroy it without drawing on their forces in the East.[44]

The British hoped that Eden's mission to Moscow would produce a treaty of friendship and assistance that would compensate for their inability to provide more direct and immediate assistance. Soon after arriving Eden discovered that the price of securing that objective was significantly higher than he had hoped to pay. Stalin demanded that Britain acknowledge the legitimacy of recent Soviet territorial annexations—the Baltic states of Latvia, Lithuania and Estonia, portions of Finland, and the Rumanian province of Bessarabia. Stalin indicated that unless Great Britain recognized Soviet 1941 boundaries, he would not sign any agreement.[45] Though the British acknowledged that his claims were not without historical justification, Government policy was against making commitments regarding postwar boundary settlements. Any such concession, it was felt, would open the way to a general free-for-all among Poles, Czechs, Greeks, and others concerning their postwar frontiers. Moreover, at the Atlantic Conference Britain had pledged to make no secret agreements which would tie American hands in the postwar settlement.[46] Nevertheless, it was clear that Stalin was making territorial recognition the test of British good will, and so important was it to the British to demonstrate their good faith, that Eden left open the possibility that Britain would accede to the Soviet demands, asking only that his Government be given an opportunity first to discuss the issue with the United States.

Eden returned to England in January to report to the Cabinet on his mission. His presentation strongly favored meeting Stalin's terms. It was of the "utmost importance," he said, that postwar as well as wartime relations with Russia be put on a better basis. The Foreign Secretary therefore recommended that Britain inform the United States that "in the interests of the broader issues of the war and of Anglo-Russian cooperation, we should like to accept M. Stalin's claim to Russia's 1941 frontiers." Strenuous objection was voiced by the head of Britain's Labor Party, Clement Attlee, who served as Lord Privy Seal. Attlee declared that the proposed action was reminiscent of the secret treaty arrangements of the First World War, implying it would have the same disastrous repercussions. It was both wrong and inexpedient. Most of the Cabinet, however, agreed with Eden that the value of improved relations with Russia should be the overriding consideration. It was, therefore, decided to have the British Ambassador in Washington present the President with a balanced statement of the pros and cons of recognition, and an explanation of why the Government felt it necessary to go as far as possible in meeting Stalin's claims.[47]

The ease with which the British retreated from the principle of refusing to discuss territorial adjustments may be attributed in part to the critical situation facing the Government in January and February 1942. The last ten days of January saw a distinct decline in public and Parliamentary confidence in the Prime

Minister, and apparently even a lessening of his confidence in himself. According to Eden the unrelieved series of British defeats in the Far East was "arousing criticism in Parliament and in the country . . . [and] seemed to many to show that the direction of our affairs was at fault."[48] Eden found the Prime Minister tired and depressed by the public reaction to military events and "inclined to be fatalistic" about the political difficulties he faced.

The failure to provide direct military aid to the Soviets was a common subject of dissatisfaction in England, especially among supporters of the Labour Party.[49] As a result, the Prime Minister was under considerable pressure either to establish the "Second Front," a project his military advisors declared impossible, or at least to give tangible evidence that Britain was disposed to make it worthwhile for the Russians to continue the war. The threat of a Russo-German separate peace was everpresent. Under such circumstances, recognition of Soviet territorial claims in Eastern Europe seemed reasonable.

It remained only to convince the United States. President Roosevelt had informed the British before the Eden talks in Moscow that the United States wished to be consulted before any Anglo–Soviet arrangement involving the recognition of disputed frontiers was concluded. The British agreed, and it was to this stipulation that Eden had appealed to justify his refusal to accede to Soviet territorial demands at the Moscow meeting.[50] Impressed by the difficulties experienced by Woodrow Wilson in 1918, Roosevelt believed that wartime political commitments would hamper efforts to secure a realistic peace.[51] The President also felt that discussion of these objectives during the war would bring out latent suspicions and tensions among the Allies, thus tending to divide the nations fighting against Hitler. Finally, Roosevelt had to consider the significant group of voters of Polish, Rumanian, Ukrainian, Lithuanian, Latvian, Estonian, and Finnish descent, as well as anti-Communists in general, who could be expected to oppose the contemplated concessions to Russia. A deal with the Soviets might turn those groups against the war effort, the President, and his party.

Roosevelt indicated his position on wartime political arrangements at a press conference held at the end of February. Questioned about references he had made to the principle of self-government in a speech delivered on the 23rd, the President replied "off the record" that "before we start determining all the details of geography, and of forms of government, and boundaries, and things like that, it [would] be just as well to win the war first, as long as you have principles."[52]

At the beginning of February the State Department, which had been closely following the Anglo–Soviet talks since their inception, produced a long memorandum summarizing the situation and outlining the Department's position on Russian demands. American policy, it declared, was to refuse to recognize any changes in European frontiers made since the outbreak of the Second World War and not to make "any commitments of a territorial nature in Europe which might hamper the proceedings of the post-War Peace Conference. . . ." To do otherwise would, according to the Department, weaken "the association of nations opposed to the Axis which thus far has been based upon the common aim of defeating the enemy." Wartime arrangements would encourage "mutual suspicion and . . . efforts of various members to intrigue in order to obtain commitments with regard to territory at the expense of other members." There was no doubt, according to the Department, that the Soviet Government:

> had tremendous ambitions with regard to Europe and that at some time or other the United States and Great Britain will be forced to state that they cannot agree, at least in advance, to all of its demands. It . . . is preferable to take a firm attitude now rather than . . . later when our position had been weakened by the abandonment of the general principles referred to above.

In transmitting this paper to the President, Secretary of State Hull suggested that Russian demands for signs of good faith would be better satisfied by American assistance than by recognition of Soviet frontiers.[53]

The President was faced with an extremely difficult situation. America's two allies were insisting on concluding a treaty which Hull and probably most other American officials thought was immoral and unwise. Moreover, the conclusion of the proposed pact would inevitably raise considerable public outcry in the United States both from those nationality groups directly affected and from all those Americans who mistrusted England or Russia or hoped that this war would be different from the last. Roosevelt sought to resolve his dilemma by in effect taking over the negotiations concerning the proposed treaty. Responding to the British message on the status of the treaty, Roosevelt told Halifax he was confident he could reach a satisfactory agreement with Stalin. The President believed that Soviet claims were based on their concern for secure frontiers, and he hoped to convince the Russians that their legitimate needs would be cared for at the conclusion of the war—without the need for immediate formal recognition of their frontiers.

The British were distressed by the President's interference in what was essentially an issue between themselves and the Russians. They were also convinced that Roosevelt's hopes of reaching an agreement were vain. Eden believed that for Stalin the issue of the frontiers transcended security considerations and involved "psychological" aspects of relations between Russia and the West. The Soviets, he thought, could never feel truly allied to a government (Great Britain) that refused to "acknowledge its right to recover from the common enemy what they consider to be their own territory." Eden also observed that American appeals to the Atlantic Charter were misplaced since each of the Russian acquisitions in 1940 was accompanied by either a plebiscite or treaty and Stalin in adhering to the Atlantic Charter did so on the assumption that the Charter did not deny the Soviets territories they had already legally acquired.[54] In spite of British doubts, of which the President was informed, Roosevelt was determined to pursue his own method of settling the issue. Time was short.

The Prime Minister's continued difficulties during February made it seem certain that the Churchill Government would soon feel obliged to agree to the Soviet demands, regardless of American wishes. On February 22nd, Donovan informed the President that his sources in London reported that "the British public was profoundly disturbed and angry over recent British military failures." Their reactions, he said, ranged from depression to defeatism as a result of what was being called the blackest week since Dunkirk. There was also, Donovan reported, a widespread tendency to criticize both the Government and the Prime Minister.[55] Churchill's troubles were exacerbated by an Order of the Day issued by Stalin on 23 February at the close of the Russian winter counteroffensive. Stalin's pronouncement indicated to the Foreign Office that Soviet war aims went no further than the liberation of Russian territory, and thus suggested that Russia might be seeking a separate peace with Germany.[56]

On the 4th and 5th of March the President received cables from Churchill in which the Prime Minister confessed his grave misgivings about the military outlook and asked American help to retrieve the situation. The second (5 March) asked that two United States divisions be sent to Australia and New Zealand to bolster the defenses of those nations so that they might feel free to keep their forces in the Middle East. The depth of Churchill's depression at this time was apparent:

> When I reflect how I have longed and prayed for the entry of the United States into the war, I find it difficult to realize how gravely our British affairs have deteriorated by what has happened since December 7. We have suffered the greatest disaster in our history at Singapore, and other misfortunes will come thick and fast upon us. . . . It is not easy to assign limits to the Japanese aggression. All can be retrieved in 1943 and 1944, but meanwhile there are very hard forfeits to pay.

Churchill also expressed concern over the situation in Russia: "The whole of the Levant–Caspian front now depends entirely upon the success of the Russian armies. The attack which the Germans will deliver upon Russia in the spring will, I fear, be most formidable." It was clear from his message that irrespective of United States objections Churchill did not feel able to antagonize the Soviets by denying their frontier claims.[57]

The Prime Minister's difficulties were a serious challenge to Roosevelt's determination to maintain the unity and effectiveness of the anti-Hitler coalition. Stimson reports he found the President obviously upset by Churchill's "gloomy and depressing cable" of the 5th.[58] His concern undoubtedly made him especially anxious to strengthen his bargaining position with the

Russians in his efforts to turn them away from their insistence on a frontiers treaty. By coincidence the Army produced just such a scheme. But before turning to the White House meeting of 5 March, during which Churchill's requests and the Army's proposal were deliberated, it is necessary to trace the development of American military thought in the weeks preceding the meeting.

FIVE

The Marshall Memorandum:
An Army Alternative
February–March 1942

I

By the end of January 1942, defeat on the battle fronts and disarray in Allied planning and strategy-making had created considerable discontent in the War Department. Stimson, Marshall, and the war planners, unhappy over the apparent aimlessness and indecisiveness of current Allied policy, tended to blame the failure of the Allies to concentrate on a single course of action. They attributed the failure to the peripheral strategy, which many of them felt the British used to rationalize the protection of their interests in the Middle East and elsewhere. The most troublesome aspect of the British approach was that it had apparently captured the support of the President, and hence determined American as well as British activities. Stimson, Marshall, and their colleagues felt the need to seize the planning initiative by devising an acceptable alternative to the British strategic scheme. During February, added impetus was given to the quest by the threat of further dispersal of American military strength posed by the plans of the Chief of Naval Operations, Admiral Ernest King.

On 18 February, with Allied forces in retreat throughout the Pacific theater, Admiral King proposed to General Marshall that the Army provide ground and air forces to garrison a number of small islands in the South Pacific. King wanted the islands fortified to protect the supply line to Australia and to serve as bases for a future offensive against the Japanese.[1] General Marshall, seeing that the initially modest request might eventually result in a full scale army commitment to offensive operations in the Pacific, objected to the scheme as implying a negation of the basic Allied strategy of "Hitler first." General Eisenhower probably expressed the attitude of the General Staff toward the King suggestion when he wrote that it appeared the Navy wanted the Army to occupy and defend "all the islands in the Pacific" so that it would have "a safe place to sail."[2] Later he commented that it looked as if the fear aroused by the Japanese advances was going "to pull us too strongly to the Australian area." The fall of Singapore and the Malay Barrier meant that the effort to sustain the proposed advanced defensive line had to be abandoned. Eisenhower felt that the resources allocated to that project should now be turned to the support of Russia, the defense of India, and the eventual invasion of the Continent from England.[3] Secretary of War Stimson was apparently thinking along much the same lines. Commenting on the danger of United States forces, especially air units, being "sucked into" the Southwest Pacific, Stimson noted in his diary that he was coming more and more to believe in basing an Allied expeditionary force in Britain "to worry the Germans at their back."[4]

The challenge posed by Navy plans, coming on top of the ARCADIA experience with the British, finally elicited an Army response. On February 28th, General Eisenhower provided the Chief of Staff a complete analysis of American strategy in relation to Admiral King's request for air and ground forces. Addressing himself to the whole question of the eventual extent of the American commitment to the Pacific theater, the Army's chief planner* conceded the desirability of maintaining a safe communications line to Australia and "the most advanced bases possible for eventual offensives" against Japan, but he pointed out that current limitations of men and material required Allied forces to concentrate on securing those objectives which were absolutely necessary for a successful prosecution of the war. Reaffirming the "Hitler-first" doctrine, he declared "necessary" undertakings to be: the protection of the British Isles and the North Atlantic sea lanes; the maintenance of an active Russian front; and the prevention of a juncture between Japanese and

---

*Eisenhower succeeded General L.T. Gerow as Deputy Chief of Staff and head of the War Plans Division on 16 February 1942.

German forces in the India–Middle East area. To secure the first two objectives and to help realize the third, Eisenhower suggested that the Army, in conjunction with British military representatives, immediately develop definite plans for operations in Northwest Europe which would "engage from the middle of May [1942] onward, an increasing portion of the German Air Forces, and by late summer an increasing amount of his ground forces." In elaborating the need for such direct and immediate contribution to maintaining the eastern front, Eisenhower pointed out that it was "not sufficient to urge upon them [the Russians] the *indirect* advantages that will accrue to them from Allied operations in distant parts of the world. . . . *Russia's problem is to sustain herself during the coming summer,* and she must not be permitted to reach such a precarious position that she will accept a negotiated peace . . . in preference to a continuation of the fight."[5]

Eisenhower's analysis had the greatest significance. It marked the end of the Army's ambivalence toward the peripheral strategy and the beginnings of unified, consistent support of the immediate concentration of American forces preparatory to an assault on German-held territory. Although thoughts of an invasion of Europe had long been entertained by both American and British military leaders, Eisenhower's paper made it an immediate objective. In doing so, the proposal answered two urgent requirements. By providing a "Second Front" in Europe it would give Russia prompt direct military assistance. Moreover, the invasion scheme itself was a planning objective toward which the United States could direct its military energies, and in relation to which all requests for men and material could be assessed. In that respect Eisenhower's plan offered the Army a way of controlling the future direction of Allied strategy. The proposal thus marked the Army's first positive step toward seizing the initiative in strategic planning.

The Army's first opportunity to halt the misdirection of the war came at a White House conference which Marshall, Stimson, and Arnold attended on 5 March. The President called the meeting to discuss an appropriate response to Churchill's desperate pleas for aid. Stimson's reaction to the Prime Minister's message was forthright and unsympathetic. He made it clear that he considered the request simply the latest in a series of British proposals which would lead the United States into a strategy of wasteful dispersion and ultimately into defeat. The dispatch of two American divisions to Australia and New Zealand (as Churchill had requested) would merely correct the most recently discovered flaw in the fundamentally unsound British strategic position and would, as Churchill himself conceded, preclude taking other steps needed to insure victory before 1944.

Rather than accept such an unwelcome possibility Stimson suggested that the United States offer a constructive alternative. The answer to Allied strategic problems, he said, "lay in sending an overwhelming force to the British Isles and threatening an attack on the Germans in France." This was "the proper and orthodox line of our help in the war as it would have the effect of giving Hitler two fronts to fight on, if it could be done . . . while the Russians were still in." A cross-Channel attack, the Secretary concluded, would have the added advantage of providing a great stimulus to "sagging" British morale.

General Arnold followed up Stimson's remarks by presenting an outline plan for actual operations against the French coast designed to demonstrate the feasibility of the proposal. General Marshall fully endorsed the concept[6] and the President also seemed strongly and favorably impressed by it. Roosevelt believed that Churchill's telegrams indicated the Prime Minister needed a "pat on the back," and he probably believed that the Army scheme would supply the needed encouragement.[7]

Less encouraging was the reaction of the British Staff Mission, the permanent representatives of the British Chiefs of Staff in Washington. They had come to the White House on the 5th to present the formal British request for a diversion of shipping to the Middle East. The President took the opportunity to ask General Arnold to restate his plan for their benefit. According to the British report, Arnold envisaged a simultaneous land and sea operation to establish a bridgehead on the Continent. Once established the enclave would constitute the locus of an air battle which would draw German air strength away from the Eastern Front. The Mission, unimpressed, thought the operation neither feasible nor likely to accomplish its objective.[8]

The First Offensive

Admiral King shared British scepticism about the Stimson-Arnold scheme. Sometime on the 5th (probably after the White House meeting) King wrote the President that while he agreed United States military efforts should be concentrated on a very few lines, he felt those lines should be drawn in the Pacific. King proposed that offensive operations against the Japanese be initiated by seizing bases in the Tonga, New Hebrides, and Ellice Islands. When those strongpoints had been taken and the sea route to Australia secured, King suggested that American forces undertake an island by island drive northwestward from the New Hebrides into the Solomons and the Bismarck Archipelago.[9]

King's views were known to the Army and were a source of considerable concern. On the 6th Stimson found Eisenhower "quite strong against King's creeping movement through New Caledonia," which he thought would accomplish nothing. Both agreed that a major obstacle to carrying out the cross-Channel proposal would be the Navy, which Stimson said was becoming "wedded to fighting in the Pacific."[10]

Roosevelt delayed replying to the Prime Minister's messages of the 4th and 5th while he considered the Army scheme and what sort of "pat on the back" he could give the Prime Minister. Meanwhile, he received two forceful reminders of Churchill's problems. On the 7th Averell Harriman, the President's special representative in England, wrote him that he was "worried" by the Prime Minister's mental outlook and political future. According to Harriman, Churchill had been badly hurt by the Singapore disaster and was apparently unable to stand up to the criticism with his accustomed vigor. Harriman also noted that a "number of astute people" felt that if the bad war news continued, the Government could not last more than a few months.[11] That same day, Churchill added substance to Harriman's observation when he wrote Roosevelt asking him for "a free hand to sign the treaty which Stalin desires as soon as possible." The increasing gravity of the war, Churchill wrote, "has led me to feel that the principles of the Atlantic Charter ought not to be construed so as to deny Russia the frontiers she occupied when Germany attacked her."[12]

Churchill's determination to delay no longer in meeting Soviet demands drew an immediate response from the President. On the evening of the 7th he cabled the Prime Minister acceding to his request of March 4th. Two American divisions would be sent to Australia and New Zealand and shipping to transport two Anzac divisions to the Middle East would be provided.[13] The following day (8 March) the President supplemented his offer by indicating that he was prepared to come to Stalin's aid by establishing a Second Front. "I am becoming more and more interested in the establishment of a new front this summer on the European continent, certainly for air and raids. . . . Even though losses will doubtless be great, such losses will be compensated by at least equal German losses and by compelling Germans to divert large forces of all kinds from Russian fronts."[14] The President's thinking on the second front was cautious. He had determined on action of some sort, but at this point he was uncertain of its exact form. He expressed concern lest growing pressure for immediate offensive action "result in some hasty action before plans to insure success were in readiness," and his circumspection led him to focus on the prospects of a large scale air offensive which he hoped might produce the desired effect on Germany and among the Allies without the costs which ground action involved.[15] Nevertheless, he had apparently decided to accept, at least in principle, the Army's plan for America's first offensive.

Roosevelt endorsed a cross-Channel operation more because of propitious circumstances than the persuasive skills of Stimson and his colleagues. At the beginning of March the President was faced with several threats to the smooth and successful Allied prosecution of the war. Morale in both England and the United States was low and demands for more aggressive leadership were increasing. Moreover, criticism of Churchill's failure to help the Russians, along with recurrent rumors of a Nazi–Soviet peace settlement, had finally obliged the Prime Minister to accept Soviet territorial demands.

In these circumstances the President sought to strengthen support of the war both at home and in Britain;[16] to silence the criticism of Allied war leadership; and to encourage and, if possible, tangibly assist the Russians during the coming German summer offensive—without compromising his policy of avoiding wartime political agreements. The solution to all these problems seemed to lie in immediate Anglo-American offensive action against Germany. Churchill's message of the 4th had confirmed the already obvious conclusion that GYMNAST was out of the question for several months at least. A substitute had to be found, and the Army's proposal provided it. Aiding circumstances in assuring its adoption by the President was the fact that, unlike GYMNAST, the Army plan enjoyed the vigorous support of most of Roosevelt's advisors (Admiral King, while preferring his own alternative, was not opposed to the operation in principle), including Harry Hopkins.[17]

While the President believed that the promise of a Second Front would divert Stalin from his preoccupation with Soviet frontiers, that issue still remained to be dealt with. In February the President had indicated to the British that he would take the matter up with Stalin directly. The nature of his approach was suggested on March 12th when he told Soviet Ambassador Maxim Litvinov that while he could not now approve of territorial settlements, he was prepared, once the war had been won, to support any legitimate claim put forth by the Soviet Union in the furtherance of its national security.[18] What else, if anything, he may have conveyed to the Russians is not known, but whatever it was, the President was confident that it would solve the frontiers problem.

On 16 March he wrote Churchill apparently in an effort to bolster his spirits. His letter sketched a rosy picture of the future course of the war and included reference to a "plan for a joint attack in Europe itself." The President also tried to set Churchill at ease regarding the Russians by telling him of his talk with Litvinov, and indicating that he expected a reply from Stalin shortly. Roosevelt, reflecting an unrealistic self-confidence, also told the Prime Minister that "I think I can personally handle Stalin better than either your Foreign Office or my State Department. Stalin hates the guts of all your top people. He likes me better, and I hope he will continue to do so."[19]

As it turned out, if indeed the President intended to head off an Anglo–Soviet treaty by personal diplomacy and the lure of a second front, his plans went awry. Whatever he told Stalin the Soviet dictator was apparently unimpressed. His reply was simply an acknowledgment of receipt of the President's views,[20] and he continued to press the British on the territorial question. As a result, before Churchill received the President's letter of the 18th,[21] the War Cabinet decided to resume negotiations over a treaty granting Soviet territorial claims.[22] As Eden pointed out:

> Under present conditions, Great Britain is unable to give military aid and assistance to Stalin in the sense of a second front, or even in the sense of any considerable supply of material. If Great Britain could undertake either of these two measures, it would be easier for Great Britain to take the position taken by the President, but in view of her inability to do so, and in view of the pressure of British public opinion, Great Britain is forced to conclude this treaty with Stalin as a political substitute for material military assistance.[23]

So at the end of March the President's efforts to preserve the principle of no wartime settlements appeared on the verge of failure.

Yet while the President's hints about a Second Front made little impression in London and Moscow, the idea was favorably received in Washington. Stimson, for one, was enthusiastic. It seemed to him that Roosevelt's espousal of a cross-Channel attack marked a significant forward step in the Army's newly begun efforts to have the United States assume the lead in strategic planning. On learning the text of the President's 7 March message, Stimson commented in his diary that it accomplished what he had been "hoping and working for" in that it took "the initiative out of the hands of Churchill where I am sure it would have degenerated into a simple defensive operation to stop up urgent rat holes, most of which I fear are hopeless."[24]

While the President's acceptance of the principle of a cross-Channel attack was indeed a significant victory, the Army's campaign for the adoption of an American grand strategy was far from over. The President had ratified the concept, but an actual plan for the operation had yet to be worked out and British acceptance obtained. Moreover, Admiral King evinced no enthusiasm for the project and it was certain that his first interest continued to lie in the Pacific.

On 14 March, the Joint Chiefs received from their planners

three possible plans for military action in the immediate future. The planning staff, unable to reconcile Army, Air Corps, and Navy differences, could only recommend that the Joint Chiefs choose between three courses: sending strong reinforcements to the Pacific at the expense of a vigorous offensive against Germany (the Navy's recommendation), accepting the loss of the Southwest Pacific while concentrating on an invasion of the Continent from bases in Britain (Air Corps), or an Army compromise calling for the provision of the minimum forces required for the defense of the South Pacific and a simultaneous buildup of forces in the United Kingdom for an assault on the Continent at the earliest practicable date. Admiral King, thinking perhaps that his Efate–Solomons offensive might be accommodated in the defensive provisions of the Army scheme[25] accepted the compromise, and as a result on 16 March a buildup of forces in Britain and the eventual invasion of Europe became the agreed upon policy of the Joint Chiefs.[26]

While it would soon be apparent that this agreement did not reflect a true meeting of the minds,[27] for the moment at least the semblance of accord made it possible to draft a tentative plan to submit to the President and ultimately to the Prime Minister. Before doing so, however, Marshall, who was aware that the British entertained serious doubts about the 1942 phase of the proposed operation, sought to reconcile the views of American and British planners on the project. Agreement with the British was especially necessary since American planners had already discovered that any operation undertaken in the summer of 1942 would have to depend primarily on British forces.[28] On 24 March, Marshall approached the British Staff Mission and it was agreed that the Combined Planners would undertake a study of cross-Channel operations. However, four days before, Stimson, worried by the continued threat of dispersions which he felt jeopardized the "vital" summer offensive, had called at the White House and arranged to have the President hear and decide on the American proposal. The date set was 25 March.[29]

Scheduling the meeting for the 25th meant that Marshall would have to defend the cross-Channel attack without the benefit of the Combined Planners recommendations. His espousal would be based on faith in the feasibility of the operation rather than on the results of careful, factual analysis. Stimson remarked that he found Marshall "troubled because he has not yet been able to get the facts and, as he has to bear the brunt of the argument, he feels that he is not thoroughly armed." The Secretary tried to overcome Marshall's doubts by telling him that they could not afford to delay in their efforts to prevent the President from "giving away what might be fatal amounts of our munitions and men."[30] The crisis in strategic planning and the momentum of Army efforts to control events apparently helped carry the reluctant General to his task.

On the 25th, Marshall, Stimson, Knox, Arnold, King, and Hopkins joined the President for lunch at the White House. Roosevelt launched the meeting with some strategic ramblings about the Middle East. When Stimson and Marshall were finally able to draw him back to the matter at hand, the Chief of Staff outlined the cross-Channel operation. Marshall's remarks are unrecorded, but it is likely that he based his comments on a memorandum given him by Eisenhower that day. Eisenhower's brief stressed the need for an immediate decision on the theater for the first major offensive. Agreement, he said, would focus Allied efforts, facilitate preparations for action in the European theater, and greatly reduce the dispersal of forces which had characterized Allied efforts over the past few months. Eisenhower believed that the preparatory buildup in the British Isles would threaten Germany's western front, thus in all probability diverting Nazi forces from Russia during the critical months ahead. At the same time the presence of American troops in England would make the British Isles secure from German attack.

Significantly, the focus of Eisenhower's memorandum was on the gathering of forces rather than on their employment; the buildup, not the invasion. As a result, Eisenhower did no violence to the logic of his argument when he recommended that if the proposed concentration in England was not accepted by Britain, the United States should abandon Europe temporarily and "go full out, as quickly as possible, against Japan!"[31]

The President showed no great enthusiasm for the Army proposal. He recommended only that it be submitted to the Combined Chiefs for further study, which may have reflected his continued reluctance to order preparations for a costly invasion before the matter had been carefully considered. In any event, his hesitancy might have resulted in a considerable delay had Harry Hopkins not then suggested that as soon as a plan was ready the American Chiefs should take it directly to London for approval by Churchill and the highest British military authorities. The President agreed.[32]

During the following week, the Army pushed ahead with the writing of an outline invasion plan. By the 27th a first draft was completed. That same day Stimson, still doubtful about the strength of Roosevelt's attachment to the Army's scheme, urged him not to delay sending the American Chiefs to London to secure British agreement. The Secretary also encouraged the President to give priority to the construction and collection of the needed landing equipment. Immediate commitment to the cross-Channel operation would, Stimson said, automatically end further dispersion of American military strength. "We shall have an affirmative answer against which to measure all such demands. . . . On the other hand, so long as we remain without our own plan of offensive, our forces will inevitably be dispersed and wasted."[33]

Although Stimson principally had in mind diversions to British projects, it was becoming increasingly evident by late March that the Navy, despite the agreement of 16 March, might pose an even greater threat. On the 29th Admiral King wrote Marshall protesting that the allocation of army aircraft to the South Pacific was inadequate. It was clear from King's message that he did not interpret the Joint Chiefs decision of the 16th as precluding the continued strengthening of American forces in the Pacific, for as he pointed out, even though the *major* objective of Allied strategy was in Europe, the most *immediate* need remained in the Pacific. King concluded, therefore, that the transfer of Army units, especially air forces, "to positions in the Pacific be given priority over movements to Europe" or other theaters.[34] The direct reply to King's message would come a week later. In the meantime, General Marshall proceeded to complete his efforts to secure top-level agreement to the principle of a cross-Channel attack.

On April 1st General Marshall received the outline invasion

plan developed by the Operations Division (OPD).* That same day the Chief of Staff, after making a number of changes[35] in the report, joined Stimson, Knox, Hopkins, King, and Arnold at the White House, where he presented it to the President. The proposal, contained in a memorandum entitled "Operations in Western Europe," began by declaring that "Western Europe is favored as the theater in which to stage the first major offensive by the United States and Great Britain." Official acknowledgment of that intention, the memorandum went on, should be made immediately even if the invasion could not be launched in 1942, in order to end the "continued dispersion of means" which was making preparations for the offensive impossible.

The ultimate objective of the proposed concentration of forces would be a cross-Channel attack carried out by approximately 48 divisions and 5,800 airplanes. The operation was to be undertaken as soon as those forces could be accumulated in England—estimated to be April 1, 1943. The memorandum, however, took cognizance of the need to provide the Russians with immediate assistance since a crisis on the Eastern front was expected before the major Allied expedition was ready. The proposal, therefore, included reference to a small-scale operation which might, under certain circumstances, be undertaken in the fall of 1942 as part of the preliminaries for the 1943 invasion. The plan recommended that from the summer of 1942 on, the Allies conduct progressively expanding air operations over western Europe, and amphibious raids against points along the coast. Such operations would furnish experience for the attack in 1943 and also because of the threat they posed would help the Soviet Union by diverting German forces to the West.† It was further suggested that the raids might culminate in a small emergency expedition to the French coast "if the imminence of Russian collapse requires desperate action," or if German forces were almost completely absorbed in Russia, or if a deterioration of German military strength made such an attack opportune.

---

*Reorganization of the War Department in March resulted *inter alia* in the creation of the Operations Division, which, now under Eisenhower's direction, assumed the functions of the WPD.

†It was also noted that these operations would have the additional value of providing "immediate satisfaction to the [American] public."

The First Offensive

The size of the 1942 operation would be determined by the number of troops which could be transported from England to the Continent at the designated time. The exact figure could not be predicted, but it was acknowledged that because of shipping shortages it would be quite small. It was estimated that by the fall of 1942 five divisions, half of them American, could be landed and supported in Europe.[36]

After carefully reading Marshall's proposal and interrogating the Chief of Staff on a number of points, the President gave his approval. He observed that the plan would mean that the United States could no longer be "treated like a sort of a stepchild" in the distribution of American production. Clearly Marshall and Stimson needed no instruction on that point.

Valuable service was rendered the Army leaders by Harry Hopkins. In an effort to insure Navy cooperation, Hopkins prodded Admiral King into explicitly accepting both the plan and its implications for the Pacific war. In response to his mordant questioning, King declared in Roosevelt's presence that he could see no reason why the operation should not be carried out. Thus the Navy was apparently brought into line. The problem of securing British agreement remained, however, and Marshall and Hopkins were assigned this task. The latter was optimistic about their chances of success, since he felt that Churchill "wouldn't dare to do anything but to go with us, as the temper of the [British] people at this time is for an 'all-out' offensive with the least possible delay."[37]

In reviewing the origins of the Marshall Memorandum we may note that General Marshall in proposing a plan for the employment of American forces had utilized a common bureaucratic stratagem. He had offered an entry in the competition for Allied strategy. If he was successful in getting his proposal simply adopted, not necessarily acted upon, the Army would have the lead and initiative in planning and with it, the advantages of front-running among the competitors. The buildup in England would be the overriding project for the coming months. Every cry for troops or planes or munitions, whether it emanated from London, Chungking, or the Office of the Chief of Naval Operations, could be matched against the needs of the cross-Channel attack and (probably) rejected. Army leadership would have a good chance of prevailing even if later events forced a modification of plans.[38]

The President for his part accepted the Marshall Memorandum because the proposal seemed to meet his political requirements. There was, however, a certain inconsistency between the Army's intentions and the President's expectations. It will be recalled that Roosevelt first encountered the proposal of a cross-Channel operation at the White House conference on 5 March. At that time General Arnold had put forward a plan for stepped-up air operations in western Europe beginning in late spring and climaxing in a landing on the Continent six weeks later. The President in his messages to Churchill on the 8th and 16th had expressed his interest in establishing a new front in Europe "this summer" and noted that definite plans were being considered. The discussions and messages of early March indicate that Roosevelt was contemplating action in 1942. The political situation in March 1942 also clearly suggests this conclusion. Morale and politics in the United States and Great Britain appeared to require immediate action against Germany. So did the problem of Soviet frontier demands. Roosevelt's understanding of the Army proposal is further suggested by the fact that his first impulse after accepting the Marshall Memorandum was to inform Stalin immediately of the new scheme.[39]

Marshall's proposal appealed to the President as a timely substitute for the defunct GYMNAST. He supported the cross-Channel attack for basically the same reasons that attracted him to the North African operation even though the military implications of each were quite different. Immediacy was the indispensable attribute of both projects. Yet the Marshall Memorandum focussed on the *buildup* and *concentration* of forces in Britain during 1942 in preparation for offensive action the following spring. Significant action in 1942, which is what the President wanted, was contingent on unforeseeable circumstances rather than scheduled as a definite necessary element of the scheme. Action in 1942 was clearly considered of secondary importance by the Army planners.

How then can we account for Roosevelt's approval? The President may have felt that the contingencies were *bound* to arise in 1942: that the Germans would either be so occupied in the East that an invasion would be relatively easy, or that the Russians would be so sorely pressed that an emergency operation would be justified. Or he may have felt that raids along the European coast and increased air attacks would be enough to satisfy his political requirements. It is also possible that, despite the inadequacy of the proposal, Roosevelt was anxious to adopt a plan which at least *promised* offensive action, content then to wait and see how events turned out. If the plan did not prove satisfactory, an alternative could be improvised later. The political situation required that Russia be given immediate *assurances* of action, not necessarily the action itself. The word was almost as good as the deed, at least temporarily.

Whatever Roosevelt's reasons for accepting the Memorandum, they had little in common with Marshall's reasons for proposing it. Ultimately this fundamental difference was to result in the collapse of the whole scheme and the revival of GYMNAST as the first American offensive.

SIX

BOLERO: A Stratagem and Its Uses, April–May 1942

I

On 4 April Hopkins, Marshall, and a small party left for London to seek official British acceptance of the "Marshall Memorandum." Before their departure the President wrote to Churchill introducing the mission and its purpose, and revealing in the process the results he sought. Clearly it was the 1942 contingency portion of the scheme which was foremost in Roosevelt's thoughts when he wrote of Marshall's proposal: "It is a plan which I hope Russia will greet with enthusiasm, and, on word from you . . . I propose to ask Stalin to send two special representatives to see me at once. I think it will work out in full accord with [the] trend of public opinion here and in Britain. And, finally, I would like to be able to label it the plan of the United Nations." The following day the President again wrote the Prime Minister expressing much the same thought: "Your people and mine demand the establishment of a front to draw off pressure on the Russians. . . . Even if full success is not attained, the *big* objective will be."[1] The President obviously thought the Memorandum contained a promise of offensive operations in 1942.

The British military were well prepared to discuss the matters which Marshall would raise since they had been actively studying the problem of a cross-Channel attack for several months. In fact, the climax to the British deliberations came at a meeting on the morning of the day the Americans arrived in England (8 April), at which the British Chiefs concluded that a cross-Channel attack in 1942 (codenamed SLEDGEHAMMER) might be successful if a German defeat in the East seemed probable or if German forces appeared overextended and committed. Despite that conclusion, however, a large element of uncertainty persisted, with the result that the Chiefs had come away from the meeting unconvinced of the feasibility of the proposal. Thus at the outset of the London talks the British military was sympathetic to the concept but doubted its chances of success.[2]

On the morning of April 8th General Alan Brooke, the Army Chief of Staff, welcomed the American mission to England. The several days of talks which ensued were amiable, the British patiently listening to the enthusiastic Americans as they generalized about the future operations. No effort was made to examine closely the feasibility of the Marshall proposal since both Hopkins and the Chief of Staff apparently wished to confine their mission to obtaining general British agreement to the *principle* of a cross-Channel attack.

Apart from the indefiniteness of the talks, their most significant characteristic was the disparate arguments used by Hopkins and Marshall, revealing something of the differing objectives sought by the President (faithfully represented by Hopkins) and the Chief of Staff. The emphasis of Hopkins' remarks was the need for American ground troops to see action against Germany as soon as possible. Although as far as the records reveal Hopkins made no explicit reference to the timing of the cross-Channel attack the nature of his comments strongly suggests that he had in mind sometime during 1942. Thus for example, on one occasion Hopkins, sensing that Churchill doubted that the operation could be carried out in 1942, pointed out that the President did not intend to immobilize "large numbers of our troops indefinitely."[3] At subsequent meetings Hopkins reiterated that point, noting that the President, the general public, and the nation's military leaders were all agreed that American troops must take the offensive as soon as possible and that western Europe was the place it could be done most quickly and most decisively. Hopkins' recorded remarks to Churchill on the proposed operation itself go no further than that.

He was somewhat more specific, however, in indicating one of the advantages he expected from immediate action. In discussions with Foreign Minister Anthony Eden, Hopkins reasserted the President's opposition to an Anglo-Soviet treaty which would recognize Russia's 1941 boundaries and suggested that the proposal Marshall had brought from Washington might be used to help the British avoid either accepting or flatly rejecting the Russian demands: "I impressed on Eden as strongly as I could the President's belief that our main proposal here should take the heat off Russia's diplomatic demands upon England." In short, all of Hopkins' remarks point to a disposition to see the "second front" politically rather than militarily and suggest that Hopkins was thinking of action commencing in 1942 rather than in 1943.[4]

The emphasis on the need for immediate action was almost totally absent from General Marshall's remarks. The Chief of Staff was interested primarily in securing agreement to the concentration of Allied resources for an eventual cross-Channel attack. Without examining the question of feasibility, General Marshall stressed the need for the prompt initiation of plans and preparations for a landing on the Continent in 1943.* Until then, he said, American troops available in England could gain combat experience by participating in raids against the Continent which hopefully would have the important additional value of diverting some German forces from the Russian front. On the matter of a second front in 1942, Marshall declared that should Soviet resistance or German strength seriously diminish, a sacrifice or opportunistic landing might be undertaken sometime in the fall of 1942, before the expected break in the Channel weather.

The British response made it clear that excluding a collapse of German resistance, any landing on the Continent in 1942 would indeed be sacrificial. General Brooke noted that although it might be possible to land a force of seven infantry and two armored divisions, it would not be strong enough to maintain a bridgehead against the scale of attack the Germans could mount against it. Moreover, it was unlikely that the expedition, once committed, could be extricated. The resultant losses, he noted, would dangerously weaken the defense of the British

---

*ROUNDUP

Isles.[5] Those conclusions and others equally depressing had already been reached by the Combined Chiefs' Planning Staff on the day before Marshall left for England. The Planners, responding to a directive asking them to determine the feasibility of invasions of the Continent, noted that by September 15, 1942 only fifteen and a half of the twenty-eight divisions needed for successful operations would be available; that the margin of fighter plane superiority over the critical battle zone would be insufficient; that a lack of landing craft would limit the assault wave to approximately one-fifth the force required; and finally that to obtain the cargo shipping and port facilities required for the operation would mean the virtual cessation of importation to England for the period of the buildup.[6]

The misgivings voiced by the British and confirmed by the Combined Planners drew no rebuttal from General Marshall. He showed no inclination to go into the details of the operations he proposed partly because he was unprepared to do so and partly because his interest lay primarily in securing preliminary agreement in principle. The superficiality of the Chief of Staff's approach was obvious to his British counterpart and caused General Brooke first to doubt Marshall's strategic soundness, and then to suspect an ulterior motive to the American Army scheme. The C.I.G.S. finally concluded that Marshall's proposal was designed as much for its effect within the American military high command as for its impact on Germany:

> He has found that King, the American Naval Chief of Staff, is proving more and more of a drain on his military resources, continually calling for land-forces to capture and hold land-bases in the Pacific. . . . MacArthur in Australia constitutes another threat by asking for forces to develop an offensive from Australia. To counter these moves Marshall has started the European offensive plan and is going one hundred per cent all out on it. It is a clever move which fits in with present political opinion and the desire to help Russia. It is popular with all military men who are fretting for an offensive policy.[7]

Brooke's interpretation of Marshall's motives is almost certainly correct as far as it goes. What Brooke did not mention, and perhaps did not see, was that the Marshall Memorandum was also designed to head off operations sponsored by the British. Churchill's influence with the President worried the Chief of Staff and his advisors more than the cries for help from King and MacArthur. Marshall hoped his plan would counter the President's susceptibility to all unsound schemes, "peripheral" or "Pacific-first."

Regardless of the motives of the Marshall mission, the British were willing to oblige their anxious guests. Although somewhat skeptical about the feasibility of the invasion-1942 portion of Marshall's proposal, Churchill and the British Chiefs were able to agree that plans and preparations for a cross-Channel attack should be undertaken immediately and the Prime Minister gave his formal approval to the American scheme on April 14th.

As General Marshall understood it, the British in accepting his outline plan had affirmed the need to keep Russia in the war and had conceded that Western Europe was the best place to undertake the first major offensive against Germany. More specifically the British, according to Marshall, agreed that "plans for major operations on the continent in 1943 should be pressed forward, and that everything should be concentrated on the main object —the defeat of Germany." It was further agreed that the Allies "may have the opportunity and may well be obliged to take action in 1942." A decision on such an emergency operation was to be made in "August at the latest" to allow sufficient time to land on the French coast and seize a port before the break in the weather expected at the end of September. Assuming that SLEDGEHAMMER proved feasible, the final decision as to whether to launch the assault would depend on the situation in Russia at the end of the summer. If Russia was being defeated it was agreed that "we may be compelled to make a supreme effort to draw off German forces." An invasion might also be called for if Germany was on the point of military collapse, a turn of events which, surprisingly enough, the Allied leaders considered a possibility in 1942. No decision was reached as to the proper course of action should the Russians stop the German summer offensive without breaking the Wehrmacht's strength.[8]

The British had thus given Marshall the agreement in principle which he sought while committing themselves to very little. In accepting the desirability of Marshall's proposal, Churchill and his military chiefs had agreed only to the buildup of American forces in the British Isles (which they welcomed) and the initiation of planning for possible future operations. They made no definite pledge to carry out any particular operation. While the discussions indicate that the British were optimistic concerning the 1943 operation, the Marshall visit seems to have done nothing to reduce their doubts concerning SLEDGEHAMMER.[9]

General Marshall was aware that the British agreement was not a firm commitment to action. In describing his discussion to the Army planners on April 13th, the Chief of Staff noted that although he thought his proposal would be "accepted in principle," he believed that in order to prevent the British from initiating "further dispersions," their determination to follow a single course of action would "have to be considerably and continuously bolstered by [the] firmness of our stand." General Marshall went on to observe that although he had encountered almost unanimous general agreement "many if not most [of the British] hold reservations regarding this or that."[10]

Still, General Marshall was probably pleased with the agreement he had obtained. The British had expressed obvious interest in an eventual invasion of western Europe, and had welcomed the concentration of American forces in the British Isles. Thus, in spite of the many questions that remained concerning SLEDGEHAMMER* and ROUNDUP,† at least BOLERO‡ appeared secure. In obtaining approval of the concentration of forces the Chief of Staff had taken a major step toward preventing the President from dribbling away American resources on what Marshall considered premature and indecisive military adventures. General Eisenhower, in commenting on the London agreement, saw that as a major achievement: "I hope that at long last, and after months of struggle by this Division [Operations] . . . we are all definitely committed to one concept of fighting. If we can agree on major purposes and objectives our efforts will begin to fall in line and we won't just be thrashing around in the dark."[11] The Army leadership, although some-

---

*Contingency invasion 1942
†Invasion 1943
‡The preparatory buildup

what uncertain, was reasonably confident that the planning initiative was now in their hands and that the task of creating a single "sound" claim on American resources had been achieved.

The President too had reason to be pleased. Help for the Russians appeared assured, and the "promise" of a second front in 1942 would eliminate both the need for meeting Russian territorial demands and the likelihood of the oft rumored Russo–German separate peace. At the same time the first American offensive in the West, or even indications that the Allies intended to seize the initiative, would go far toward boosting American (and British) public support for the war effort while quieting public criticism of the Administration's military policy.

The President was not long in finding "political" uses for the London agreement. Even before the meetings had produced formal British acceptance, the President had initiated efforts to use the promise of a second front to influence Anglo–Soviet relations. On the day that Marshall and Hopkins arrived in London, Eden, responding to continued Soviet pressure, had arranged for Foreign Minister V. M. Molotov to come to London to sign a treaty.[12] Aware that Anglo–Soviet negotiations were about to resume, Roosevelt cabled Stalin asking him to send Molotov to Washington in the immediate future to hear the President's views on a "very important military proposal involving the utilization of our armed forces in a manner to relieve your critical western front." The President noted that he had sent Hopkins to London to consult with the British on the scheme and that he wanted to speak to Molotov "before we determine with finality the strategic course of our common military effort."[13] On 20 April Stalin agreed to send Molotov to Washington "for an exchange of views on the organization of a second front in Europe in the near future."[14] and two days later the President told Churchill that he hoped Molotov would make it a point to go to Washington before going to London to participate in the final stage of Anglo–Soviet treaty negotiations. Obviously the President hoped to use the stopover to expand on the promise of a second front in an effort to dissuade Molotov from pressing the British for recognition of Soviet territorial gains. However, Stalin insisted that a preliminary exchange of views between the United Kingdom and the Soviet Union was essential before Molotov went to Washington to take up the question of the second front.[15] The President's failure to meet Molotov first was a blow to his plans, but it did not end his hopes of using a second front promise and his powers of persuasion to head off Soviet demands.

During the first week in May Ambassador Winant advised the President that Churchill and Eden felt Stalin had made the issue of frontier recognition "the basis of trust in Britain." While the British leaders did not believe that failure to accede to Stalin's request would lead to a Russian separate peace,[16] the Prime Minister felt that acceptance of the Russian position was necessary and, according to Winant, had reluctantly decided to grant Stalin's request for recognition of Russian boundary claims. Winant therefore had prevailed upon the British to arrange for Molotov to make his planned trip to the United States after discussions had taken place but before the treaty was signed. Winant pointed out to the President that he would thus have a chance at the Soviet Foreign Minister before final action on the treaty.[17] With this last slim opportunity in the offing, the issue rested awaiting Molotov's arrival in London two weeks hence.

While the "promise" of a second front failed to have the hoped for effect on Anglo–Soviet negotiations, the mission to London did have an almost immediate impact on the President's other major concern—American public opinion. For news of the Marshall-Hopkins trip became public just in time to dispel some of the gloom generated by a recent spate of bad news from the fighting fronts. *Time*, calling the week ending April 19th the "blackest since Singapore," commented that the "Allied peoples needed the antidote of aggressive action, or at least the promise of action," which they found in the Marshall-Hopkins mission: "anxious millions forthwith believed what they wanted to be told: that their forces were about to take the offensive and open a second front in Europe."[18] Statements by various Allied leaders, including General Marshall[19] and Lord Beaverbrook,[20] were interpreted by the press in the light of the mission to London to indicate that offensive operations were being planned and that a second front would be opened before the year was out. A survey by the Office of Facts and Figures covering the third week in April revealed that a substantial number of the nation's most influential newspapers had discussed the subject of a possible Allied offensive editorially and that "all considered that the visit of General Marshall to London presaged its launching."[21] The press, which had been looking for signs of offensive action by the United States since the end of February, found them in the London talks.

While the optimism generated by the Marshall mission went a long way toward satisfying Roosevelt's hopes of stimulating the public's offensive-mindedness, the episode soon seemed to have created more problems than it solved. Roosevelt should have anticipated that while the news of an impending offensive might be enough to boost the spirits of the editors and news commentators, it would take combat itself to give the public the involvement and identification with the war which he sought. Moreover, the widespread belief that offensive action was imminent increased the pressure on the Administration to produce such action. The public was unaware of the conditional terms of the London agreement, or the problems which the 1942 operations involved. An offensive was wanted. The mission to London, the apparently official talk of seizing the initiative, and growing Communist-inspired propaganda in favor of a second front made it seem that an offensive was both possible and imminent. Expectations were high but so was the danger of an adverse reaction should the offensive be delayed.

The discussion of immediate offensive action increased throughout the late spring and summer as the news media alternately anticipated and demanded a full scale offensive.[22] As early as mid-April, shortly after the return of Marshall and Hopkins, there were signs that the belief in the coming offensive was in danger of having unfortunate results. On the 25th OFF pointed out that the "strong talk of an offensive . . . shows signs of backfiring unless something happens soon. . . ." The agency noted that there would be no let up in talk of the offensive, and that "writers and editors are beginning to seek the reasons why it is not launched." The most common explanation offered, OFF found, was the "miscalculation and ineptitude" of British and American strategists."[23] There were indications of possible political ramifications as well. The Republican party, obviously aware of the enthusiasm for the rumored offensive, seized the opportunity presented by the London meetings to go on record in support of immediate military action. A resolution adopted by the Republican National Committee demanded "the relentless and unreserved prosecution of an offensive war,"[24] thus serving notice that if President Roosevelt was unwilling or unable to take the fighting initiative, the GOP could provide the leadership which would.

Altogether, from the President's point of view, the Marshall Mission was far from an unalloyed triumph. The success of the London meeting proved no less equivocal in practice for General Marshall. For despite the agreement on Allied strategy, in the two months following the Mission the Army leadership was repeatedly faced with the same sort of diversionary challenges which had been in large part responsible for the Marshall Memorandum and the trip to England. While it is true that the BOLERO decision combined with the lack of activity in the western desert and a current shortage of shipping had quieted the British threat, General MacArthur and the Australian government (in spite of the provisions of JCS23 and the London understanding—see page 108 above) now joined Admiral King in insisting on a further buildup of American forces in the Pacific area, thus threatening the planned concentration of Allied force against Hitler. Marshall's response was to invoke the London agreement and the need to measure every proposed American commitment against it.

Before describing Marshall's use of BOLERO to answer demands for the expansion of Pacific operations, it might be well to examine an unrelated and relatively minor episode which provided the first occasion for the application of the London agreement. Sometime after General Marshall's return from London, Roosevelt asked the Chief of Staff if the Army might be able to give the Russians a number of transport planes which they had requested. On 27 April Marshall replied, strongly opposing the scheme. Basing his opposition on the needs of the contingency invasion of the Continent in 1942 (SLEDGEHAMMER), the Chief of Staff argued that "to supply transport planes to Russia at this time will directly endanger [the] success of the invasion plan." Marshall pointed out that "a principal reason for original British reluctance to agree to an invasion of Europe in

1942 was the fact, in their opinion, that essential material means could not be made available in time." The greatest service to Russia, Marshall continued, was "a landing on the European continent in 1942, and we must not jeopardize that operation or risk the sacrifice of the troops engaged by scattering the vital material required for what we know will be a hazardous undertaking." Marshall concluded by urgently recommending that no commitment of transport planes be made to the Soviet Union.[25] Thus, not even the needs of the Russians, whose succor was the proclaimed immediate objective of the cross-Channel attack, were to be permitted to interfere with the concentration of United States forces. The transport episode was settled to Marshall's satisfaction, but a far more serious challenge to the concentration of American military energies was yet to come.

During the third week in March, General MacArthur landed in Australia to assume command of all Allied forces in the Southwest Pacific. MacArthur celebrated his arrival by announcing that he intended to organize an offensive that would drive the Japanese out of the Philippines: "The President . . . ordered me to break through the Japanese lines for the purpose, as I understand it, of organizing the American offensive against Japan. . . . I came through and I shall return." MacArthur modestly qualified his declaration by noting that the success of his mission depended "primarily upon the resources which our respective governments place at my disposal." No general, MacArthur observed, "can make something from nothing."[26]

Clearly MacArthur intended his remarks to pressure the Administration into support of his plans, and the public response which they evoked seemed at first to promise success. For his arrival in Melbourne and his interpretation of United States policy were enthusiastically received by the people and press in both Australia and the United States.[27] *Time* gave expression to the triumphant excitement: "The man who knows how to stop the Japanese took command this week of the last place in the Southwest Pacific to stop them. When Douglas MacArthur reached Australia, the United States and all the United Nations breathed a sigh of relief and hope. *By God, they got him out!*"[28] And a week later: "The world had learned of his arrival. . . . From sick Allied hearts, a wave of hope rose, the wave became a flood, a kind of prayerful madness. . . . Statesmen, the Press, plain men everywhere cried that MacArthur would put an end to retreats; MacArthur would take the offensive; MacArthur could win the war."[29] The Office of Government Reports confirmed *Time*'s conclusions in part, noting that "all media are jubilant over the transfer of General MacArthur to Australia." The press, however, was also concerned lest the hopes generated by the General be unfilled because of Washington's failure to give him necessary material support.[30] MacArthur and the requirements of his command had captured public support.

The new Supreme Commander of the Southwest Pacific Area was not long in making his requirements known to the War Department. Early in April MacArthur told General Marshall he was concerned about the weakness of the Allied position in Australia. When Washington failed to respond to the hint with an offer to reinforce the Australian garrison, the General took his problem first to the press and then to "higher authorities." In mid-April American correspondents in Australia learned, presumably from MacArthur's staff, that the General had still not been given the authority to commence plans and preparations for his campaign against the Japanese. The "oversight" quickly became public knowledge.[31] At the end of the month, Australian Prime Minister Phillip Curtin, acting as he said at MacArthur's request, asked Churchill to supplement the forces in Australia with two British divisions, an aircraft carrier, and additional space on the shipping coming from America. The request was akin to a demand since Curtin's message implied that if the British troops were not forthcoming he would insist that Australian forces be withdrawn from India, which was then hastily preparing to meet an expected Japanese attack.[32]

The President seems to have entertained the idea of making some kind of concession to MacArthur. On the 29th he told a meeting of representatives of the Allied governments involved in the Pacific theater that he hoped to increase the number of planes and troops based in Australia,[33] although Churchill had already been informed that he should treat the Curtin message as reflecting only the views of the Australian Government. General Marshall feared that the President's remarks might indicate that he was disposed to in some way support the Curtin-MacArthur proposal and on May 3rd he wrote the President strongly opposing the reinforcement of Australia. The Chief of Staff pointed out that his "mission to England was greatly embarrassed by the fact that we could propose only two and a half divisions to participate in the cross-Channel attack by September 15th." The allocation of 25,000 troops to Australia would not only prevent increasing the numbers that might participate in SLEDGEHAMMER, but would reduce that number to the point that "our recent proposal to the British Government for 1942 has, in effect, largely been cancelled."[34] The President agreed, and the MacArthur menace was averted for the time being.

No sooner had Marshall responded to the MacArthur challenge than he faced a threat from another quarter. On May 4th Admiral King complained to the Chief of Staff about the inadequate defenses of certain American island bases in the Pacific. Repeating the position he had consistently taken, the Navy Chief pointed out that although basic American planning called for defending Allied positions in the Pacific, he was not convinced "that the forces now there are sufficient to hold . . . against [a] determined Japanese attack which they can initiate very soon." While King said he agreed in principle to the concentration of forces for the European assault, at the same time he felt that "the mounting of BOLERO must not be permitted to interfere with our vital needs in the Pacific. As important as the mounting of BOLERO may be, the Pacific problem is no less so, and is certainly the more urgent—it must be faced now."[35] Although King's arguments suggest that he was principally interested in defense, it has since become clear, and was probably apparent to General Marshall at the time, that the Admiral intended to use the buildup of men and supplies in the Pacific for an offensive campaign which would eventually require far more support than his initial modest requests.[36]

Obviously General Marshall's struggle to concentrate United States military efforts on a single objective had not been ended by the London agreement. General Eisenhower probably expressed the Chief of Staff's consternation over recent developments when he wrote: "Bolero is *supposed* to have the approval of the President and the Prime Minister, but the struggle to get everyone behind it, and to keep the highest authority from wrecking it by making additional commitments of air–ships–troops elsewhere is never ending." Eisenhower thought that very few people in the Administration realized the seriousness of the military situation.[37]

General Marshall answered the proposals of Admiral King and General MacArthur in a single statement to the President; once again pressing the London agreement into service. On 6 May Marshall sent the President the message he had received from King on the 4th along with his reaction to the proposals for a Pacific buildup: "My view, and I understood it to be your decision prior to my visit to England, was that our major effort would be to concentrate immediately for offensive action against Germany from the British Islands. The most pressing need, in the opinion of the Army General Staff, is to sustain Russia as an active, effective participant in the war. That issue will probably be decided this summer or fall. . . . We believe that this may be done by combined British and American operations in Western Europe. . . . Only by complete and whole-hearted acceptance by all concerned . . . can BOLERO have any chance of success." Marshall went on to point out that the allocation of air units to Australia and the South Pacific Islands would delay the initiation of the American air offensive in Western Europe by two months, while the dispatch of ground forces to MacArthur's command would prevent the United States from participating in the initial stages of the cross-Channel attack. This being the case, Marshall declared, the President would either have to issue definite instructions to the Joint Chiefs that BOLERO remained the "primary objective of the United States" or formally notify the British that the London agreement could not be honored.[38]

Being obliged to choose between two mutually exclusive alternatives was not at all agreeable to the President. He generally preferred to let his warring subordinates work out their disagreements through discussion and compromise, thus allowing him to avoid favoring one side at the risk of antagonizing the other. Roosevelt would probably have liked to solve the problem by reasserting his commitment to BOLERO while insisting that the demands of the Pacific could be met by extra effort. However, the size of the forces required by MacArthur's and King's demands could not be reconciled with BOLERO, certainly not to Marshall's satisfaction. Marshall's "ultimatum" probably made Roosevelt realize that the three-way dispute endangered the plan for putting troops into action against Germany in 1942 and would have to be resolved by choice not compromise.

A decision in favor of General Marshall and SLEDGEHAMMER was a certainty. The President was of course anxious to have American action in the European theater, and he also would have liked to provide the Russians with direct aid. Moreover, in inviting Stalin to send Molotov to Washington the President had informally committed himself to a "second front" in 1942, and recent difficulties in supplying the Soviet Union made that commitment appear especially important.

The bulk of Allied assistance to Russia was transported by two routes. About three-quarters came by convoy around the North Cape of Scandanavia and into the Soviet ports of Murmansk and Archangel. Most of the remainder came by ship through the Indian Ocean to the complex of underdeveloped port facilities around Basra at the head of the Persian Gulf, and thence by rail and road into the Soviet Union.[39] During the first few months of Russian participation in the war, the northern convoy route had proven satisfactory. In February 1942, however, the Germans began to build up their naval and air forces in northern Norway to take advantage of the long daylight of the Arctic summer to interdict the northern convoy route. As the Germans stepped up the scale of their attacks, the losses of cargo and escorting naval vessels increased dangerously, and the British, who supplied most of the ships, found that the Murmansk run was severely undermining their ability to meet other commitments.

Roosevelt learned of the convoy predicament in late April, and fearing that the situation might cause the British to cut back on the Arctic convoys, urged Churchill not to "seek at this time any new understanding with Russia about the amount of our supplies" since such news would have "a most unfortunate effect" on Stalin. On 2 May Churchill rejected the President's suggestion, declaring that "we are absolutely extended, and I could not press the Admiralty further." Roosevelt reluctantly accepted Churchill's limitations on future deliveries to Russia, but indicated that he would prepare the Russians by suggesting that BOLERO was partially responsible for the cutback. The President apparently felt that the Russians would find a reduction more palatable if it were in some way linked to the second front.[40]

On the fourth, having already informed the Soviet Ambassador of the problems concerning the northern convoy route, the President cabled Stalin hinting at the possibility that "grave difficulties with the Northern convoy" might oblige the Allies to curtail the volume of goods flowing into the Soviet Union. Roosevelt sought to soften the impact by reminding Stalin of Molotov's scheduled trip to Washington, saying that he was looking forward to the meeting and hoped the Soviet Foreign Minister would stay at the White House when he arrived. The far from subtle implication was that Roosevelt intended to resolve most Soviet problems during his discussions with Molotov, presumably by announcing that a second front was on the way.[41]

The possible cutback of shipments to Russia was a source of great concern to the President. For not only were the supplies badly needed, but thus far they were the only tangible evidence of Allied support for the Soviet effort. As such, the President saw them as an important (possibly the most important) indication of Allied "good faith."

It is important to bear in mind that Roosevelt's exchange with Churchill and Stalin over the convoy problem took place just a few days before General Marshall wrote the President (6 May) insisting that he choose between BOLERO and the projects suggested by King and MacArthur. As a result, at the time Roosevelt was faced with the Marshall ultimatum he had already in effect told the Russians that a second front was in the offing. Therefore when confronted with a choice between Marshall and King he had little choice but to support the Chief of Staff. In so doing he took the opportunity to clarify and formulate the current strategic situation.

On the 6th Roosevelt met with the Chief of Staff to discuss his request. In the course of their conversation the President outlined two basic courses of action open to the United States in the current situation. The first called for the United States to: "1) Proceed with Sledgehammer and stay in France if we can. 2) Get all U.S. troops in action as quickly as possible; 3) Proceed in all other theaters as now planned; 4) Keep up aid to Russia but via Basra." The second possible course was to: "1) Abandon Sledgehammer 1942; 2) Slow up Bolero 1943 [ROUNDUP] for the coming three months; 3) Take all planes now headed from U.S. to England and reroute them to (a) Middle East or Egypt (majority), (b) S.W. Pacific (minority); 4) Send 5 Divisions to England slowly; 5) Send 5 divisions to Middle East fast; 6) Speed up Bolero preparations by October—so that Bolero-Roundup will be ready April 1943; 7) Keep up aid to Russia, but via Basra."[42]

Significantly both courses suggested by the President called for American troops to go into action against Germany in 1942. The second, proposing their use alongside the British in the Libyan campaign, had the obvious disadvantage of not providing the diversion on the Continent. Further, joining the British in the desert would have neither American Army support nor the beneficial domestic political impact of the cross-Channel attack.[43]

There was, of course, no doubt as to which alternative the President intended to choose. His written reply to Marshall (dated 6 May) emphatically asserted that he did not want BOLERO "slowed down," explaining that when he had suggested that reinforcements might be sent to the Pacific he meant only if it "could properly be done" without interfering with plans for the European theater.[44] The President expanded on this topic in a long memo dated 6 May and addressed to Stimson, Marshall, Arnold, Knox, King, and Hopkins (MacArthur was sent a separate conciliatory explanation). Setting forth his analysis of the requirements of the current military situation, Roosevelt reaffirmed his determination to see American troops in action against Germany in 1942, declaring that he had been disturbed by "American and British naval objections to operations in the European Theatre prior to 1943." He thought it was "essential that active operations be conducted in 1942" in order to assist the Soviet Union and suggested that a second front of limited scale would be sufficient to draw German forces from the East. According to the President, once air supremacy had been secured over the northwestern coast of Europe the Allies might conduct comparatively small hit-and-run commando raids; or "super commando operations" carried out by forces numbering up to 50,000 troops which might remain in France for about a week; or establish a permanent bridgehead which could be reinforced, made secure, and used as a point of entry for a larger force in 1943. In any event, the need to sustain Russia, the President declared, required that action be initiated in 1942, not in 1943. To do so, the Allies had to be prepared to launch what Roosevelt called "an operation of desperation."[45]

Even as the President's commitment to SLEDGEHAMMER hardened, continuous study of the project was confirming the initial estimates of its impracticality. At a May 5th White House conference concerning the landing craft situation, the President was told that the large landing craft needed to put artillery and tanks on French beaches would not be available by the fall. In regard to the smaller personnel-carrying types planned for the assault, the British naval representative predicted that a large proportion would not survive the Channel crossing and that the men who did make it across in such boats would be in no condition to fight. A major obstacle to the President's efforts to secure the critically-needed large landing craft for SLEDGEHAMMER was Admiral King, who objected to the expansion of landing craft construction on the grounds that it seriously interfered with the production of anti-submarine and escort vessels which King considered vitally important.[46] Undeterred, the President directed Lt. General Brehon Somervell (Chief, Services of Supply) to submit a study to him showing "What we can do—not what can't we do—by September 1942 . . . in assembling landing craft to effect the BOLERO channel crossing." A week later Somervell reported that according to his best estimates, by early September there would be enough landing craft of appropriate types in Britain to carry an expedition of about 21,000 men, 3,000 vehicles, and 300 tanks to France.[47] That large a force would constitute a sizeable raid, but could by no stretch of the imagination be considered a second front.

The President's refusal to be dissuaded by estimates that repeatedly indicated the impracticality of a landing in France in 1942 was based in large measure on his desire to assist the

Soviet Union to withstand an expected second German on-slaught. The Russians had survived the initial German thrust launched in June 1941 and in the first week in December had begun a counteroffensive that had succeeded in making modest gains. However, during the spring of 1942 the Russian drive had shown signs of petering out, and by the second week of May the Germans had once again taken the initiative with some impor-tant local successes. The President's concern over Russian pros-pects reflected the informed consensus in Washington based on estimates of the comparative overall strength of the opposing forces in the East. On balance it appeared that despite its severe losses the German Army still had the ability to force the Soviets to sue for peace during the coming six months. Should the Russians quit the war the Western Allies would be obliged to seek peace with Hitler or face a protracted military struggle of doubtful outcome. A second front, it was argued, would draw off sufficient German forces to tip the balance in favor of the Rus-sians and was therefore a military necessity.

While this argument certainly appealed to Roosevelt, his in-terest in the second front, as has been suggested, went beyond the tangible military assistance which the project would render the Soviets. The fact that he clearly recognized SLEDGEHAMMER might amount to no more than a series of commando raids suggests that whatever hopes he may have entertained for the operation achieving positive decisive results vis à vis Russia, he saw the second front primarily as a symbol or token of America's commitment to all-out aggressive war against Germany. Its value as such was manifold. The promise of a second front in 1942 would bolster public support for the war in both Britain and the United States. Moreover, it was the sign of good faith that Roosevelt hoped would dissuade the Russians from press-ing their territorial claims on the harassed and vulnerable Churchill; or from feeling betrayed and angered at the cutback in the Arctic convoys. Finally, that same token of good faith—of common commitment—might well be the deciding factor for Stalin if during the coming months he was faced with the choice of negotiating a disadvantageous settlement with Hitler or con-tinuing a costly struggle. When viewed as a token, even a landing which was driven into the sea without having drawn a single German foe from the Eastern front could be considered a success.

The President anticipated that his forthcoming meeting with Soviet Foreign Minister Molotov would give him an opportunity to assure the Soviets personally that the Allies intended to open a second front on the Continent in 1942. This he hoped would dissuade the Russians from pressing their treaty claims on the British (if the preliminary commitments to a second front had not already done so); ease the pain of the forced cutback of the Arctic run; and steel Stalin's resolve in the coming test with the Axis. By May, however, hope of obtaining all of these objectives must have strained even Roosevelt's powerful optimism.

Prospects for influencing Anglo–Soviet negotiations appeared especially dim. At the end of March, faced with Russian refusal to discuss important military matters until the frontier question was settled, the British Government decided to sign a treaty with the Soviet Union recognizing Soviet territorial claims excepting the area seized from Poland. In reaching that decision, Churchill and Eden were influenced by the lingering fear that if they did not give in to Russian demands Stalin might, if occasion arose, take the Soviet Union out of the war. A more positive consideration was official feeling that the proposed treaty would help form the base of hoped for postwar collaboration between the two countries. Finally, it was recognized that the issue was more one of principle than of substance since in all probability Russia would reoccupy the territory in question should she succeed in defeating Germany.[48]

At the beginning of April Eden had invited Molotov to London for final treaty negotiations, and he was scheduled to arrive in the British capital during the latter part of May. In the meantime negotiations between the Foreign Office and the Soviet Ambassador, Ivan Maisky, proceeded in an effort to resolve the major issues before Molotov's arrival. The discussions, however, revealed that the Russians had increased their demands and so the talks made little progress. The Soviet Government now wanted not only a free hand in the Baltic States but also the exclusion of the United Kingdom from Soviet–Polish frontier negotiations, and prior British agreement (by means of a secret protocol) to as yet unseen Russian treaties with Finland and Rumania.[49]

The British Government, though willing to accede to Russia's initial demands, was reluctant to expand its commitment along the lines now suggested. Thus, when Molotov arrived in London on the 20th there was some doubt as to whether discussions would actually result in agreement. In his opening talks with the British, Molotov implied that he would make no concession on Russia's latest demands, adding, however, that he attached more importance to the second front than to the treaty. On the 22nd Churchill and representatives of the British Chiefs briefed the Soviet Foreign Minister on current Allied plans and preparations. According to Churchill's account, Molotov was told that the Allies were planning an assault on the French coast for later in the year which they hoped would draw German air forces from the east. Churchill made it clear, however, that it was unlikely that "any move we could make in 1942 . . . would draw off large numbers of enemy land forces from the eastern front."[50] Not surprisingly this presentation failed to diminish Molotov's insistence that the Anglo–Soviet treaty include the boundary settlement provisions which the Russians had recently put forth.

Having reached an impasse in the negotiations, the British now attempted to break the deadlock by suggesting that the Political and Military Treaties be dropped altogether in favor of a Treaty of Mutual Assistance, such as the one Eden had proposed in December, which would make no mention of the thorny frontier problem. At this point the American Ambassador in London, Gilbert Winant, met with Molotov and told him very frankly of the adverse American public reaction that was likely to greet the signing of the Political Agreement which the Soviets had been pressing for. On the other hand, Winant noted, the Treaty of Mutual Assistance would be welcomed in the United States. On the following day, Molotov cabled the text of the proposed Mutual Assistance pact to Moscow along with what he had recently learned of British and American attitudes toward the proposals. Commenting on these developments, Eden noted that it was "quite evident" that Maxim Litvinov, the Soviet Ambassador in the United States, had not kept his government informed of American opinion, suggesting that if the Russians had been aware of the hostility toward the proposed boundary settlement, Stalin would not have pressed the issue. That night Molotov told Eden that he liked the Treaty of Mutual Assistance better than he had expected, and from that point the issue moved swiftly to resolution. On the 26th, amidst much secrecy, the Anglo–Soviet treaty was signed.[51]

The reasons for the abrupt Soviet change on the frontiers issue are not known. It is likely that, as Eden later speculated, Molotov became convinced during his stay in England that a frontiers treaty would seriously antagonize the United States and thereby diminish chances of securing a second front in 1942. This would explain why Molotov went back to the Mutual Assistance treaty which made no provision on frontiers, rather than accepting the draft Political-Military treaty which the British had agreed to in April, which did recognize most of the Soviet boundary claims. The key event seems to have been Winant's talk with Molotov on the 23rd. As the Ambassador himself observed ". . . it wasn't until I told him myself [of Roosevelt's very real opposition to a Frontiers Treaty] that he agreed to abandon his position and recommend to Stalin the draft [Mutual Assistance] Treaty which I had worked on with Eden."[52] Very likely Roosevelt's messages suggesting military action in 1942, and reports from Litvinov of intense agitation of the issue in the United States, convinced Molotov that he would be able to extract from the President the commitment he had been unable to obtain from the Prime Minister—if Russia demonstrated its good will by dropping the frontier issue.

Molotov arrived in Washington on the afternoon of 29 May, and that evening conferred for the first time with the President and Hopkins at the White House. The Foreign Minister came right to the point. The outcome of the German offensive was doubtful, he said, but it was possible that Moscow and Rostov would be lost and the Red Army forced to withdraw beyond the Volga. Should that happen, they would not be able to engage anywhere near the number of Germans presently involved in operations in Russia, and the brunt of the German war effort would be directed against the western Allies. Turning to the matter of the second front, Molotov declared that what was needed was an operation that would draw forty of Hitler's divisions to the West. This he thought could be accomplished by an Allied expeditionary force of thirty infantry and five armored divisions; he made no mention of diverting Axis air units. Phrasing his request in the most positive terms, Molotov declared that if the Allies acted immediately, the Red Army could defeat Germany within a reasonably short time.

The President asked Molotov whether the desired diversion might be obtained by an expedition of ten divisions (the maximum estimated to be available for operations in 1942) which might undertake the cross-Channel attack "perhaps not with any idea that they should attempt to establish themselves on the continent permanently, but merely to create an intensive diversion with the possibility that they might eventually be forced to withdraw, even at the expense of another Dunkirk." After all, the President observed, "the Germans would not know for a while how much of a force we were sending, whether the first ten divisions were not really the prelude to large debarkations." Molotov showed no enthusiasm for the President's proposal, and reiterated his Government's contention that thirty-five divisions "was the minimum force that could do the job with some prospect of permanent success."

The President admitted the force of Molotov's arguments but asked him to bear in mind that he "had to reckon with" military advisors who were inclined to prefer "a sure thing in 1943 to a risky adventure in 1942," observing that the same principle might apply to Churchill as well.[53] It should be pointed out that while the President was probably correct in saying that the American military and the British Prime Minister preferred to wait until the spring of 1943 before launching the cross-Channel attack, his remark was somewhat misleading. It was not caution that limited SLEDGEHAMMER to ten divisions, but the impossibility of gathering sufficient landing craft to carry more than ten divisions across the Channel before October 1942.

On the following day Marshall joined the President, Hopkins, and Admiral King at the White House for another meeting with Molotov. At the President's suggestion the Soviet Foreign Minister repeated his analysis of the Russian military situation for the benefit of Marshall and King. Molotov indicated that there were two possible courses which events might take in Russia in 1942: 1) The Red Army might be able to withstand the coming German onslaught in and around its present defensive positions without a decisive weakening of Red Army strength; or 2) The Russians might be driven back beyond the Volga River with severe losses, thus indefinitely crippling Soviet offensive power, throwing the burden of defeating Hitler on the West, and consequently prolonging the war. Should the Allies be able to "create a new front and to draw off forty German divisions from the Soviet front," Molotov reiterated, "the Soviets could either beat Hitler this year or insure beyond question his ultimate defeat." Molotov now bluntly inquired if the Allies were prepared to launch an attack which would divert forty German divisions. The President turned to General Marshall and asked "whether developments were clear enough so that we could say to Mr. Stalin that we are preparing a second front." To this diluted revision of Molotov's inquiry the Chief of Staff was able to reply honestly in the affirmative, and the President then authorized Molotov to inform Stalin "that we expect the formation of a second front this year."

If Molotov thought that he had been guaranteed the thirty-five division front he had sought, then the President had clearly misled him, for Roosevelt was aware that a force of such size could not be put into France in 1942. In suggesting that Soviet expectations would be met Roosevelt may have had in mind a bridgehead of up to ten divisions in the fall of 1942 which might be enlarged by the following spring to the thirty-five divisions envisaged by Molotov. If this was Roosevelt's thinking, the record of their conversations does not indicate that he made the point clear to the Soviet representative.

While Molotov was probably deceived by the President's declaration, General Marshall's subsequent elaboration of Allied plans should have warned the Foreign Minister that the Allied concept of a second front did not entirely conform to his own. The object of the second front, General Marshall told Molotov, was "to create as quickly as possible a situation on the continent under which the Germans would be forced into an all-out air engagement" by the presence of an Allied force in France. While the Soviets based their considerations on the number of German divisions (forty) which they would like to see diverted from their front, the Allies, Marshall explained, had to base their actions on "the number of men we could ship across the Channel in order to provoke an all-out battle for the destruction of the German air-force." Marshall, using the argument raised some weeks earlier by Roosevelt, declared that America was limited by the necessity of sending tonnage to Murmansk. Marshall's point was valid only in regard to the large scale invasion contemplated for 1943. Operations in 1942, as we have seen, were hampered by the landing craft shortage, not by the shipping shortage.[54]

On June first the President and Hopkins held a final meeting with Molotov before the Soviet diplomat left for London on his way back to Moscow. The President took the occasion to elaborate on the downward revision of the program of lend-lease aid to Russia which had been suggested to Molotov on the previous day. Both Roosevelt and Hopkins stressed that the cutback was designed to free shipping for the buildup of forces in England. The President noted that "every ship we could shift to the English run meant that the second front was so much the closer to being realized." After all, he observed, "ships could not be in two places at once," and every ton taken from the run to Murmansk could be used to increase the forces building up for the invasion of the continent. "The Soviets could not eat their cake and have it too." All this was of course true, but largely beside the point. No mention was made of the real reason for the proposed cutback on the Murmansk run—the difficulties experienced by the British in convoying the shipping in the face of increased German opposition. While it is undoubtedly true that the President and his military advisors wanted to increase the shipping available for BOLERO, it is also true, as indicated above, that an increase would not have significantly affected the size of the 1942 effort.

Molotov, now apparently for the first time grasping the meaning of the attempt to link the second front and the Murmansk run, objected to the President's remarks: "The second front would be stronger if the first front still stood fast." Moreover, he asked with what seemed to the interpreter "deliberate sarcasm," what would happen if the Soviets cut down their requirements and then no second front eventuated? With that question in mind Molotov now insisted that the President give him a firm commitment to a second front in 1942. The President had already suggested that the munitions cutback was necessitated by BOLERO. If the Russians were to be deprived of supplies because of the second front buildup, it was understandable that they should expect assurances that the cross-Channel attack would indeed take place. Under the circumstances Roosevelt probably would very much have liked to oblige. However, he resisted the temptation to give Molotov a categorical commitment and instead instructed the Foreign Minister to tell Churchill and Stalin that "we expected to establish a second front," and that "we could proceed toward its creation with the more speed if the Soviet Government would make it possible for us to put [more] ships into the English service."[55] The President had again suggested that a second front would be exchanged for Soviet acceptance of curtailment of the Arctic run. On this misleading note the series of conferences between the Soviet representative and the President came to an end. Only a formal announcement on the result of the meetings remained to be worked out.[56]

While Molotov had every reason to conclude that he had received a promise of a second front, the American remarks contained so many reservations and conditions that at the conclusion of the meetings Allied intentions were probably not really very clear. Roosevelt was aware that the talks had been confusing and less than satisfactory from the Russian point of view and he told Marshall and King that in view of the dangerous situation on the Russian front he would like to make "a more specific answer to Molotov in regard to a second front." As a result, despite Marshall's objections the President accepted Molotov's suggestion that the public statement on the meetings contain the phrase: "in the course of the conversations full understanding was reached with regard to the urgent tasks of creating a Second Front in Europe in 1942." The communique containing this phrase was issued on June 11.[57] The President realized that this vague promise was needed to give the meeting the psychological value which he sought.

Roosevelt had hoped for a great triumph of personal diplomacy at the meetings but found the Russian Foreign Minister unimpressed by gestures of good will and tokens of cooperation. The discrepancy between Molotov's statement of Soviet needs and Allied capabilities must have come as a shock, making the President all the more anxious to provide some sign of Allied good will. In a letter to Churchill following the conferences, Roosevelt spoke of the need for launching operations before a break in the weather with the immediate objective of provoking an air battle which would result in either drawing German planes off the Russian front or in creating an opportunity for expanded ground operations leading to the establishment of a permanent bridgehead on the Continent.[58]

In spite of his inability to promise the Russians the level of military assistance they sought, Roosevelt had reason to be pleased with the meetings. For one thing, he had laid the groundwork for breaking the bad news to the Russians concerning the northern convoys. More importantly, the Soviets had been given the morale booster which the President thought they needed. As he told Churchill, he was "especially anxious" that Molotov carry back some "real results" and be able to give Stalin "a favorable account" of his mission since he (the President) was inclined to think that the Russians were at present "a bit down in the mouth."[59]

Roosevelt's concern over Stalin's attitude is the key to understanding the conference in Washington. For it was concern lest the Russian government pressure the British into recognition of Soviet boundaries which had led to the meeting initially, and it was concern for demonstrating Allied good faith and avoiding Russian displeasure that had led the President to link the curtailment of the Arctic convoys to a second front in 1942. His sensitivity to Soviet attitudes and his consequent reluctance to confront Stalin with unalloyed resistance to Soviet claims led Roosevelt during the Washington talks to complete the transformation of SLEDGEHAMMER from a doubtful operation of limited means and objectives into a "second front" for 1942, designed by implication to draw forty German divisions from the Eastern front. Significantly the evolution of this self-deception suffered little hindrance from General Marshall.

The Chief of Staff was dubious enough about the possibilities of launching a serious invasion of the Continent in 1942 to protest against the mention of any date in the communique describing the results of Molotov's visit. However, he made no real effort to shatter the President's growing illusions concerning the second front. For it was Roosevelt's faith in SLEDGEHAMMER which kept the President from turning a sympathetic ear to Admiral King, or General MacArthur, or Winston Churchill, or to anyone else with a scheme for the immediate employment of American military forces. If the probability of launching a cross-Channel attack in 1942 was once seriously impaired, the door would again be open to the multitude of competing projects that had characterized Allied military planning at ARCADIA and before. The spectre of GYMNAST continued to haunt General Marshall's thinking.

SEVEN

SLEDGEHAMMER Under Attack:
Marshall on the Defensive
June–July 1942

I

The response to the Second Front announcement in both the United States and in Russia was all that Roosevelt could have hoped for. In America, public enthusiasm for an immediate second front grew markedly following the Molotov visit, especially since renewed German offensive operations in Russia and the desperate struggle of the Red Army tended to dominate the headlines during June. Even isolationist elements of the nation's press, previously indifferent to the European war and hostile toward the Soviet Union, joined the chorus of demands for immediate Allied action.[1] In the Soviet Union itself the press and radio followed up the June 11th announcement with repeated and unqualified references to the coming Allied invasion of the Continent, stimulating considerable enthusiastic discussion of the subject among the Soviet people.[2]

However, in both the United States and the Soviet Union it was clear from the outset that the enthusiastic response had a potential for untoward results. By the end of July, officials of the Office of War Information[3] reported that an "angry impatience" over Allied military inactivity had superceded the initial "thunderous revival of demand" for a second front. OWI warned that the failure to produce a second front could lead to serious repercussions in public opinion.[4] In the Soviet Union much the same situation appeared, as Western observers there warned of the danger of a negative reaction should the Allies fail to launch the promised assault. American Ambassador William H. Standley informed the President of the overly optimistic construction being put on the second front communique in Russia and noted that: "If such a front does not materialize quickly and on a large scale, these people will be so deluded [sic] in our sincerity of purpose and will for concerted action that inestimable harm will be done to the cause of the United Nations."[5] Thus the key to the long-range success or failure of the Washington talks lay in the ability of the Allies to fulfill the commitment which Roosevelt had made.

There was no reason for President Roosevelt to be alarmed by any of this. He had been led to believe that a cross-Channel assault on some scale during 1942, although difficult, was not impossible. The SLEDGEHAMMER concept had been neither carefully considered nor defined in the Marshall Memorandum, and little had been done in Washington since the April meetings to alter the situation. Instead, during April and May the pressures of a variety of divergent immediate problems gradually transformed SLEDGEHAMMER from its original purpose as a possible expedient for use in case of a grave emergency in Russia or an exceptional opportunity in France, into a scheduled operation (of limited size) largely political in purpose. Thus during this period the increasing value of SLEDGEHAMMER as a concept tended to inhibit careful consideration of it as a reality, with the result that, at the White House at least, there was a total lack of appreciation of the difficulties which a landing on the Continent in 1942 entailed. His thinking colored by optimism born of this ignorance, the President probably welcomed the enthusiasm generated by the June 11th communique as a sign of the offensive spirit he had long sought to foster.

The British military perspective was, of course, quite different and it was this difference which was to undermine and ultimately destroy the American sponsored commitment to Russia. Experienced in amphibious warfare both in putting troops ashore and evacuating them under fire, the British were more aware than the Americans of the difficulties of such operations. Having been in the war longer and having experienced it at first hand, they were less prone to impatience and less susceptible to the blandishment of desperate measures, especially where the burden of sacrifice would fall primarily on British troops as was the case for SLEDGEHAMMER. Finally, Churchill and his military chiefs were free from the blinding effects of "political" commitment which characterized the attraction of General Marshall and the President to SLEDGEHAMMER. As a result, when the second front communique threatened to force Great Britain into an operation of doubtful merit, Churchill decided that the time had come to apprise the Americans of the reality of the military situation as it applied to operations in 1942.

Churchill and most of his senior officers had long entertained strong misgivings concerning the feasibility of a cross-Channel attack during 1942. Careful study of the proposal following the London Meeting failed to dispel their doubts. On 8 May the British Chiefs concluded that "on account of its dependency on the weather, the difficulties of maintenance [logistics] and the lack of sufficient landing craft, 'Sledgehammer' with the resources available, is not a sound military operation." Accepting that assessment, the Chiefs decided that the operation was possible only if German morale disintegrated, eliminating the likelihood of serious opposition. An emergency attack in the event of an imminent Soviet collapse was dismissed as suicidal with no prospect of materially aiding the Russians.[6] The result was a decision to hold plans for SLEDGEHAMMER in readiness for use only in case of German collapse.

The substance of these findings was passed along to the Prime Minister on May 27th. Churchill also learned from the Chiefs that in the event that heavy fighting continued in Russia, with no decision in sight and no significant impairment of German combat ability, the forces that the Allies could bring to bear in the initial assault wave (4,300 men and 160 tanks) would not be sufficient to establish a beachhead. This probably confirmed Churchill's own estimate of the situation. He thereupon decided against any major invasion effort in 1942, observing that an Allied disaster would in no way help the Russians, but would seriously jeopardize future efforts.[7]

Having substantial grounds for believing that SLEDGEHAMMER would be a pointless disaster, Churchill now undertook to break the spell which the operation had apparently cast over the President's thinking. On the 28th a telegram from the Former Naval Person to Roosevelt began the campaign of friendly persuasion: "We are working hard with your officers, all preparations are proceeding ceaselessly on the largest scale. Dickie [Mountbatten] will explain to you the difficulties of 1942 when he arrives.[8] I have also told the Staffs to study a landing in the north of Norway . . . which seems necessary to ensure the flow of our supplies next year to Russia." The Prime Minister's message also mentioned that the long delayed British offensive in the western desert had begun and concluded with the words which were to introduce the final stage in the several months of deliberations over the site and timing of the first offensive: "We must never let 'Gymnast' pass from our minds. All other preparations would help, if need be, towards that."[9]

The assignment of Lord Louis to the task of opening the assault on the SLEDGEHAMMER myth was a good one. Mountbatten had made a very favorable impression on Roosevelt at their first meeting and his charm, youthful vigor, and distinguished war record assured him an attentive hearing from the President. Moreover, Mountbatten as head of Britain's Combined Operations was an authority on amphibious operations. As a result, his opinion was bound to carry considerable weight with the President.

While Lord Louis made ready for his visit to Washington, the Prime Minister proceeded with an examination of the alternatives to SLEDGEHAMMER. Before leaving, Mountbatten told Churchill that he shared the conclusions reached by the Force Commanders and the Chiefs of Staff as to the impracticability of SLEDGEHAMMER and suggested that a large scale raid on the port of Dieppe was the most ambitious action the Allies could undertake against the Continent in 1942. Churchill was now thoroughly convinced that no substantial landing in France should be made on a sacrifice basis, that is, without the intention of staying, and he was equally convinced that no permanent landing was possible in 1942.[10] He did, however, agree to a large scale raid (RUTTER). This now famous raid on Dieppe had been considered since early April. It was to be small (equivalent to less than a division), intended to remain on the Continent less than one day, and was related to SLEDGEHAMMER-ROUNDUP only in that it was hoped it would provide lessons and experience to be applied to the larger operation. Churchill called it a "butcher and bolt" raid. The raid was carried out in August—with disastrous results. It accomplished few of its tactical objectives and suffered 60 percent casualties. It did, however, provide costly lessons in the problems of assaulting the Continent: so costly that had the raid taken place before the final decision on the second front (end of July) its results would almost certainly have quickly ended the debate over the feasibility of SLEDGEHAM-MER.[11]

On June 4th, Churchill discussed with General Brooke a variety of likely substitutes for SLEDGEHAMMER, including in addition to an Anglo–American invasion of North Africa (GYMNAST), several operations designed to help secure the convoy route to Murmansk and Archangel. Churchill placed great faith in one of these, an invasion of Northern Norway (codenamed JUPITER), which he hoped would enable the British to break the German air and naval blockade of the Russian Arctic ports.[12] As for action along the French coast, Churchill suggested the preparations continue for possible use in the event of a German collapse. He emphasized, however, that SLEDGEHAMMER "should be dependent not on a Russian failure but on a Russian success and the consequent proven German demoralization in the west."[13]

In the midst of these discussions Soviet Foreign Minister Molotov arrived in London on his way home from his meetings with the President. Molotov brought with him the Second Front communique which he expected the British to endorse. Public release of the document was to await his arrival in Moscow. The Prime Minister and Foreign Secretary Eden did not share Molotov's obvious satisfaction over the results of the Washington meeting, especially since they had not given advance approval to the second front commitment, even though Britain would have to supply most of the manpower. Nevertheless, not wishing to repudiate the President's work, Churchill agreed to subscribe to the document. Before doing so, however, he made it quite clear to Molotov that he did not share American certainty concerning the prospects of the second front operation, and in discussions with the Russian representative on 9 and 10 June, and in an *aide-memoire* supplied him on the 10th, both the Prime Minister and Eden sought to hedge the Anglo-American commitment by stressing the difficulties of SLEDGEHAMMER and its uncertain feasibility. In his *aide-memoire* Churchill noted that while preparations for a major landing in France were under way "it would not further either the Russian cause or that of the Allies as a whole if, for the sake of action at any price, we embarked on some operation which ended in disaster. . . ." SLEDGEHAMMER would be carried out, Molotov was told, only if it appeared "sound and sensible" at the time of its scheduled launching.[14] In discussing these remarks with the Cabinet, Churchill made it clear that he had not committed Britain to carry out SLEDGEHAMMER and that Molotov understood this. He also indicated that he personally did not believe that the conditions under which the operation might be carried out were likely to arise.[15]

While those events were taking place in London, the Prime Minister's effort to woo the President from his attachment to SLEDGEHAMMER had already achieved substantial success. On June 9th Mountbatten dined with Roosevelt and Hopkins at the White House. After dinner the discussion turned to SLEDGEHAMMER, and Mountbatten outlined the difficulties of carrying out an effective assault on the Continent in 1942. He pointed out that no landing within Allied capacity could draw any German troops from the Russian front since there were some twenty-five German divisions already in France and a shortage of landing craft prevented the landing of an expedition large enough to overcome even that force. Roosevelt was apparently at a loss to rebut his argument and could only remind Mountbatten of the Prime Minister's alleged agreement to undertake a sacrifice landing that summer should things go badly on the Russian front.[16] The President said he was especially concerned that Mountbatten's pessimistic report might presage the immobilization of a million American troops in England, a possibility which he found intolerable. In this connection Roosevelt expressed interest in a delayed cross-Channel attack perhaps as late as December 1942 aimed at the capture of a port such as Cherbourg. Roosevelt also noted that he had been impressed by the injunction which had concluded Churchill's telegram of 28 May ("we must never let GYMNAST pass from our minds"). Indeed the President, his interest in the idea apparently revived, suggested that six American divisions might be sent straight to North Africa either to fight alongside the British in Libya, or to join a

British force in a landing in Morocco. Thus in a few hours of informal conversation Mountbatten had begun the overthrow of more than two months of General Marshall's efforts. Once again the Prime Minister threatened to destroy the Army's grip on Allied strategy.[17] Apparently hoping to follow through on his initial success, Churchill now informed the President that he wished to come to Washington for further talks on Allied plans. Not content with stirring the President's interest in GYMNAST, Churchill was probably anxious to purge the President of any lingering interest in a sacrifice operation.

The purpose and success of Mountbatten's mission was quickly known to General Marshall, and when he learned of the forthcoming visit of the Prime Minister he began at once to shore up his defenses. Anticipating that GYMNAST would prove to be the chief rival to BOLERO-SLEDGEHAMMER, the Chief of Staff instructed the army planners to produce an up-to-date appraisal of the North African invasion. Their findings left Marshall convinced of the pernicious results to be expected from the scheme and more determined than ever to prevent its realization. Armed now with counterarguments both old and new, General Marshall was ready to meet the latest challenge. The opportunity for the Chief of Staff to express his views came on 17 June when the President called Stimson, Knox, Marshall, King, and Arnold to the White House to prepare for the talks with the British that were to commence the following day.

Although the principal immediate cause of both the Churchill visit and the White House strategy session on the 17th was British objections to SLEDGEHAMMER, several important changes in the military situation during June had to be taken into account. In the Pacific the American Navy had won a decisive engagement with a huge Japanese naval force off the island of Midway (8 June). The victory had two important but contradictory implications for future Allied operations in the Pacific: it clearly ended the ability of the Japanese to expand their conquests in the Pacific significantly, and thus made the current Allied position in the Pacific secure without the need for important reinforcement; on the other hand the magnitude of the success suggested that the victory should be exploited by a rapid expansion of offensive operations in the Pacific.[18]

The First Offensive

Recent news from the Middle East was of a different nature. During the spring both the British 8th Army under General Claude Auchinleck and Field Marshall Erwin Rommel's Afrika Korps had been preparing for the next round in the drawn out struggle for the southern coast of the Mediterranean. Rommel struck first. After a period in which it appeared that the German effort had been checked, the battle turned against the British on June 12 and 13 when they suffered a severe defeat in the battle of Knightsbridge. Auchinleck's forces then began a retreat toward the Egyptian border that threatened the complete elimination of British military power west of Suez.

So stood the military situation of 17 June. Eventual victory in the Pacific seemed almost certain, the situation in the Middle East was grave, and the supreme test along the Russian front was expected shortly. On this date and in these circumstances, the President called together Secretaries Stimson and Knox and the three military Chiefs for an afternoon conference at the White House. The Commander-in-Chief opened the meeting by announcing that the arrival of Churchill and the British Chiefs on the morrow warranted some preliminary discussion, particularly of possible diversionary efforts for the relief of Russia during 1942. The President went on to say that while he favored a cross-Channel attack, he now had doubts that it could be undertaken in 1942. The main objective, he said, was to "get something done in 1942 which would help the Russians," and a landing on the Continent could not be effected until April 1943. As a result, he was considering two alternatives to the cross-Channel attack. The first was a landing in North Africa, which he felt would meet with only token opposition.[19] There was no reason, according to the President, that the United States could not launch an invasion of Northwest Africa by 10 September 1942. The President did not explain his choice of the date. His suggestion of an all-American force probably reflected the widely-held conviction that the French garrison would resist British or Gaullist forces but would welcome the Americans.

A second alternative to SLEDGEHAMMER suggested by the President was the deployment of American troops to the Middle East in direct support of British forces currently facing the Germans at the Egyptian–Libyan border. This suggestion reflected the President's concern at signs of imminent British collapse. The State and War Departments had been warned repeatedly from Cairo by Ambassador Alexander Kirk and by Col. Bonner Fellers (the War Department's observer in the area) of the danger of a British rout unless they were provided with direct American support.[20]

While both General Marshall and Secretary Stimson shared some of the President's concern over recent Allied reverses, they were acutely dismayed by his suggestion of American participation in African operations. Marshall responded with a restatement of the familiar arguments against the operation. Basing his remarks on a paper prepared for him shortly before the meeting by the Operations Division, the Chief of Staff noted that the scheme lacked several prerequisites for success; sea transport, escort ships, and air support. His fundamental objection, however, was that the operation would involve the United States in an entirely new, indecisive theater, thus delaying the rapid buildup of forces in England for the crucial assault on the Continent.

Stimson strongly supported Marshall's presentation but both were probably surprised to find that Admiral King did not join in the attack on GYMNAST.[21] Instead King cut much of the ground from under the Army position by unexpectedly declaring that he could furnish the convoys for the operation if necessary by drawing ships from the Pacific. As far as air support was concerned, General Arnold thought that the strength already scheduled for use in the Middle East would suffice for the GYMNAST operation.

The discussion at the White House settled nothing. Roosevelt did not at that time indicate a strong preference for any particular course of action. Instead he simply asked his military advisors to think about the alternatives he had suggested with a view toward recommending the best course of action for helping the Russians in 1942. On the latter point he was uncharacteristically pessimistic. General Arnold notes that for the first time in his knowledge the President expressed doubts about winning the war, declaring "that right now if the Russians held until December he would give odds that we would win the war, but on the other hand if the Russians folded up by December it would be very doubtful that we could win the war and we would have less than an even bet."[22] The President concluded the meeting by asking Marshall to arrange for the reception of the British military delegation due to arrive with the Prime Minister on the 19th. The President's schedule called for General Marshall and his colleagues to confer with the British military representatives in Washington while he entertained the Prime Minister in the more agreeable surroundings at Hyde Park.

Stimson and Marshall hastened to make use of the short time remaining before Churchill's arrival to put their case before the President in writing. On the 19th Stimson sent the President an eloquent and persuasive review of BOLERO and its strategic advantages. BOLERO-SLEDGEHAMMER was in the Secretary's view the surest way of breaking Hitler's grip in Russia in 1942 and of bringing ultimate victory. An attack on France, Stimson declared, was "the easiest road to the center of our chief enemy's heart." That being so, "an immense burden of proof rested upon any proposition such as GYMNAST which posed even the slightest risk to BOLERO." He concluded his plea for SLEDGEHAMMER by reminding the President that the cross-Channel attack "in its inception and in its present development is an essentially American project, brought into this war as the vitalizing contribution of our fresh and unwearied leaders and forces," and should not be abandoned in favor of alternatives posed by the presumably weary British.[23]

General Marshall was equally active in defending BOLERO. Following the meeting of the 17th, he succeeded in convincing Admiral King that GYMNAST should be opposed, and on the 19th the Navy Chief revised his previous position and joined Marshall in a memorandum to the President condemning the operation. After restating the arguments against North African operations the Chiefs declared that "the advantages of implementing the GYMNAST plan as compared to other operations, particularly 1942 emergency BOLERO operations [SLEDGEHAMMER], lead to the conclusion that the occupation of Northwest Africa this summer should not be attempted."[24]

While the President, now in the company of Churchill at Hyde Park, considered their views, Marshall undertook to bring General Brooke and the British military into the anti-GYMNAST camp. It proved surprisingly easy. The British professionals, pleased by the buildup of American forces in Britain, optimistic about a return to the Continent in 1943, and worried about the further scattering of badly strained Allied resources in the coming months, were strongly committed to BOLERO and dead set against GYMNAST. At meetings in Washington on the 19th and 20th the American and British Chiefs found themselves happily in accord. They agreed that their efforts should concentrate on accumulating Allied forces in Britain looking toward a full scale attack in Northwest France in the spring of 1943. Any other offensive operation in 1942 was to be undertaken only if it did not delay the 1943 invasion (ROUNDUP); or if it was forced upon the Allies by emergency conditions not currently existing. GYM-NAST was specifically ruled out because it would seriously diminish the availability of men and equipment, especially cargo and troop shipping, needed to sustain operations elsewhere, particularly in the Middle East. It would also markedly slow up BOLERO. The problem in that regard was that GYMNAST called for the transport of forces directly from the United States to the African coast, and as such required the protracted diversion of shipping to the transAtlantic crossing. On the other hand, any operation against the European continent would be based in England, thus maintaining a concentration of base organization, lines of communication, and air strength. Nevertheless, while the Combined Chiefs rejected GYMNAST and supported BOLERO-ROUNDUP, they did not endorse SLEDGEHAMMER as a scheduled operation. Instead, their final recommendations noted that since any 1942 operation would have some adverse effect upon the hoped for 1943 invasion, it should be undertaken only in case of necessity or exceptional opportunity.[25]

This general agreement, though significant, glossed over an important divergence of views. The Americans, though joining the British in preferring to husband Allied resources for 1943, supported SLEDGEHAMMER as the next best alternative. The British for their part were strongly opposed under any circumstances to operations on the Continent in 1942. At discussions on the 20th General Brooke made it clear that although the concept of a sacrifice operation on the Continent to relieve pressure on Russia had been exhaustively examined, the British Chiefs had been unable to discover any plan they could approve.

Thus, while the British Chiefs could see the fallacies of GYMNAST, they were not prepared, as General Marshall was, to impart strategic value to SLEDGEHAMMER.[26]

While Marshall may well have preferred a British commitment to SLEDGEHAMMER, he was probably satisfied with the agreement reached by the Combined Chiefs. Though it only delayed the decision on operations in 1942, it did strongly endorse the concentration in England looking toward an invasion of the Continent in 1943. Moreover it seemed to spell the end of GYMNAST. However, as the Chiefs had feared, the concurrent discussions at Hyde Park made the professional deliberations in Washington academic.

Churchill had indeed already gone far toward convincing Roosevelt not only that SLEDGEHAMMER was impracticable but that some other 1942 operation had to be substituted for it at once. While affirming his commitment to the concept of a cross-Channel attack and supporting continued preparations for a possible landing in the fall, Churchill declared that he opposed any operation certain to suffer high losses. If that happened, he said, it would not help the Russians whatever their plight, but would endanger the Frenchmen who came to the aid of the invaders and gravely delay the main operation in 1943. "We hold strongly to the view that there should be no substantial landing in France this year unless we are going to stay." No British military authority had been able to devise such a plan. In the event that no feasible cross-Channel operation could be produced, Churchill asked: "Can we afford to stand idle in the Atlantic theatre during the whole of 1942?" Shouldn't the Allies be preparing some substitute such as GYMNAST which would at least indirectly take some of the weight off Russia?[27]

That same day Roosevelt, probably inspired by Churchill's remarks, replied to the Marshall-King memorandum of the 19th by asking the American Chiefs what they proposed as a substitute for GYMNAST in 1942 to aid the Soviets. "On the assumption that the Russian Army will be hard pressed and retreating . . . at what point or points can American ground forces prior to September 15, 1942 . . . execute an attack on German forces or in German controlled areas which can compel withdrawal of German forces from the Russian front?"[28]

That night, June 20th, without waiting for a reply, Roosevelt cut short the sojourn at Hyde Park and returned with Churchill to Washington to confer with their military advisors on the problem. General Marshall, aware that he would have to answer the President at a meeting the following morning, directed the Operations Division to prepare a response. The resultant memo produced by the planners on the 20th enumerated and ruled out all the alternatives to SLEDGEHAMMER mentioned thus far. They insisted instead that an attack on the French coast was both feasible and the only significant action within the Allies' capability in 1942. The planners acknowledged the dangers which their proposal involved but declared that "pinpricks" at the periphery of German power (e.g. GYMNAST) would not divert the Germans from their operations in Russia. To accomplish that, calculated risks would have to be taken. In further justifying continued loyalty to BOLERO-SLEDGEHAMMER the planners noted that "Allied strategy prior to the accepted Bolero Plan appears to have been based upon political considerations, emotionally engendered commitments and uncoordinated deployments."[29]

On Sunday, June 21st, General Marshall, fortified with the planners' report and the support of the Combined Chiefs, met with Churchill, Hopkins, and the President at the White House prepared to fight to keep BOLERO intact. Churchill started off the meeting with a "terrific attack" on SLEDGEHAMMER.[30] His undoubtedly eloquent arguments were answered by Marshall supported by Hopkins and, on this occasion, by the President himself. After lunch the four men were joined by General Brooke and General H. L. Ismay and the discussions resumed, apparently following along the same lines. Midway in the talks, however, news arrived from London which cast gloom over the meeting and diverted interest temporarily from the topic at hand.[31] The British garrison at Tobruk, numbering it was believed 25,000 men (actually 33,000) had succumbed to German seige. The capture of Tobruk gave Rommel a good sized port close to the front lines which would facilitate the resupply of the Axis forces in the desert. Churchill and Brooke were crestfallen, and the Americans, already much concerned by the situation in the Middle East, turned to consoling them. Marshall at this point repeated a previously tendered offer to send the First American

The First Offensive

Armored Division to the Middle East, but Brooke, aware that the force was only partially trained and that its deployment would entail the complications of setting up a separate front, declined in favor of taking the initial delivery of the new Sherman tanks which had been intended for use by the American division. The request was quickly and graciously honored by the President with Marshall's approval, and the details were left for the Chiefs to work out.

The discussion now returned to the issue of Allied relief for the Red Army and a compromise was quickly reached which held that plans and preparations for ROUNDUP were to continue with all speed and energy and a determined effort made to devise a feasible plan for a cross-Channel attack in 1942. If none could be found, however, the possibility of an invasion of French North Africa was to be conscientiously explored. Offensive operations in 1942 were endorsed as an absolute necessity.[32]

The agreement of the 21st was a tactical victory for General Marshall and the Army since it recognized the overriding importance of BOLERO and the cross-Channel attack, and put off a decision concerning GYMNAST. Marshall could still hope that during the next few months some other operations which did not detract from ROUNDUP might be found, or that GYMNAST would be ruled out by changes in the military situation, or by a failure to achieve the required political conditions.

But if the Anglo–American agreement had preserved BOLERO for the time being, still discussions and events during the British visit had clearly influenced Roosevelt's thinking in a way that boded ill for the continued concentration of Allied efforts on the cross-Channel attack. The President's faith in SLEDGEHAMMER had been badly shaken, his concern for the situation in the Middle East aroused, and his interest in GYMNAST revived. Even before the British departed, the impact of recent events on the President's thinking was apparent. After dinner on the 21st, Roosevelt, Hopkins, Marshall, and King met again with Churchill and the British military representatives in a session which lasted past one the following morning. A variety of subjects was covered, but toward the end of the meeting Marshall was "terribly taken aback" to hear the President offer to have American troops take over the whole front between Tehran and Alexandria. Roosevelt apparently intended the move to release British forces for the campaign in the desert while building up the defense of the Middle East against a possible German breakthrough in the Caucasus. Marshall, according to Stimson's second-hand account, refused at that late hour to discuss a scheme which directly challenged all of his hopes and plans for the coming months, and in the Secretary's words, "he walked out."[33]

On the 22nd, with Stimson and Knox present, discussions between Roosevelt and Churchill resumed. The President again repeated his offer to send a large American force to secure the rear of the British position in the Middle East, but Churchill, much to Stimson's relief, did not pick up on the suggestion and the proposal was dropped. Marshall's immediate response, if any, to the renewed proposal is unrecorded; however, that same day he did draft a memorandum for the President on the question. The Chief of Staff flatly opposed the idea for a variety of reasons. On logistical grounds he noted that the area was 12,000 miles from the United States and that as a result "for every man we place in the Middle East we could put three in Western Europe." He opposed it on administrative-political grounds: "it is doubtful that they [the British] would consent to our control of operations in that area." And finally he opposed it because it was far afield from the point at which the ultimate offensive must come: "The decisive theater is Western Europe. That is the only place where the concerted effort of the bulk of the U.S. and British forces can be brought to bear on the Germans. A large venture in the Middle East would make a decisive American campaign in Western Europe out of the question."[34]

On the 23rd Marshall struck out again at the diversionary threat. The Prime Minister had submitted a memorandum to Roosevelt on the 20th which questioned the SLEDGEHAMMER scheme, challenged the Americans to devise an alternative, and revived the idea of GYMNAST. Marshall now provided the President with his answer. The success of SLEDGEHAMMER, he suggested, was largely a matter of will. The difficulties posed by the operation could be overcome, Marshall said, by imaginative and resourceful planning. "Any military operation against odds may lead to disaster," but the project was worth the risks involved since it would at very least bring about a major air battle over Western Europe, which he felt was in itself probably the greatest single aid that could be rendered to Russia. GYMNAST he again dismissed as an indecisive diversion from the main theater.[35]

In spite of the efforts of his military advisors, Roosevelt's faith in SLEDGEHAMMER had been shaken, and the central question from that point forward was—If not SLEDGEHAMMER, what then? GYMNAST appeared to be the answer.

Stimson's diary entries for 23, 24, and 25 June reveal that both Marshall and the Secretary were beset by "anxiety and pressure" as a result of the President's "irresponsible attitude toward . . . Bolero."[36] Marshall now again faced the problem, as he saw it, of keeping "political considerations and British face-saving diversions from interfering with strategy. . . ."[37]

On the evening of the 25th the British left for home. A decision on the basic issue they had come to discuss, the viability of SLEDGEHAMMER, had been postponed. The more immediate problem in the Middle East emphasized by the fall of Tobruk had been dealt with—large amounts of material, but not American troops, were to be dispatched posthaste to the British desert forces. For the time being General Marshall, despite frustration and misgivings, reported to his War Department colleagues that his "struggle to keep diversions of our forces to other theaters from interfering with Bolero" had been successful.[38]

II

General Marshall's success was, however, short lived. Roosevelt and Churchill had decided at the June meetings that plans and preparations for SLEDGEHAMMER would be pressed ahead with the utmost energy until September, when a decision on the feasibility of the operation would be made. Returning to England Churchill and the British Chiefs reexamined SLEDGEHAMMER, particularly the effect on overall strategy of continuing preparations for the assault. Objections to the proposed invasion were many. Even the best prepared invasion of the Continent would be risky, but preparations for the proposed operation were inadequate in almost every respect. Deliveries of landing ships to England were considerably below expectations,[39] American troops scheduled for use in the operation could not be trained in amphibious warfare in time, and wind and weather in the Channel in early September were "uncertain." Moreover, incidental costs of the enterprise were high. The diversion of shipping would deny Britain 750,000 tons of needed imports, including food, and would so derange coastal shipping as to curtail the supply of coal available to England's factories and homes in the coming winter.

The strategic costs were if anything even more discouraging. Whether or not the operation was successful, SLEDGEHAMMER would, contrary to the views expressed by the Americans, significantly restrict the main invasion thrust scheduled for the spring of 1943. The British estimated that if SLEDGEHAMMER failed, the losses and dislocations entailed would delay the launching of ROUNDUP for two or three months. If SLEDGEHAMMER succeeded in establishing a bridgehead, the large scale attack in 1943 now contemplated would be ruled out by the necessity of committing Allied resources piecemeal to sustain and expand the small tenuous enclave established by SLEDGEHAMMER.

Most of those problems had been anticipated for some time, but it was now clear to the British that nothing was going to happen in the several weeks remaining before the scheduled assault to circumvent or mitigate them. On the contrary, continued preparations for an operation that should not, and almost certainly would not, take place were beginning to delay training and other preparations for the strategically far more important landings in 1943. In those circumstances the British Chiefs recommended that since the Prime Minister and the President had already decided that offensive action in 1942 was essential, agreement with the Americans should be sought on substituting GYMNAST for SLEDGEHAMMER as the first Allied offensive. On July 7th the War Cabinet accepted those conclusions, authorizing the Prime Minister to lay them before the President.[40]

On the 8th Churchill reopened the whole second front issue with a message to the President in which he contended that the conditions which would make SLEDGEHAMMER a sensible enterprise were unlikely to occur. Churchill went on to declare that French North Africa offered the best chance for effecting the relief of the Russian front in 1942, a concept which he said had "all along been in harmony with your ideas." In fact, he said, "it is your commanding idea, here is the true Second Front of 1942." Churchill also suggested that the Allies should not be put off by a failure to receive a guarantee of a friendly French reception.[41] General Marshall, who was already aware that British military authorities were unenthusiastic about SLEDGEHAMMER, now learned with certainty from Field Marshal Dill that the June meetings had resolved nothing and that Churchill had decided to revive the whole second front controversy.

The Chief of Staff's response was immediate and drastic. Discussing Churchill's declaration with Admiral King, Marshall proposed a drastic reversal of American strategy: "If the British position must be accepted," he said, "the U.S. should turn to the Pacific for decisive action against Japan." That, he noted, would tend to concentrate rather than scatter U.S. forces and would be highly popular throughout the United States, as well as with the Chinese and the personnel of the Pacific Fleet and the Pacific War Council. Moreover, next to BOLERO, which it would destroy, the operation would have the greatest effect on relieving the pressure on Russia. Admiral King agreed entirely, and after further discussion the Chiefs dispatched a memorandum to the President expressing their views.[42]

Stimson vigorously supported the scheme, believing that the ultimatum would avoid a new series of "painful negotiations," since the British would give in rather than see the Americans abandon Europe for the Pacific theater.[43] The King-Marshall memorandum reaffirmed their attachment to BOLERO-SLEDGEHAMMER as the best course of Allied action for 1942, and rejected GYMNAST as neither feasible nor desirable. They then exploded their bombshell: "If the United States is to engage in any other operation other than forceful, unswerving adherence to full Bolero plans, we are definitely of the opinion that we should turn to the Pacific and strike decisively against Japan . . . assume a defensive attitude against Germany . . . and use all available means in the Pacific."[44] In a separate memo Marshall indicated that he hoped the new position would be put to the

British at once with the object of forcing them "into acceptance of a concentrated effort against Germany." However, if the ultimatum did not have that effect, Marshall recommended that his alternative be pursued.[45] A draft message to Churchill which the OPD prepared for possible use by the President informed the Prime Minister that "I [Roosevelt] believe that if we are not agreed to go all-out for SLEDGEHAMMER, even as a desperate measure, the United States should turn to the Pacific," even though such action would "definitely prolong the war and may prevent an Allied victory over Germany," and would be welcomed by Hitler.[46] The reference in the proposed message to the prolongation of the war and the benefits to Germany of the Pacific alternative, and indeed the tone of much of the documentation dealing with the episode, suggests that the proposal may have been a bluff; i.e. that Marshall intended only to frighten the British and would not have pressed for that course of action should Churchill have remained obdurate. Many years after the event both Marshall and Stimson declared that this was the case.[47] Very likely Marshall looked upon the alternative *primarily* as a bluff. If, however, the Chief of Staff had been given a choice between GYMNAST and the Pacific it is possible that he would indeed have turned to the Pacific.[48]

For several months Marshall had been under considerable pressure from King and others to meet the demands of the Pacific theater. Although considerable American effort had in fact gone into the area, since April the Chief of Staff had kept the demands of the Pacific within bounds and maintained the priority of the coming operations in Europe. This he had done in the main by repeated reference to the overriding importance of BOLERO. The revival of GYMNAST and its obvious potential of delaying the European confrontation until 1944 would leave Marshall with very little basis for opposing a stepped up commitment of men and material to the Pacific theater. Disheartened at the impending loss in the strategy-making struggles of the past several months and discouraged by the unpleasant prospect of continuing to resist Admiral King without his most formidable weapon, Marshall may well have been inclined to heed the call of the Pacific-firsters.

Recent events in the Pacific had already set in motion a train of circumstances heading in that direction. It will be recalled that in the spring Admiral King had sought reinforcement of the American garrisons in the South Pacific. This was needed, he said, primarily for defensive purposes; to secure the supply route to Australia and to contain the Japanese advance to the southeast. However, he also hoped to use the strengthened bases in the South Pacific as jumping off points for an offensive in the fall of 1942 which would advance from the New Hebrides westward through the Solomons and Bismarcks. King's plans had been stymied although not destroyed when General Marshall brought the issue before the President as a choice between "the Pacific theater versus BOLERO" and secured the President's declaration that he did not want BOLERO interfered with. King had not given up, however, and after the important American naval victory at Midway in the first week of June, he renewed his appeal for Army support. On 25 June he sent a memorandum to Marshall in which he urged the necessity of following up the Midway victory with offensive operations in the Solomons beginning on the first of August. The Chief of Staff apparently agreed, for on the 26th he accepted the King proposal, and on 2 July a JCS directive was issued calling for the initiation of operations in the New Britain–New Ireland–New Guinea area. The discovery on 5 July that the Japanese were starting construction of an airfield on Guadalcanal focused the attention of the Navy planners on that island. On July 10, the day that Marshall proposed the Pacific alternative, he had received a memorandum from Admiral King regarding recent aggressive Japanese movements and proposing actions to counter the expected Japanese occupation of points in the Solomon Islands. Marshall responded positively to King's memorandum, noting that the speed with which the Japanese were preparing to act led him to believe that they had guessed American plans in the South Pacific, and that as a consequence the execution of Navy plans should be expedited. Preparations were stepped up and, after a short postponement, the King offensive got under way with Marine landings at Guadalcanal and Tulagi on 7 August.[49]

Marshall's true intentions in the Pacific at that moment are not known. Perhaps he had not yet formed any. But if his expressed interest was only a bluff, he had certainly fooled Stimson who found the General's advocacy of the Pacific alternative forceful and optimistic. In fact, on the basis of his discussions with Marshall the Secretary of War was moved to contemplate the results of the new plan hopefully, commenting that at least it would enable the United States to "take the offensive in a very important part of the world." Personally he hoped that the threat to the British would work and that BOLERO would be revived. But he noted: "If it is not revived, if they persist in their fatuous defeatist position as to it, the Pacific operation while not so good as Bolero will be a great deal better . . . than a tepidly operated Bolero. . . ."[50]

The President responded to the Marshall-King memorandum on 12 July by asking them for a "detailed comprehensive outline" of their Pacific alternative including its effect on the deployment of men and material in the European theater.[51] Marshall, who was out of town when the President's request reached his office, hurriedly returned and, after discussions with his staff, produced a short reply. He acknowledged that no detailed plan for major offensive operations in the Pacific was currently available, but insisted that such plans were in the process of being developed.[52] On the 14th the President rejected the Pacific alternative telling Marshall that he would confer with him and King on the matter when he returned to Washington the following day.[53]

The Joint Chiefs convened that day (14 July) to consider the President's message. According to notes made by General Wedemeyer it was generally agreed that should the British finally veto SLEDGEHAMMER, operations in the Pacific were the preferred alternative. At the same time, however, it was acknowledged that "apparently our political leader would require major military operations *this year in Africa.*"[54]

The following morning at meetings with Stimson, Marshall, King, Arnold, and Hopkins, the President was by turns sympathetic to and critical of the Marshall-King plan. He gave every indication of fully supporting BOLERO-ROUNDUP, was unhappy over the apparent ease with which the British had given up SLEDGEHAMMER, and concerned that it might be a portent of a subsequent abandonment of the cross-Channel attack in 1943. At the same time, however, he completely rejected the Pacific alternative, telling Stimson that "he did not like the manner of the men [Marshall and King] in regard to the Pacific" since their proposal was "a little like 'taking up your dishes and going away.' " The President's distaste for the proposal was so intense in fact that he later told General Marshall that although he knew the proposal was "something of a red herring, the purpose for which he thoroughly understood . . . he thought the record should be altered so that it would not appear in later years that [Marshall and King] had proposed what amounted to the abandonment of the British."[55]

During their discussions with the President on the 15th both Stimson and Marshall spoke out vigorously against expeditions to either the Middle East or to North Africa, and Marshall at least apparently thought that he had some success. However, the President in a later conversation with Hopkins again stressed the importance of striking at Germany in 1942 and indicated that operations in North Africa and the Middle East would suit the purpose. In evaluating the two alternatives the President noted that while GYMNAST had the great advantage of providing a purely American battle sector, the Middle East offered the likelihood of deployment without resistance.[56]

The President hoped to have those questions settled with the British immediately and decided to send Hopkins, together with Marshall and King, to London for the purpose. On July 16th, he presented them with a set of instructions based on a draft prepared by Hopkins the night before. The object of the mission, according to the President, was agreement on definite plans for Allied action during the current year, and tentative plans for operations during 1943. Roosevelt urged the mission to press for the adoption of SLEDGEHAMMER, to be conducted in a manner designed principally to divert German Air Forces from the Russian front. If the cross-Channel attack was found to be "finally and definitely out of the picture" the Americans were instructed to determine "another place for U.S. troops to fight in 1942."[57] So, the employment of American troops in the European theater during 1942 continued to be the President's principal concern, but the security of the Middle East now joined the relief of the Red Army as the President's principal military objectives for the year. His directions to the mission reveal a deep concern for the consequences of the loss of the Middle East, which he envisaged as including a possible juncture between German and Japanese forces, the loss of all of French Africa including Dakar, and the consequent threat to South Atlantic shipping and the east coast of South America.[58] The President was therefore anxious that his representatives not only provide for the use of American troops in 1942, but that they also determine the best method of "holding the Middle East" by either (a) sending forces to the Persian Gulf, Syria, and Egypt, or (b) a landing in North Africa "intended to drive in against the backdoor of Rommel's armies," or both.

Roosevelt concluded his instructions by reemphasizing his dedication to the principle of Germany first, the need for American troops to face Germans in 1942, and by indicating that he expected the mission to achieve total agreement within a week of its arrival in London.

Some aspects of the President's thinking at this point are apparent. He was concerned about Soviet survival, and with good reason. The situation on the Russian front at the beginning of July was extremely critical. During May and June the Germans had resumed full scale offensive operations in Russia, concentrating on the southern sector of the front to achieve a breakthrough into the Caucasus.[59] However, the President's concern transcended the possiblity that the Soviets would leave the war. Such an event would of course have been a serious blow to the Allies, but the more immediate danger that the German drive into the Caucasus might reach the Iranian border, thereby jeopardizing the entire Allied position in the Middle East, seemed to have made an even greater impression on Roosevelt at this moment. He was acutely conscious of the effect the loss of the area might have on both the European and Pacific theaters. The fact that his instructions repeat the proposal, first made during the June discussions and rejected by Marshall and Stimson, of an American front from Iran to Egypt, reflects this concern.[60] The President's strategic thinking was now for the first, and perhaps the only, time strongly influenced by military considerations.

Yet while Roosevelt's instructions to Marshall, King, and Hopkins reflect an uncharacteristic concern for defense, his position in regard to Allied strategy remained preeminently political—and aggressive. He was still anxious to satisfy the increasing public sentiment for immediate offensive action without vitiating his commitment to the Germany-first strategy. Moreover, he hoped that even token American military action would have the important effects of bolstering Churchill's sagging spirits[61] and encouraging Stalin's will to resist.[62] In total, the President's instructions reflect both a continuing sensitivity to the psychological (morale) factors of the war, and a heightened concern for the immediate future of the Allied cause.

Thus, on July 16th with the German armies threatening in Russia and the Middle East in what was surely the beginning of the blackest period of the war for the Allies, the American mission set out for London to settle finally on the site and timing of the first American offensive action in the West.

EIGHT

TORCH: The Politics of
Strategy Making, July 1942

I

Before leaving for England, Marshall cabled Eisenhower informing him of the purpose of the trip, and instructing him and his staff to "be prepared on our arrival with [a] searching analysis of [the] SLEDGEHAMMER situation; . . . and with [a] specific outline of how SLEDGEHAMMER might be carried out." Significantly, Marshall described his task not as an effort to reach agreement with the British on where offensive operations might be undertaken in 1942 but rather to determine whether or not SLEDGEHAMMER was feasible, without regard to alternatives: "My mission primarily is to ascertain from you, [Gen. Mark W.] Clark, and [Gen. John C. H.] Lee* whether or not it is believed possible to carry out SLEDGEHAMMER and advise the President accordingly."[1] This limited interpretation of the President's intent, a misreading in which he persisted during and for some time after the London talks, probably reflected Marshall's hope that he could somehow avoid GYMNAST or some other diversion, and maintain the integrity of BOLERO.[2] The dichotomy between his views and those of the President remained. Roosevelt's primary goal was action for American troops in the European theater during 1942. Marshall's was the preservation of BOLERO. For about three months SLEDGEHAMMER had made those goals appear compatible. However, should the British definitely veto SLEDGEHAMMER, the President would look elsewhere for action

*Members of Eisenhower's staff in London.

in 1942, and BOLERO would be destroyed. Marshall was determined to prevent it.

Marshall, King, Hopkins, and their party arrived in England on the morning of 18 July to begin discussions with Churchill and the British military during which the Chief of Staff hoped to convince the British to continue plans and preparations for SLEDGEHAMMER. His efforts were hampered from the first by the realization that military circumstances argued against his position. The factual portion of Marshall's presentation relied to a great extent on the work of General Eisenhower and his staff, and the results of their work were not encouraging. Intensive studies begun by the London group on the 16th had left its members rather pessimistic concerning the Allies' prospects for affecting the outcome of the battle on the Russian front.[3] On the 17th the group completed a first draft of a paper, "Conclusions as to the Practicability of SLEDGEHAMMER," for General Marshall's use. In it the planners indicated that a shortage of suitable landing craft would limit the initial assault on the French Coast to approximately one division, and that "the danger of early defeat by enemy forces already in France, even assuming a successful landing of the leading division, is always present." Eisenhower personally guessed that the chances of a fairly successful landing, assuming that surprise was achieved, were "about 1 in 2," while the chances of finally establishing a force of six divisions in France with supporting air and other arms were about one in five. Predictions concerning the effectiveness of even a tactically successful landing were equally pessimistic. The Army planners, who it should be recalled were attempting to justify the operation, estimated that while a "successful" SLEDGEHAMMER "should have some beneficial moral effect on the Russian Army and nation . . . its material effect would probably be of little consequence." However, they pointed out that an unsuccessful attack, while it "may depress and discourage the Russians" would at least "convince them that we are trying to assist."

The report ended on a somewhat inconclusive note, leaving to future determination, perhaps after discussions with the British, the question of whether the Russians were in as desperate straits as they appeared to be, and secondly whether a reasonably successful SLEDGEHAMMER would effectively help them. In that regard it is not clear whether Eisenhower included "morale building" under the category of effective assistance, but in any event he recommended that if the answer to both these questions was yes, SLEDGEHAMMER should be launched at the earliest possible date; while if either answer was no, all effort should be concentrated on ROUNDUP. Finally Eisenhower again advised that should the Russian front collapse before a landing was effected American efforts should turn to the Pacific.[4]

The final position paper submitted to Marshall by Eisenhower on the 19th, while more positive in tone, was still reserved in its support of SLEDGEHAMMER. It recommended an Allied invasion of France in October 1942 provided the Germans had by that time denuded their western defenses in a final effort to defeat the Soviets. This he thought would give the operation a good chance of achieving tactical success and of affecting the outcome in Russia. The late date was dictated by the need for maximum time to prepare for the attack—in spite of the acknowledged fact that weather conditions would normally prevent the launching of an invasion after 15 September.[5] Eisenhower suggested that Marshall recommend that intensive preparations for SLEDGE-HAMMER, which so far as possible avoided interference with ROUNDUP, be resumed immediately and that in early September an evaluation be made of the Russian situation. Then, on the basis of the evaluation, a decision as to the wisdom of going ahead with the operation might be reached.[6] Marshall apparently accepted Eisenhower's recommendations.

Though initially the Americans believed they could reach agreement with the British on the basis of Eisenhower's proposal,[7] that impression was very shortly dispelled. Even before the Americans arrived, General Brooke had expressed the conviction that "1942 is dead off and without the slightest hope." The only real issue, he felt, was whether ROUNDUP would be possible, and that depended on the ability of the Soviets to hold out through the winter.[8] On the 18th, shortly after the mission arrived, the British Chiefs and the Prime Minister agreed that while they would entertain any plan that held out any promise of success, they themselves had found no such scheme.[9] In such circumstances they decided to tell the Americans that the only feasible operation for 1942 was GYMNAST, which they said might be expanded to include landings inside the Mediterranean as well as at Casablanca.[10] The eastward landings would not only increase the operation's chance of success, but would also contribute directly to the battle in the Western desert by threatening the rear of Rommel's position.

The first formal session of the Combined Chiefs London meetings met on July 20th. An opening American suggestion of a September attack against Cherbourg, "if conditions then are such as to make it appear desirable,"[11] was rejected by the British on the grounds that, as Eisenhower had already suggested, it would require at least three months to mount any sizable operations against the Continent. The early attack having been disposed of, Marshall now proposed landings in October aimed at establishing a base for full scale operations early in 1943.[12] The October attack, while stronger than the earlier effort, was riskier because of the increased weather hazard. Moreover, the later date made it all the more certain that the operation would have little material impact on the situation in Russia since it was generally conceded that the battle there would be well on its way to resolution in October.

In discussions on the following day (21 July) Marshall concentrated on the benefits of the later landings. However, since they did not answer the original purpose of SLEDGEHAMMER (immediate tangible aid to the Soviets) the Americans played down that objective and emphasized instead the contribution that a late SLEDGEHAMMER would make to ROUNDUP, and the intangible benefits that would accrue to the United Nations from the operation. The arguments used by the Chief of Staff to support the October SLEDGEHAMMER stressed the idea that the plan preserved the BOLERO-ROUNDUP strategy and avoided further dispersion of Allied forces. Marshall also pointed out that SLEDGEHAMMER would provide valuable experience for the full scale invasion the following spring, and while he conceded that it would interfere with training for ROUNDUP, he thought that "careful planning and intensified effort" could minimize this problem.[13] Brooke and his colleagues were unconvinced, and insisted that operations against the Continent in 1942 would be pointless suicide.[14]

The major burden of defending the late (mid-October) landing had then fallen to General Eisenhower. Aware of the obvious difficulties that the scheme involved, his advocacy was tentative and conditional. Eisenhower believed that the final decision on the operation rested on an evaluation of the situation in Russia —an evaluation which he apparently felt unable to provide. He told the Chief of Staff, however, that should he decide that "the Russians were in bad shape and that an attack on the French coast would have a material effect in assisting [them], we should attempt the job at the earliest possible date—regardless." Eisenhower admitted that the delay until October heightened risks because of increasingly adverse weather conditions and the possible reinforcement of the German garrison in France, but he still gave the expedition a "fighting chance." Analyzing the current discussions, Eisenhower conceded that there was a tendency to be influenced by "the mere passion for doing something." While he thought that he himself was free of that fault, he did insist that action for its own sake had its merits since "the British and American armies and . . . people need to have the feeling that they are attempting something positive. We must not degenerate into a passive and [sic] mental attitude."[15]

The British, however, apparently more concerned about casualties than mental attitudes, remained unmoved. The showdown came on the 22nd when the Americans presented the British Chiefs with a memorandum proposing an attack on the Cotentin peninsula as a preliminary to a large scale offensive in France in 1943. Once again the British replied by pointing out some of the flaws in the scheme. They noted that the Germans had about twenty-seven divisions in France, six to ten of which could immediately be used to seal the peninsula at its base. German reinforcements could then be brought up from as far away as Russia (where German divisions outnumbered Russian by approximately 284 to 250) without seriously affecting other operations. Moreover, according to the Chief of the Air Staff, the Allied air forces that could operate over the battlefield would be outnumbered by the Germans approximately six to one, and could not adequately protect the expedition. One result would be that the port facilities of Cherbourg, which were essential for resupply of the proposed expedition, would be bombed into a "heap of ruins" in six months time. Further complicating the resupply problem was the fact that few transports could cross the Channel during the gale weather that frequently struck in October and after. In short, the bridgehead, even if successful, would not survive the winter and hence would not provide the base for expanded operations on the Continent in 1943.

The Americans, although perhaps convinced, would not abandon SLEDGEHAMMER. Instead they declared the meeting deadlocked and decided to refer the issue to the President for his decision as to the next step. General Marshall admitted that he did not think SLEDGEHAMMER could be launched before October and that the operation was unsupportable on purely military grounds. However, he explained he felt he had no choice, since the alternative to undertaking SLEDGEHAMMER was the adoption of a defensive posture in the European theater again exposing Allied operations to the hazards of diversionary pressures, including GYMNAST.[16] The Americans, though convinced of the sacrificial nature of SLEDGEHAMMER, refused to give up the operation. Further discussion, they now admitted, was pointless.

II

Following the conference of the 22nd, the Americans informed the President that the British had refused to accept SLEDGEHAMMER. Roosevelt replied immediately, declaring that he was not wholly surprised and that he was standing by his July 16 directive "that some other offensive be worked out for American ground forces in 1942." The only condition he imposed on selecting the alternative was that it "ought not to be at such a distance as to require [a] very long sea trip." He went on to suggest in order of desirability based on their chances of success, their political and military usefulness, and the possibility of speedy execution, the following operations: (a) An expanded operation against French Africa including Algiers, which had been suggested by the British at the meeting on the 20th. (b) An attack against the Casablanca area (old GYMNAST) limited initially to American troops. (c) Landings in Northern Norway (JUPITER), which was a favorite target of Churchill's and had probably gained favor with the President as a result of the enforced suspension of the Northern convoys. (d) A buildup in Egypt, where the front had by now stabilized at El Alamein,[17] and, finally, (e) The defense of the northern flank of the Middle East area. The last had apparently slipped from Roosevelt's favor during the preceding week, possibly because he had become conscious of the supply and shipping problems which the great distances involved. The President concluded his reply with a request for speedy action on his suggestions, citing a report from the American legation in Berne which indicated that the Vichy government had undertaken the construction of an air field and coast defenses in Morocco, and recommendations from pro-Allied French sources that action be taken before French Africa was made impregnable. The Berne report, a paragraph of which was included in the President's telegram, insisted that an invasion force of 100,000 to 150,000 troops could seize all of French Africa in 1942, and that such an attack should take precedence over an attack against continental France.[18]

On the same day that Roosevelt's instructions went out to Hopkins, Marshall, and King (23 July), Secretary of War Stimson learned of the stalemate in the London talks. He went immediately to the White House, where he found the President disappointed over the rejection of SLEDGEHAMMER and inclined to attribute it to British timidity which he blamed on war weariness. Stimson was less disposed to excuse the British action. That afternoon he wrote the President advising him to hold Churchill to his June agreement to wait until September before he made any final decision on SLEDGEHAMMER. Although aware that Roosevelt had already cabled instructions to the American mission to move for a decision on an alternate site for Allied operations in 1942, Stimson urged the President, in effect, to disregard the British and continue as before with preparations for action in 1943. At the same time the Secretary cabled General Marshall informing him of his action, encouraging him to do the same.[19]

In London, the results of the conferences left the Americans disappointed and dejected; General Eisenhower declaring that he felt as though his efforts over the preceding seven months had been in vain.[20] However, neither Marshall nor Eisenhower thought that the President's directive to find an alternative to SLEDGEHAMMER ruled out their hopes for ROUNDUP. On the 23rd Eisenhower surveyed the strategic situation in light of recent developments and suggested that the Chief of Staff refuse to consider any "avoidable reduction in preparations for ROUNDUP . . . as long as there remains any reasonable possibility of its successful execution." Elaborating on that idea, Eisenhower recommended that "no major operation which will interfere with BOLERO-ROUNDUP be launched until the result of the Russian campaign can be estimated with reasonable accuracy. We believe this will be possible by October 1942."[21] That same day Harry Hopkins, aware that the thoughts of his military companions were not in line with the President's, cabled Roosevelt urging him to clearly express his preference about the future course of action.[22] As if in direct response to Eisenhower's evaluation, the President replied on the 24th that the continued concentration on ROUNDUP would mean the "abandonment of GYMNAST or any other new assignment of American troops in 1942," and that "therefore if the American objective of putting ground forces into useful action in 1942 is maintained, ROUNDUP as planned must be abandoned as the primary objective at this time." Having clearly restated the fundamental basis of his approach to the military situation, the President went on to express his preference for GYMNAST, and to reassert the need for speedy action in that direction.[23]

The President, however, still did not *order* the adoption of African operations and the abandonment of proposals which stood in their way. Obviously he preferred to exercise no more than general guidance in the determination of the next phase of the war, leaving the "decision" to Marshall and King. His hopes of leading by indirection were, however, in vain.

On the 24th the Combined Chiefs met again in London to work out the final memorandum on their conversatons. It is not known whether the President's message of the 24th reached Marshall before the meeting, but in any event the American position did not reflect the President's "recommendations." Marshall, with strong support from King, insisted that preparations for ROUNDUP should continue as long as the operation appeared at all possible. They further argued that preparations for SLEDGEHAMMER continue until at least October 1st for purposes of deception and to await a possible opportunity to develop SLEDGEHAMMER into a full scale invasion. The American Chiefs agreed with the British that once large forces had been committed to GYMNAST, ROUNDUP was out. They therefore proposed that a decision on the North African operation be deferred until September 15th. If at that time the situation indicated "such a collapse or weakening of Russian resistance as to make ROUNDUP appear impracticable" the decision for GYMNAST should be made.[24] Brooke and his colleagues accepted the American proposal.

The British were aware that Allied agreement along the lines suggested by the Americans left the issue of whether GYMNAST would be carried out dependent on a future assessment of events in Russia and that "there was thus no definite decision to proceed with either operation." Some War Cabinet members feared that such indefiniteness might "hamper effective and timely preparations for TORCH," as GYMNAST was now called. However, their suggestion that the agreement be rephrased to indicate that TORCH would be carried out unless the situation in the fall strongly favored ROUNDUP was opposed by the Chiefs, who wished to propitiate the Americans on that point. The British Chiefs thought the Americans realized that it was unlikely that ROUNDUP could be carried out and that they were resigned to TORCH. They were conscious that Marshall and King had been forced to modify their views greatly during the last week, and thought "it would be undesirable to press for further alterations" in the Combined Memorandum.[25]

The cabinet agreed to the Chief's position and the memorandum was transmitted to the President for his approval. The meaning of the document was sufficiently obscure to prompt Hopkins to send the President a separate note to clarify the decision. Hopkins was concerned that the Combined Chiefs paper "seems to me to postpone a flat and final decision to go for GYMNAST." Hopkins thought the document should be altered so that the decision on GYMNAST was made at once rather than postponed until sometime as late as September 15th: "I fear that if a firm decision is not made now to go for GYMNAST and a reasonably early date [for its launching] fixed [Hopkins recommended October 30th], delay and procrastination may take place." He went on to suggest somewhat generously that the difficulty lay in the language employed, rather than in the intent of the users.[26] Advice of a different sort came to the President from Stimson, who was disturbed because the proposed agreement appeared to rule out SLEDGEHAMMER, call ROUNDUP into question, and make GYMNAST a distinct possibility. The Secretary, both in an interview with the President on the morning of the 25th and in an angry letter dated that same day, vigorously opposed the new course of action, which he felt was a "dangerous diversion and a possible disaster."[27] Stimson's message irked the President; his pique lasted over the next several days, finally leading him to dictate a memorandum which he deposited in his files attached to the Secretary's letter of the 25th. In uncharacteristic bad temper, Roosevelt declared for the record that Stimson's message was "not worth replying to in detail because it is contradictory in terms and fails to meet the objectives as of the Summer of 1942." Specifically he criticized the Secretary for insisting on SLEDGEHAMMER although it had been found impracticable, and for not offering an alternative for 1942. Stimson, he declared, "abandons any offensive by U.S. ground troops in the European or African Theaters in 1942 and would merely build up for a European offensive in 1943 and some kind of Pacific offensive at the same time. In this he gives, in effect, no help to Russian resistance in 1942."[28]

The President had already made his decision and sent it to London. However, he ignored Hopkins' warning concerning the Combined Chiefs' agreement and his imprecise reply to the American Chiefs again left the issue unresolved. The phrasing of his message suggests that he assumed a decision had in fact been made to proceed with GYMNAST. Thus he instructed the mission to go ahead with planning for GYMNAST landings to take place not later than October 30 and asked Hopkins to tell the Prime Minister that he was "delighted that the decision had finally been made and that orders were now 'full speed ahead.' "[29] The response left Marshall room to believe that though planning for GYMNAST should proceed, priority need not be given the African scheme over ROUNDUP and that a final decision had not yet been rendered. The result was to allow the

Chief of Staff to conclude that GYMNAST was not quite in and ROUNDUP not yet out.

On the afternoon of the 27th Marshall, King, and Hopkins returned to Washington. Stimson was on hand to greet them. On the ride into town from the airport Marshall briefed the Secretary on the results of the trip. Later that evening further information was provided him by a member of Marshall's staff. As a result of these conversations Stimson, now up-to-date on Marshall's stratagem, felt a good deal happier about the decision: "Though SLEDGEHAMMER was beaten by the British War Council . . . Marshall did succeed in insisting that preparations for SLEDGEHAMMER and BOLERO should go on until it became absolutely clear that the Russian Army was beaten. That leaves quite a loop hole in which public sentiment may restore some of the British leaders' morale."[30]

The obvious conflict between the President's concern for the immediate initiation of plans and preparations for a North African expedition, and CCS 94,* which left the issue undecided, could not long remain unresolved. On 30 July the Combined Chiefs of Staff met in Washington for their first meeting following the London discussions. Admiral William D. Leahy, who had been recalled as American Ambassador to France, now sat as the President's representative on the Joint Chiefs of Staff, having been appointed "Chief of Staff to the Commander in Chief" on 20 July.[31]

Discussions among the Chiefs concerning the timing of the North African operation, now known as TORCH,† quickly revealed a difference of opinion as to whether or not a final decision concerning the operation had been made. Admiral Leahy, supported by Sir John Dill, expressed the belief that the President and Prime Minister had definitely decided to undertake TORCH. Moreover, they thought that the two leaders were under the impression that all preliminary arrangements were already underway toward launching the operation at the earliest possible date. Marshall, with King's support, replied by pointing out that the terms of CCS 94 made no final choice between ROUNDUP

---

*Designation of the Combined Chiefs decision of the 24th.
†Codename GYMNAST was changed to TORCH by the CCS on 25 July.

and TORCH and therefore had not committed the Allies to all-out preparation for the North African project. Technically Marshall was right—the President had not chosen to launch TORCH and abandon ROUNDUP. He had not seen the issue as a distinct choice, feeling instead that preparations for ROUNDUP on a reduced scale could proceed without interfering with the effort to launch TORCH. However, as Marshall would shortly discover, that did not mean that he wished the African planning held up awaiting a final decision concerning the feasibility of the cross-Channel attack. At this point Leahy made his first important contribution to Allied military policy-making by declaring that the difference of opinion among the Combined Chiefs would have to be submitted to the President for resolution.[32]

That evening brought the climax to two years of thinking and planning on the site of America's first offensive in the West. At a White House meeting attended by Admiral Leahy, General Arnold, Brig. General Walter Bedell Smith, and the President's naval aide Captain John L. McCrea, the President announced in no uncertain terms that TORCH would go ahead at full speed and that no other operations including specifically ROUNDUP should be permitted to stand in its way: "The President stated very definitely that he, as Commander-in-Chief, had made the decision that TORCH would be undertaken at the earliest possible date. He considered that this operation was now our principal objective and the assembling of means to carry it out should take precedence over other operations as, for instance, BOLERO."[33]

The President's decision of the 30th was firm and unequivocal and clearly constituted the end of all reasonable doubt on the nature of the Allied military policy for the immediate future. There were, however, important loose ends that remained to be tied before TORCH could reach the final stages of preparation. Involved were two major issues: exactly when the attack would take place, sometime in October or in early November; and at what points the troops would go ashore, inside the Mediterranean or outside, or both, and how far inside and at how many locations? A tremendous volume of discussion concerning those issues—between General Eisenhower in London, who was now in charge of the TORCH operation; and General Marshall in Washington; among the Combined Chiefs; and between

Churchill and Roosevelt—characterized Allied military planning between the July 30th decision and September 3rd when the site and size of the Allied landings were finally decided.[34] During this time General Marshall tended to drag his feet on preparations for TORCH, apparently hoping that something would happen to revive ROUNDUP. Nothing did, and support for his diehard stance diminished. As preparations for the North African attack gained momentum, Marshall's position became increasingly unsupportable and unsupported, and even General Eisenhower came to favor a vigorous prosecution of TORCH. His efforts finally culminated in the successful assault on North African shores, 8 November 1942.

NINE

Conclusion

Deliberations on the site and timing of the first Anglo-American offensive in the western theater of operations were from first to last colored by the larger political purposes of the major actors. So singleminded were Marshall and Roosevelt in concentrating on the politico–military effects of the first offensive that the immediate results of the operation received hasty consideration. Originally conceived as a contingency operation designed to relieve German pressure in the east, discussions of the project indicated early and consistently that the likelihood of effecting such results was quite small. The SLEDGEHAMMER attack would in fact have been a disaster. An Allied invasion of France, on the scale and at the time such an attack was feasible (less than ten divisions, sometime in October 1942), would have involved sending thousands of men to almost certain death or imprisonment with little prospect of establishing a permanent bridgehead in France or of drawing significant German forces off the eastern front. The sobering effect of this assessment was lost as American military leaders allowed themselves to be misguided by wishful thinking and their pursuit of grander objectives. The result was that planning continued in an atmosphere of self-imposed ignorance, redeemed only near the last instant by the refusal of the British to proceed. The episode, which should never have been, left a residue of suspicion among the Allies that was never totally erased.

Responsibility for the fumbling American strategy-making

and its near disastrous results rests mainly with the Chief of Staff. He was in a position to know the facts that made SLEDGE-HAMMER a false vision, yet continued to press for the operation long after the high costs and probable negative results were apparent. To the extent the President depended on Marshall for military advice on the first offensive, he was ill-served. Confronted by the danger that the British and the U.S. Navy would take advantage of the President to the detriment of Allied strategy and Army interests, Marshall, encouraged by his subordinates, gave first priority to putting American military power on the right track. Instead of acting as an advisor, Marshall adopted, albeit reluctantly, the role of advocate, acting with a singlemindedness and an occasional lack of candor that diminished his value to the President.

The President, for his part, by his actions and outlook pushed Marshall along the route he took. It was Roosevelt's insistence on immediate action that largely accounts for the Chief of Staff's loyalty to SLEDGEHAMMER. Roosevelt's concern for morale in the United States and in the Allied countries now seems excessive. More importantly his expectation that his manipulation of military activities could significantly affect national attitudes without interfering with the proper prosecution of the war appears vain.

The Allies' good fortune in not undertaking the premature invasion of France must be credited to the British. Continuous study of the problem convinced the British Chiefs and the Prime Minister that the operation would be costly and ineffective, and it was Churchill's refusal to go further with preparations for the assault that finally killed the scheme. Nevertheless, the British are not free of responsibility for creating the situation they were to save at the last minute. They offered little objection to the SLEDGEHAMMER plan when the Americans first proposed it in April, though they were even then very skeptical. They chose instead to go along with the scheme until a final decision was unavoidable. Here as in so much of the deliberation concerning the first offensive, the rationale is found in the apparent subordination of professional judgment to ulterior purposes. For Britain, the prospect of an American buildup in the British Isles outweighed the fact that the forces were being accumulated for

Conclusion

a seriously ill-conceived operation.

In short, all of the men involved in Allied strategy-making in 1942, confronted with the dilemma of matching a scarcity of men and material to a wide range of possible actions and purposes, had become embroiled to a greater or lesser extent in a complex, confused, sometimes devious political process.

Works Cited

Unpublished Papers and Records

Arnold, Henry H. Manuscripts Division, Library of Congress, Washington, D.C.

Department of State. National Archives, Washington, D.C.

Eisenhower, Dwight D. Papers. Eisenhower Project, The Johns Hopkins University, Baltimore, Maryland.

Great Britain, Records of the War Cabinet, 1941–42. Public Records Office, London.

Hopkins, Harry. Franklin D. Roosevelt Library, Hyde Park, New York.

Kittredge, Tracy. "U.S.–British Naval Cooperation, 1940–1945," draft typescript. Navy Historical Division, Office of the Chief of Naval Operations, Washington, D.C.

Mellett, Lowell. Franklin D. Roosevelt Library, Hyde Park, New York.

Office of Civilian Defense. National Archives, Washington, D.C.

Office of Facts and Figures. National Archives, Washington, D.C.

Office of Government Reports. National Archives, Washington, D.C.

Office of War Information. National Archives, Washington, D.C.

Roosevelt, Franklin D. Franklin D. Roosevelt Library, Hyde Park, New York.

Stimson Diary and Papers. Yale University Library, New Haven, Connecticut.

World War II Records. National Archives.
 Combined Chiefs of Staff (CCS)
 Joint Chiefs of Staff (JCS)
 Office of the Chiefs of Staff (OCS)
 War Department Chief of Staff Army (WDCSA)
 Operations Division (OPD)
 War Plans Division (WPD)

Works Cited

Books

Arnold, Henry H. *Global Mission.* New York: Harper & Brothers, 1949.

Blum, John M. *From the Morgenthau Diaries.* Vol. 2, *Years of Urgency, 1938–1941.* Boston: Houghton Mifflin Co., 1965.

Brereton, Lewis. *The Brereton Diaries.* New York: William Morrow and Co., 1946.

Bryant, Arthur. *The Turn of the Tide.* Garden City, N.Y.: Doubleday & Co., 1957.

Butcher, Harry C. *My Three Years With Eisenhower.* New York: Simon and Schuster, 1946.

Cantril, Hadley, ed. *Public Opinion 1935–1946.* Princeton, N.J.: Princeton University Press, 1951.

Casey, Lord. *Personal Experiences, 1939–1946.* New York: David McKay Co., 1962.

Chandler, Alfred D. Jr., ed. *The Papers of Dwight David Eisenhower.* Vol. 1, *The War Years.* Baltimore: Johns Hopkins University Press, 1970.

Churchill, Winston S. *The Second World War.* Vol. 3, *The Grand Alliance.* Vol. 4, *The Hinge of Fate.* Boston: Houghton Mifflin Co., 1950.

Cline, Ray S. *Washington Command Post: The Operations Division. United States Army in World War II,* edited by Kent Roberts Greenfield. Washington, D.C.: Office of the Chief of Military History, 1951.

Conn, Stetson, and Byron Fairchild. *The Framework of Hemisphere Defense, United States Army in World War II,* edited by Kent Roberts Greenfield. Washington, D.C.: Office of the Chief of Military History, 1960.

DeJong, Louis. *The German Fifth Column in the Second World War.* Chicago: University of Chicago Press, 1956.

Divine, Robert A. *The Reluctant Belligerent.* New York: John Wiley & Sons, 1965.

Eden, Anthony. *The Memoirs of Anthony Eden: The Reckoning.* London: Cassell & Co., 1965.

Eisenhower, Dwight D. *Crusade in Europe.* Garden City, N.Y.: Doubleday & Co., 1948.

Foreign Relations of the United States, 1941 and 1942. Washington, D.C.: State Department Series, 1968.

Foreign Relations of the United States, The Conferences at Washington, 1941–1942, Washington, D.C.: State Department Series, 1968.

Freedman, Max, annotator. *Roosevelt and Frankfurter: Their Correspon-*

Works Cited

dence, *1928–1945*. Boston: Little, Brown and Co., 1967.

Frye, Alton. *Nazi Germany and the American Hemisphere.* New Haven: Yale University Press, 1967.

Gallup, George. *A Guide to Public Opinion Polls.* Princeton, N.J.: Princeton University Press, 1944.

Gwyer, J.M.A., and J.R.M. Butler. *Grand Strategy.* Vol. 3, *June 1941– August 1942: History of the Second World War,* United Kingdom Military Series. London: H.M. Stationery Office, 1964.

Harrison, Gordon A. *Cross-Channel Attack. United States Army in World War II,* edited by Kent Roberts Greenfield. Washington, D.C.: Office of the Chief of Military History, 1957.

Howe, George F. *Northwest Africa: Seizing the Initiative in the West. United States Army in World War II,* edited by Kent Roberts Greenfield. Washington, D.C.: Office of the Chief of Military History, 1957.

Hull, Cordell. *The Memoirs of Cordell Hull.* New York: Macmillan Co., 1948.

Ickes, Harold. *The Secret Diary of Harold L. Ickes.* Vol. 3, *The Lowering Clouds.* New York: Simon and Schuster, 1954.

Ismay, Hastings. *The Memoirs of General Lord Ismay.* New York: Viking Press, 1960.

Jones, S. Shepard, and D.P. Myers, eds. *Documents on American Foreign Relations.* Vol. 3, *July 1940–June 1941.* New York: Harper & Brothers, 1941.

Kennan, George F. *Memoirs, 1925–1950.* Boston: Little, Brown and Co., 1967.

King, Ernest J., and Walter M. Whitehill. *Fleet Admiral King: A Naval Record.* New York: W.W. Norton & Co., 1952.

Langer, William L. *Our Vichy Gamble.* New York: Alfred A. Knopf, 1947.

Langer, William L., and S. Everett Gleason. *The Undeclared War 1940– 1941.* New York: Harper & Brothers, 1953.

Leahy, William D. *I Was There.* New York: McGraw-Hill Book Co., 1950.

Leighton, Richard M., and Robert W. Coakley. *Global Logistics and Strategy 1940–1943. United States Army in World War II,* edited by Kent Roberts Greenfield. Washington, D.C.: Office of the Chief of Military History, 1955.

Lilienthal, David E. *The Journals of David E. Lilienthal.* Vol. 1, *The TVA Years, 1939–1945.* New York: Harper & Row, 1964.

Long, Breckinridge. *The War Diary of Breckinridge Long,* edited by Fred L. Israel. Lincoln, Neb.: University of Nebraska Press, 1966.

Macmillan, Harold. *The Blast of War 1939–1945.* London: Macmillan & Co., 1967.

Works Cited

Matloff, Maurice and Edwin M. Snell. *Strategic Planning for Coalition Warfare 1941–1942*. United States Army in World War II, edited by Kent Roberts Greenfield. Washington, D.C.: Office of the Chief of Military History, 1953.

Moran, Lord (Sir Charles Wilson). *Churchill: The Struggle for Survival, 1940–1965, Taken from the Diaries of Lord Moran*. Boston: Houghton Mifflin Co., 1966.

Morison, Elting E. *Turmoil and Tradition*. Boston: Houghton Mifflin Co., 1960.

Morison, Samuel Eliot. *History of United States Naval Operations in World War II*. Vol. 4, *Coral Sea, Midway and Submarine Actions*. Boston: Little, Brown and Co., 1962.

Morton, Louis. *The War in the Pacific, Strategy and Command: The First Two Years*. United States Army in World War II, edited by Kent Roberts Greenfield. Washington, D.C.: Office of the Chief of Military History, 1962.

Nicholson, Harold. *Diaries and Letters of Harold Nicholson*. Vol. 2, *The War Years, 1939–1945*. New York: Atheneum Publishers, 1967.

Pearl Harbor Attack. Hearings before the Joint Committee on the Investigation of the Pearl Harbor Attack, 79th Congress, 1st and 2nd Sessions. Washington, D.C.: U.S. Government Printing Office, 1946.

Pendar, Kenneth. *Adventure in Diplomacy*. New York: Dodd Mead & Co., 1945.

Playfair, I.S.O. *The Mediterranean and Middle East*. Vol. 3, *British Fortunes Reach their Lowest Ebb*. History of the Second World War, United Kingdom Military Series. London: H.M. Stationery Office, 1960.

Pogue, Forrest C. *George C. Marshall*. Vol. 2, *Ordeal and Hope, 1939–1942*. New York: Viking Press, 1966.

Pratt, Julius W. *Cordell Hull, 1933–1944*. New York: Cooper Square Press, 1964.

Robertson, Terence. *Dieppe: The Shame and the Glory*. Boston: Little, Brown and Co., 1962.

Roosevelt, Elliott, ed. *FDR: His Personal Letters 1928–1945*. New York: Duell, Sloan and Pearce, 1946.

Rosenman, Samuel I., ed. *The Public Papers and Addresses of Franklin D. Roosevelt*. Vol. 10, *The Call to Battle Stations, 1941*. Vol. 11, *Humanity on the Defensive, 1942*. New York: Macmillan Co., 1950.

———*Working With Roosevelt*. New York: Harper & Brothers, 1952.

Sherwood, Robert E. *Roosevelt and Hopkins: An Intimate History*. New York: Harper & Brothers, 1948.

Slessor, Sir John. *The Central Blue*. London: Cassell & Co., 1956.

Works Cited

Stalin, Joseph. *Stalin's Correspondence with Churchill, Roosevelt and Truman, 1941–1945.* New York: E.P. Dutton & Co., 1958.

———*The Great Patriotic War of the Soviet Union.* New York: International Publishers Co., 1945.

Standley, William H. and Arthur A. Ageton. *Admiral Ambassador to Russia.* Chicago: Henry Regnery Co., 1955.

Stilwell, Joseph W. *The Stilwell Papers,* edited by T.H. White. New York: William Sloane Associates, 1948.

Stimson, Henry L. and McGeorge Bundy. *On Active Service in Peace and War.* New York: Harper & Brothers, 1948.

Watson, Mark S. *Chief of Staff: Prewar Plans and Preparations. United States Army in World War II,* edited by Kent Roberts Greenfield. Washington, D.C.: Office of the Chief of Military History, 1950.

Wedemeyer, Albert C. *Wedemeyer Reports!* New York: Henry Holt & Co., 1958.

Welles, Sumner. *Seven Decisions That Shaped History.* New York: Harper & Brothers, 1950.

Werth, Alexander. *Russia at War 1941–1945.* New York: E.P. Dutton & Co., 1964.

Weygand, General Maxime. *Recalled to Service: The Memoirs of General Maxime Weygand.* New York: Doubleday & Co., 1952.

White, Dorothy S. *Seeds of Discord: DeGaulle, Free France, and the Allies.* Syracuse, N.Y.: Syracuse University Press, 1964.

Wilson, Theodore A. *The First Summit.* Boston: Houghton Mifflin Co., 1969.

Winant, John G. *Letter from Grosvenor Square.* Boston: Houghton Mifflin Co., 1947.

Woodward, Llewellyn. *British Foreign Policy in the Second World War. History of the Second World War,* United Kingdom Military Series. London: H.M. Stationery Office, 1962.

Articles

Cantril, Hadley. "The Public Opinion Polls: Dr. Jekyll or Mr. Hyde?" In *Public Opinion Quarterly* 4 (June 1940).

Coakley, Robert W. "The Persian Corridor as a Route for Aid to the USSR." In *Command Decisions,* edited by Kent Roberts Greenfield. New York: Harcourt, Brace and Co., 1959.

Gorlitz, Walter. "The Struggle for Stalingrad, 1942–3." In *Decisive Battles of World War II: The German View,* edited by H.A. Jacobsen and J. Rohwer. New York: G.P. Putnam's Sons, 1965.

Works Cited

Leighton, Richard M. "Overlord Revisited: An Interpretation of American Strategy in the European War, 1942–44." In *American Historical Review* 68 (July 1963).

Robinson, Claude E. "Recent Developments in the Straw-Poll Field." In *Public Opinion Quarterly* 1 (July 1937).

Steele, Richard W. "Preparing the Public for War: Efforts to Establish a National Propaganda Agency, 1940–41." In *American Historical Review* 75 (October 1970).

Notes

Abbreviations used in these notes: **ACofS**: Assistant Chief of Staff; **CNO**: Chief of Naval Operations; **CofS**: Chief of Staff; **FDRL**: Franklin Delano Roosevelt Library; **N.A.**: National Archives; **OCS**: Office of the Chief of Staff; **OF**: Official File; **OFF**: Office of Facts and Figures; **OGR**: Office of Government Reports; **OPD**: Operations Division; **OWI**: Office of War Information; **PPF**: President's Personal File; **PSF**: Personal Secretary's File; **SLC**: Standing Liaison Committee; **SW**: Secretary of War; **WDCSA**: War Department Chief of Staff U.S. Army; **WPD**: War Plans Division

Chapter One

1. See Harold L. Ickes, *The Secret Diary of Harold L. Ickes,* vol. 3, *The Lowering Clouds;* and John M. Blum, *From the Morgenthau Diaries,* vol. 2, *Years of Urgency, 1938–1941,* chaps. 5–8.

2. Julius W. Pratt, *Cordell Hull, 1933–1944,* vol. 1, chaps. 10–13, especially pp. 361–365.

3. See Hadley Cantril, "Present State and Trends of Public Opinion," *New York Times,* 11 May 1941, sec. 4, p. 3:3. Polls on the public's attitude toward the war are numerous but also ambiguous. However, most do reveal the public's ambivalence and confusion concerning America's stake in the European war, a persistent and widespread belief that "this is not our war," and a reluctance to become actively involved. See Hadley Cantril, *Public Opinion 1935–1946,* pp. 939–943, 949–950, 954–955, 966–978.

4. Stimson Diary (MS.), 26 January 1941, Yale University Library; and Memo, Knox for FDR, reporting at President's request on number of Brazilians of German origin (received 28 January 1941), in Personal Secretary's File [PSF] "Knox," Franklin D. Roosevelt Library, Hyde Park [FDRL]. See also Cordell Hull, *The Memoirs of Cordell Hull,* chaps. 35, 42, 48, and 59; and Alton Frye, *Nazi Germany and the American Hemisphere.*

5. Louis DeJong, *The German Fifth Column in the Second World War,* pp. 39–143.

6. Stetson Conn and Byron Fairchild, *The Framework of Hemisphere Defense,* p. 33.

7. Robert E. Sherwood, *Roosevelt and Hopkins,* p. 11.

8. The bill, signed into law in March 1941, became known as the Lend-Lease Act.

9. S. Shepard Jones and D. P. Myers (eds.), *Documents on American Foreign Relations,* vol. 3, *July 1940–June 1941,* pp. 17–26.

10. Ibid., 3:26–34.

11. Office of the Chief of Staff [OCS], Notes on Conferences, 16 April 1941, folder 13, W.W. II Records, National Archives.

12. Ibid. Quoted in Maurice Matloff and Edwin M. Snell, *Strategic Planning for Coalition Warfare 1941–1942,* p. 52.

13. Conn and Fairchild, *Hemisphere Defense,* pp. 106–107.

14. See Matloff and Snell, *Strategic Planning,* pp. 52–53; Forrest C. Pogue, *George C. Marshall,* vol. 2, *Ordeal and Hope, 1939–1942,* p. 133.

15. Memo, Chief of Staff [CofS] for Secretary of War [SW], 16 April 1941, OCS, Notes on Conferences, folder 13, W.W. II Records.

16. Jones and Myers, *Documents,* 3:43–47; *New York Times,* 25 April 1941, p. 12:2, p. 6:5; Samuel I. Rosenman (ed.), *The Public Papers and Addresses of Franklin D. Roosevelt, 1941,* pp. 132–138. On 26 April Admiral Stark, responding to the increased talk of American military action, warned the commander of the Pacific Fleet that the "Clamoring for an all out [offensive] in the Atlantic" might require him to transfer additional units from the Pacific to the Atlantic. Letter, Stark to Kimmel, 26 April 1941, *Pearl Harbor Attack,* Hearings before the Joint Commit-

tee on the Investigation of the Pearl Harbor Attack, 79th Congress, 1st and 2nd Sessions, part 5, p. 2212.

17. Letter, Leahy to FDR, 21 April 1941, PSF "France" [closed]; Confidential Memo, Biddle for FDR, 26 April 1941, PSF "Great Britain" [closed]; FDRL.

18. Stimson Diary (MS.), 8 May 1941.

19. Memo, FDR for Knox, 9 May 1941, PSF "Navy" [closed], FDRL.

20. *New York Times,* 20 May 1941, p. 1:4.

21. Draft message by Welles, 19 May 1941, PSF "Welles—1940–41" [closed], FDRL. Welles supported a bolder policy toward Germany than was generally accepted in the State Department.

22. Stimson Diary (MS.), 20 May 1941.

23. Memo, "O. W." [Col. Orlando Ward] for CofS, 24 May 1941, OCS, Notes on Conferences, folder 15, W.W. II Records.

24. Report, G-2 to Asst. Chief of Staff [ACofS], War Plans Division [WPD] (on State Department Evaluation of 12 May 1941), 20 May 1941, WPD 4300–20, W.W. II Records.

25. Memo, Chief of Plans Group, WPD (Col. C. W. Bundy), for ACofS, "Prevention of Axis Penetration to South America," 22 May 1941, sent to CofS 27 May 1941. WPD 4224–155, W. W. II Records.

26. Hull's position is not known. There is, however, no record of his having objected, and his statement of 24 April suggests he supported action.

27. Letter included in Memo, WPD for CofS, "Analysis of Plans for Overseas Expedition, Rainbow 5," 31 May 1941, WPD 4175–22, W.W. II Records.

28. Described in Memo, Col. C.W. Bundy for ACofS, WPD "Conference in CofS Office, Morning of May 23, 1941," 23 May 1941, WPD 4422–3, W. W. II Records; Letter, Stark to Kimmel, 24 May 1941, in *Pearl Harbor Attack,* pt. 5, p. 2113.

29. Murphy to Welles, 21 May 1941, in *Foreign Relations of the United States, 1941,* 2:344–346.

30. Rosenman, *Public Papers 1941*, pp. 181–194. The references to the proximity of danger had been suggested to the President by his friend and frequent unofficial advisor, Justice Felix Frankfurter. He had suggested that the President's speech emphasize the direct American interest in the war by repeating his remarks to Congress of 29 December 1940, when Roosevelt had emphasized the proximity of points in Africa and the Western Hemisphere. Letter dated 24 May in *Roosevelt and Frankfurter: Their Correspondence 1928–1945*, annotated by Max Freedman, pp. 599–600.

31. Telegram dated 29 May 1941 in *Foreign Relations, 1941*, 2:843–844. The dispatch of Marines to Iceland was ordered by the President on 16 June and accomplished 7 July. See Mark S. Watson, *Chief of Staff: Prewar Plans and Preparations*, pp. 487–488.

32. *Foreign Relations, 1941*, 2:844–845.

33. See Watson, *Chief of Staff*, p. 487.

34. Tracy Kittredge, (draft typescript) U.S–British Naval Cooperation, 1940–1945, vol. 1, sec. 4, pt. C, chap. 16, p. 326. Churchill formally requested the Iceland operation 3 June. Conn and Fairchild, *Hemisphere Defense*, pp. 123–124. John G. Winant, *Letter from Grosvenor Square*, p. 145.

35. See for examples in *Foreign Relations, 1941*, vol. 2: Leahy to State, 4 June 1941, pp. 361–362; 5 June 1941, p. 367; 7 June 1941, pp. 370–371.

36. The Joint Army and Navy Board was the highest agency of interservice cooperation. It was the forerunner of the Joint Chiefs of Staff, created early in 1942.

37. Draft Memo, CofS for Chief of Naval Operations [CNO], "Joint Plan for Occupation of . . . Brazil" (27 May 1941), WPD 4224–155, W.W. II Records.

38. Stimson Diary (MS.), 19 June 1941.

39. "Notes for a Diary" by Gen. L. T. Gerow, 19 June 1941, Operations Division [OPD], Executive Office file [exec] 10, item 1, W.W. II Records.

40. See for examples: Memo, CofS for Under Sec. State, "Axis Operations in the American Narrows the Dakar-Natal Area," 14 July

1941, OCS 21135–68; SW for Sec. State (no subject), 30 August 1941, OCS 21134–78; Gerow Diary, 31 August 1941, OPD, exec. 10, item 1, tab "G"; Minutes of the Standing Liaison Committee, Chief of Staff U.S. Army [WDCSA], Standing Liaison Committee [SLC], vol. 2, tab 34. All in W.W. II Records.

41. See Matloff and Snell, *Strategic Planning,* p. 53.

42. Stimson Diary (MS.), 23 June 1941; and Letter, Stimson to FDR, 23 June 1941, in President's Personal File [PPF] 20, FDRL.

43. William L. Langer and S. Everett Gleason, *The Undeclared War,* p. 587.

44. The effect of the deterioration of the British military position in Egypt on the attitude of French African officials is mentioned in a State Department memo, 30 June 1941, in *Foreign Relations, 1941,* 2:386; and in William D. Leahy, *I Was There,* pp. 54–55.

45. Murphy to State, 10 July 1941, *Foreign Relations, 1941,* 2:389.

46. State to Leahy, 13 July 1941, ibid., pp. 391–392.

47. *Fortune* used standard professional polling techniques, and *Fortune's* results were comparable to those of other polls, i.e., an average error during 1940–1942 of about 2.5 percent. *Fortune's* election forecasts for the 1936 and 1940 elections were accurate within 1 percent. See George Gallup, *A Guide to Public Opinion Polls,* p. 56.

48. Letter, Russell Davenport to Hopkins, 10 July 1941, in Hopkins Papers, box 298, FDRL. Notation indicates that the letter containing the poll results was shown to the President on or before the 13th. At about the same time the President received a report by a French officer (Lt. Col. Dassonville) proposing a plan for armed American intervention in French North Africa. Stimson, to whom the President referred the report, wrote the President on the 22nd roundly condemning the proposal and recommending that it be given no further consideration. Letter, SW to President, 22 July 1941, Classified Files of the Secretary, file 1722, in National Archives.

49. Sherwood, *Roosevelt and Hopkins,* pp. 316–317.

50. The Atlantic meetings are discussed in full in Theodore A. Wilson, *The First Summit.* Wilson suggests that Roosevelt intended his

meeting with Churchill as the dramatic event needed to arouse and unify the American people. See especially p. 23.

51. Letter, Major General J. E. Chaney (London) to General Marshall, 18 June 1941, WPD 4402–141, W.W. II Records.

52. Neither the dispatch of a small contingent of Marines to supplement the British force in Iceland, nor the token American garrison in Greenland were considered politically or militarily hazardous.

53. Memo, Stark for Sec. Navy, 12 November 1940, WPD 4175–15, W.W. II Records. The background of the document is described in Watson, *Chief of Staff*, pp. 118–123.

54. Matloff and Snell, *Strategic Planning*, pp. 34–37; Sir John Slessor, *The Central Blue: Recollections and Reflections*, pp. 344–349.

55. Kittredge, *Naval Cooperation*, vol. 1, sec. 4, chap. 14, pt. A, pp. 343–346; and Slessor, *Central Blue*, pp. 344–347, 349.

56. For examples of the partial acceptance of the peripheral strategy see Memo, Anderson for L. T. Gerow, "Military Agreement with British," 18 February 1941, OPD, exec. 4, item 11, W.W. II Records; and Slessor, *Central Blue*, p. 349.

57. RAINBOW 5 was approved by the Joint Board on 14 May, and sent to the President on 2 June. Following his policy of super caution toward making military commitments before the formal advent of hostilities, the President returned the document and the ABC agreement to the Board without approval or disapproval. General Marshall assumed that this denoted tentative acceptance of the plan. RAINBOW 5 is discussed at length in Matloff and Snell, *Strategic Planning*, pp. 43–47.

58. Discussion of Atlantic Conference military talks based on: Memo, Bundy for CofS, "Notes on Atlantic Conference," WPD 4402–64; and Memo, Commander F. Sherman for CNO, 18 August 1941, "Notes on Staff Conference, 11–12 August 1941," OPD, exec. 4, item 10; both in W.W. II Records. Sherwood, *Roosevelt and Hopkins*, pp. 354, 358; J. M. A. Gwyer and J. R. M. Butler, *Grand Strategy*, 3:125–128.

59. Bundy Notes, WPD 4402–64, W.W. II Records.

60. Gwyer and Butler, *Grand Strategy*, 3:127.

61. See Pogue, *Marshall*, 2:148–154; Langer and Gleason, *Undeclared*

War, p. 574; and Robert A. Divine, *The Reluctant Belligerent*, pp. 130–131. Public morale, as the combative spirit was known, was low. Service as the Arsenal of Democracy and other bloodless activities seem to have been accepted, but the dedicated spirit of self-sacrifice which the Administration sought was largely absent. A *New York Times* article commenting on this situation at the end of August attributed the mood to several factors, including: the lack of a formal state of war, the feeling that the Administration was not candid about its policies, hostility toward the British Empire and the Soviet Union, and the general feeling that the current situation was not serious and posed no threat to American security. Article by Frank L. Kluckhohn, 31 August 1941, sec. 4, p. 8:1. Not even the loss of American lives in U-boat attacks on American vessels in October stirred the American people. "Since there were no drafted men in the Navy . . . there was no great popular indignation against Hitler for the attacks on the destroyers. . . . The American people were merely waiting, in a seemingly apathetic state, comparable to that of the British people during the 'Phony War' period. . . ." Sherwood, *Roosevelt and Hopkins*, pp. 380–381.

62. Press Conferences, 19 August 1941, FDRL. The quotation from Lincoln may be found in Carl Sandburg, *Abraham Lincoln: The War Years*, 1:553.

63. Stimson Diary (MS.), 29 August 1941.

64. Letter, Marshall to President, 6 September 1941, PSF "War Department;" and Memo, President for Marshall, 23 September 1941, ibid., FDRL.

65. See Richard W. Steele, "Preparing the Public for War: Efforts to Establish a National Propaganda Agency, 1940–41," *American Historical Review*, 75, no. 6 (October 1970): 1640–1653.

66. Walter Lippmann, "The Case for a Smaller Army" (condensed from N.Y. *Herald-Tribune*), *Readers Digest*, November 1941, p. 39.

67. This position is set forth in a letter, Sec. War to President, 23 September 1941, Classified Files of the Secretary, file 1700, N.A. Major Albert C. Wedemeyer was directly responsible for drawing up the Program.

68. Pogue, *George C. Marshall*, 2:76–78.

69. Memo for the Record by "WTS" (Col. W. T. Sexton), "Informa-

tion for the President," 20 September 1941, OPD, exec. 4, item 7, tab "K", in W.W. II Records.

70. See folder "Information Used by the CofS at Conference with President, Sept. 22, 1941," OCS, Notes on Conferences, W.W. II Records.

71. Sherwood, *Roosevelt and Hopkins,* pp. 410–418.

72. Ibid., p. 418.

73. Stimson's words as he recalled them were: "there was a long distance between getting into war and crushing Germany." Stimson Diary (MS.), 25 September 1941; and Letter, SW to President, 23 September 1941 (handed to President on 25th), in Classified Files of the Secretary, file 1700, N.A.

74. Stimson Diary (MS.), 29 September 1941.

75. *Colliers* article described in *New York Times,* 3 October 1941, p. 4:3.

76. Ambassador Leahy reported on 25 September that there was increasing feeling in France that at the conclusion of the current campaign in Russia the Germans would renew their demands for facilities in Africa, and that these demands might be accompanied by an ultimatum. Leahy to State, in *Foreign Relations, 1941,* 2:439. Petain expressed similar thoughts to Leahy on 4 November, ibid., p. 454.

77. Memo (draft), CofS for President, "Ground Forces," 7 October 1941, OPD, exec. 4, item 7, tab "K", W.W. II Records.

78. Memo, SW for President, 7 October 1941, WPD 4511–5, W.W.II Records. Stimson may have waited until his meeting with the President on October 9 to hand him this memo. If Marshall's purpose was to put off African operations without ruling them out, Stimson appears to have been working at cross purposes, for he warned the President on the 8th, and again on the 9th against any United States operation in West Africa. After the last encounter Stimson thought he had talked the President out of the West African project but noted that "there are other side-tracks of which I am even more afraid." Stimson Diary (MS.), 9 October 1941.

Chapter Two

1. Stimson Diary (MS.), 7 October 1941.

2. Ibid., 10 October 1941.

3. Letter, Mountbatten to FDR, 17 October 1941, PSF "Great Britain 1941," FDRL.

4. Winston S. Churchill, *The Second World War*, vol. 3, *The Grand Alliance*, p. 542.

5. Elliott Roosevelt, *FDR: His Personal Letters 1928–1945*, 2:1223. The President may have had in mind the dispatch of an American force to Tangier in the International Zone of Spanish Morocco. (Churchill, *Grand Alliance*, p. 552.) At about the same time William Donovan (the Coordinator of Information) began work, probably at the President's suggestion, on a study of the "strategic situation with regard to the Iberian Peninsula and North and West Africa in the event of our more active participation in the Atlantic." (Report, Baxter to Donovan, sent to FDR by Donovan 23 October 1941, PSF "C.O.I.—Donovan" [closed], FDRL.

6. Churchill, *Grand Alliance*, p. 540.

7. Ibid., p. 544.

8. Ibid., pp. 551–552.

9. William D. Leahy, *I Was There*, p. 56.

10. Ibid., p. 57; and Leahy to State, 7 November 1941, *Foreign Relations, 1941*, 2:456.

11. See Memo, Miles (G-2) for CofS, "American Assistance for the Defense of French No. Africa," 21 October 1941, WPD 4511–18, W.W. II Records.

12. State to Leahy, 10 November 1941, *Foreign Relations, 1941*, 2:456–457.

13. Murphy to U. Sec. State, 19 November 1941, ibid., pp. 466–468.

The substance of this message was repeated by Murphy and other U.S. diplomatic representatives in North Africa several times during November. See especially message, Murphy to State, 21 November 1941, in Hopkins Papers, box 317, folder VI, FDRL.

14. Churchill, *Grand Alliance*, p. 544.

15. Memo, FDR for Watson, 17 November 1941, in Official File [OF] "Bullitt," FDRL.

16. Telegrams, Cairo to State, 18 September 1941, Hopkins Papers, box 304, FDRL.; Cairo to State, 25 September 1941, 740001 1EW/15436, in State Department Records, N.A.

17. See Letter, FDR to Churchill, 25 November 1942, apprising the latter of Bullitt's mission, in PSF "Churchill," FDRL.

18. FDR for Bullitt, 22 November 1941, PSF "Bullitt 1941–1942" [closed], FDRL. In February 1919 President Wilson had sent Bullitt to Moscow to gather information on which to base a policy toward the Bolsheviks. It is also interesting to note that in November 1939, while Bullitt was serving as U.S. Ambassador to France, Roosevelt suggested that he go to Algiers and Tunis for a "couple of weeks" and make a report on the general situation in North Africa. He did not go. FDR to Bullitt, 28 November 1939, PSF "France-Bullitt, 1939–40" [closed], FDRL.

19. Harold Ickes, *The Secret Diary of Harold L. Ickes*, 3:615.

20. Stimson Diary (MS.), 30 October 1941.

21. Ibid., 12 November 1941. The substance of this complaint is repeated in the diary for 1 December 1941.

22. Memo, C. W. Bundy for CofS, 28 November 1941, WPD 4511–26, W.W. II Records.

23. See below, pp. 23–24.

24. Stimson Diary (MS.), 11 and 17 December 1941.

25. Minutes of the Standing Liaison Committee, 20 December 1941, WDCSA, SLC, vol. 2, tab 40, W.W. II Records.

26. Memo, Lovett for SW, and covering memo for Arnold, "Need for Protection of West Africa Bases . . .", 18 December 1941, Office

of the Secretary of War, "White House" file, W.W. II Records. On the following day Stimson. impressed by the urgent need "to save West Africa," consulted Colonel Lee S. Gerow of the War Plans Division on the possibility of American military action in the area, only to learn that because of shortages of ammunition the Army at present "could do nothing to stop Germany from cutting American communications across Africa." Memo for the Record on his meeting with SW by Col. L. S. Gerow, 19 December 1941, WPD 4511–30, W.W. II Records. Stimson also approached Harry Hopkins on the subject. Stimson Diary (MS.), 19 December 1941.

27. Memo, SW for President, "Suggested Analysis of Basic Topics . . .", 20 December 1941, WPD 4402–136, W.W. II Records. Memo with covering note also found in Hopkins Papers, box 308, FDRL.

28. The agenda is quoted in Maurice Matloff and Edwin M. Snell, *Strategic Planning for Coalition Warfare 1941–42*, p. 97.

29. "Notes on Agenda Proposed by British," 21 December 1941, OPD, exec. 4, book 2, W.W. II Records.

30. Ibid.

31. The failure of the Germans to defeat Russia had an important bearing on Franco-German relations. See William L. Langer and S. Everett Gleason, *Undeclared War*, p. 771.

32. See Kenneth Pendar, *Adventure in Diplomacy;* William L. Langer, *Our Vichy Gamble*, pp. 205–206; Telegram, Vichy to State, 4 December 1941, 851.00/2534, State Dept. records, N.A.; *New York Times*, 13 December 1941, p. 8:8.

33. It may be noted that Donovan was supplying the President with information (intelligence) bearing on both the success of his mission in building up a pro-Allied force in Africa and on the feasibility of following through on that mission by the commitment of armed force. To have recommended against intervention would have put Donovan in the position of suggesting that his espionage activities were either a failure or to no purpose.

34. Memo, Donovan to FDR, 15 December 1941, PSF "Donovan Reports," FDRL.

35. Ibid., 21 December 1941. On the 12th the American Minister in Cairo cabled the State Department requesting "that consideration

be given to the possible operation of American units in West and North Africa against Axis territory and forces within striking distance." Kirk to State, 12 December 1941, *Foreign Relations, 1941, 3*: 297. It is possible that this message was shown to the President, for another message from Kirk (22 December 1941, 740.0011EW39/17883) referring to his of the 12th was definitely sent to the White House.

36. See below, p.p. 41–42.

37. SW, "Memo of Decisions at White House Sunday, Dec. 21, 1941," in Stimson Diary (MS.), 21 December 1941. See also Stetson Conn and Byron Fairchild, *The Framework of Hemisphere Defense*, pp. 168–171.

Chapter Three

1. See Hadley Cantril, "The Public Opinion Polls: Dr. Jekyll or Mr. Hyde?", *Public Opinion Quarterly,* 4 (June 1940): pp. 212–217; and Claude E. Robinson, "Recent Developments in the Straw-Poll Field," ibid., 1 (July 1937): pp. 45–56.

2. In 1940 Roosevelt told the Australian Ambassador that he carefully followed the results of all public opinion polls, both published and unpublished. From a 6 May 1940 diary entry in Lord Casey, *Personal Experiences. 1939–1946,* p. 31.

3. A survey and analysis conducted in the summer of 1942 by the Office of Public Opinion Research, Princeton, noted that people did not hesitate to admit prewar noninterventionist points of view, and that public opinion analysis showed no "profound conversion or change of conviction among pre-Pearl isolationists." Hadley Cantril, "Pre–Pearl Harbor Interventionists and Non-Interventionists," a confidential report dated 3 August 1942, entry 171, box 256, Records of the Office of Government Reports [OGR], N.A. This analysis confirmed an earlier report based on opinion sampling between 7 December 1941 and the end of February 1942 which revealed that the irreducible minimum of opposition to Administration foreign policy had been reached immediately before the war, and its numbers had not been appreciably reduced by American entry into the war. "Survey of Intelligence Materials, no. 12," (2 March 1942), prepared by the Bureau of Intelligence, Office of Facts and Figures [OFF], in PSF "OFF," FDRL.

4. These figures were available to the President in "Survey of Intelligence Materials, no. 9" (February 9, 1942), in PSF "OFF," FDRL.

5. The President almost certainly knew of all these results. He had available: a Cantril poll based on polling 10–16 December forwarded to him by Lowell Mellett on 19 December, see memo, Mellett to President, box 5, Mellett Papers, FDRL; a confidential report by Frederick Williams and Hadley Cantril "What People Think about Peace . . .", dated February 14, 1942, forwarded to President by Mellett on the 26th, in OF 788, box 6, FDRL; "Survey of Intelligence Materials, no. 9" (9 February 1942), in PSF "OFF," FDRL. Results on ignorance of war aims from "Intelligence Report, Trends in American Public Opinion Since Pearl Harbor" (11 September 1942), in PSF "OWI," FDRL.

6. Letter, Donovan to FDR, 14 December 1941, PSF "Donovan Reports," FDRL.

7. Memo, Kintner to MacLeish, 24 December 1941, folder "Committee on War Info.," box 35, Records of the Office of War Information [OWI], N.A.

8. Letter, MacLeish to Grace Tully [Pres. Roosevelt's secretary], 27 December 1941, folder "Victory Program," box 52, OWI records, N.A. OFF's suggestions were incorporated in the President's address.

9. The Committee on War Information (CWI) comprised MacLeish, several members of his staff, and high-level representatives of the War, Navy, and Justice Departments, the Treasury, Lend-Lease Administration, and the Office of the Coordinator of Information. Lowell Mellett also participated, in effect providing liaison with the White House. Each week OFF supplied the CWI with a survey of the deficiencies encountered or anticipated in the public's knowledge and acceptance of Administration policy and objectives. The OFF would then suggest remedies for the problems, which if accepted by the Committee would be implemented by the information offices of the departments and agencies represented on the Committee. A serious flaw in this arrangement was the lack of White House policy guidance. As a result OFF and its successor OWI had to guess what Administration policy was and more than once were in the position of advocating a policy contrary to the position adopted on the issue by the President.

10. "Meeting of the Committee on War Information," 29 December 1941, in Correspondence of the Director, box 13, entry 78, OGR

records, N.A. Deliberations of the CWI were routinely available to the President.

11. Samuel I. Rosenman, *Working With Roosevelt*, p. 308. Roosevelt made this remark to Rosenman during the preparation of the fireside chat delivered on 9 December.

12. Samuel I. Rosenman (ed.), *The Public Papers of Franklin D. Roosevelt, 1941*, pp. 529–530. The reader will note the repetition of the prewar theme pointing up the danger of an Axis attack on the Western Hemisphere by way of French Africa. The President in this speech could not know whether the European Axis would declare war on the United States and hence was anxious to justify American involvement in the European war. The theme of a single war directed from Berlin is, however, found in subsequent speeches.

13. Dates and percentages naming Japan: December 26–30, 31.7%; January 28–February 4, 30.5%;February 16–23, 37.5%. The percentage naming Germany dropped from 58.8 to 41% in the same period. The difference is accounted for by those answering "both" or "don't know." In "Survey of Intelligence Materials, no. 12" (2 March 1942), in PSF "OWI," FDRL.

14. Henry L. Stimson and McGeorge Bundy, *On Active Service in Peace and War*, p. 430.

15. Former Naval Person to President, 11 December 1941, 740.0011EW39/17332/½, State Dept. records, N.A.; and Winston S. Churchill, *The Second World War*, vol. 3, *The Grand Alliance*, pp. 632, 641–643.

16. J. M. A. Gwyer and J. R. M. Butler, *Grand Strategy*, 3:325–336.

17. The German drive on Moscow ended on 6 December when the Soviets launched their winter counter-offensive.

18. Rommel's forces were in full retreat during December. The British captured the key port of Benghazi on the 24th.

19. Text of this paper in Gwyer and Butler, *Grand Strategy*, 3:325–336.

20. Ibid., p. 343.

21. The British position as thus outlined was very much like that

recently accepted by General Marshall, especially inasmuch as it made no provision for immediate offensive action by the Allies. Text of the final paper in Gwyer and Butler, *Grand Strategy*, 3:345–348.

22. The absence of General Brooke (recently appointed Chief of the Imperial General Staff) probably made it much easier for the Prime Minister to dominate his other military advisors. Brooke, who had the strong character needed to oppose Churchill's schemes, had been obliged to remain in England during the ARCADIA talks. Lord Moran (Sir Charles Wilson), *Churchill: The Struggle for Survival, 1940–1965*, pp. 21–22.

23. Churchill, *Grand Alliance*, p. 664.

24. Account of meeting in Churchill, *Grand Alliance*, pp. 663–665; and Gwyer and Butler, *Grand Strategy*, 3:353–354.

25. The President used a memo from Stimson (20 December 1941) as the basis for his remarks. This memo, which Stimson submitted to the WPD for comment, is found in OPD, exec. 4, item 13, W.W. II Records. See also Stimson Diary (MS.), 23 December 1941; Gwyer and Butler, *Grand Strategy*, 3:354–355. While there is no evidence that the Army leaders had made their objections to GYMNAST known directly to the President, Roosevelt was certainly aware that they gave other projects higher priority. On the 22nd, Stimson at the request of the Chief of Staff had once again urged Roosevelt to appoint a special envoy to go to Brazil to obtain President Vargas' permission to station American Army troops at air bases in the northeastern portion of the country. The President was thus aware that the Army leadership considered the defense of Brazil and the trans-African supply route far more important than Northwest Africa. Stimson Diary (MS.), 22 December 1941; and memo of the Secretary's phone call in OF 26, box 15, FDRL. The President again turned down the Army's request that he take a hand in the problem of Brazil.

26. He may have had in mind the use of Black African units of the French Army, since it was assumed in the War Plans Division that Caucasians could not fight for long in the West African climate.

27. Pencilled notes taken at meeting by General Marshall, and his expanded version of what took place (produced after the meeting), both in WPD 4402-136, W.W. II Records. See *Foreign Relations of the United States, The Conferences at Washington 1941–1942*, pp. 69–80. Gwyer and Butler, *Grand Strategy*, 3:354–357.

28. Diary entry for 25 December 1941, in Arthur Bryant, *The Turn of the Tide*, pp. 229–230.

29. These points may be found in Memo, Ridgway for Marshall , 23 December 1941, OPD, exec. 8, bk. 1, tab "Misc."; Memo, Bundy for CofS, 28 November 1941, "Conference with Mr. Bullitt," WPD 4511–26, W.W. II Records.

30. Forrest C. Pogue, *George C. Marshall*, vol. 2, *Ordeal and Hope, 1939–1942*, pp. 133–134.

31. Memo entitled "More Important Factors in Current Strategic Situation," signed "S.D.E.", 16 December 1941. Sent to CofS by ACofS, WPD on 17 December 1941, WPD 4622–37, W.W. II Records.

32. Ibid., and Memo by Embick [no addressee, date, or subject], in folder "Dec. 1941 ARCADIA Papers, Post-ARCADIA Collaboration, GYMNAST," in OPD, exec. 4, item 13, W.W. II Records. Quoted at length in Maurice Matloff and Edwin M. Snell, *Strategic Planning for Coalition Warfare 1941–1942*, pp. 104–105.

33. Richard M. Leighton and Robert W. Coakley, *Global Logistics and Strategy 1940–1943*, pp. 152–153. These conclusions were brought to the President's attention on the 26th in a Memo, CofS for President, 26 December 1941, WPD 4511–32, W.W. II Records.

34. Churchill, *Grand Alliance*, p. 649.

35. Churchill, *Grand Alliance*, p. 665.

36. "Notes on Informal Conferences held during Visit of British Chiefs in Washington," OCS Minutes, WDCSA 334 (1–28–42); and Memo, CofS for President, 26 December 1941, WPD 4511–32, both in W.W. II Records. See *Foreign Relations, Conferences 1941–1942*, pp. 100–106.

37. See Leighton and Coakley, *Global Logistics*, pp. 205–207, and appendix A-6, p. 725.

38. It is interesting to note that in July 1942 General Marshall was satisfied with a proportionally smaller force for the far more hazardous SLEDGEHAMMER (invasion of France in 1942) because he was anxious to justify the operation.

39. General Marshall apparently believed that the "British greatly

exaggerated the importance of North Africa" since he reported Embick's observation on this point to Admiral Stark (27 December). Minutes of the conference in Stark's office 27 December 1941, in "Notes on Informal Conferences held During Visit of Brit. Chiefs in Wash.," WDCSA 334 (1–28–42), W.W. II Records.

40. Diary entry for 1 January 1942 in Moran, *Churchill*, p. 22.

41. Entry for 31 December 1941, ibid., p. 21. Even Hopkins was concerned about the effect of Churchill's influence on Roosevelt. See Pogue, *George C. Marshall*, 2:255–256, 270.

42. Memo, Donovan to FDR, 27 December 1941, PSF "Donovan Reports," FDRL. See William L. Langer, *Our Vichy Gamble*, pp. 208–209.

43. Minutes of White House Conference, 28 December 1941, in "Notes on Informal Conf. Held During Visit of Brit . . .," WDCSA 334 (1–18–42), W.W. II Records. Published in *Foreign Relations, Conferences 1941–1942*, pp. 126–130.

44. General DeGaulle's Free French controlled a large area of central Africa and had a force of about 6,000 men fighting alongside the British in the Middle East. See Dorothy S. White, *Seeds of Discord: DeGaulle, Free France, and the Allies*, chap. 11, ff.

45. General Arnold's "Notes on White House Conference," 1 January 1942, in box 180, Arnold Papers, Library of Congress. Published in *Foreign Relations, Conferences 1941–1942*, pp. 152–154, 249–250.

46. Joseph W. Stilwell, *The Stilwell Papers*, entry for 3 January, pp. 20–21.

47. "Notes on Conference at Office of the SW, January 4, 1942," in Stimson Papers Correspondence, 1942, Yale University Library; see also Stimson Diary (MS.), 4 January 1942.

48. Stimson had responded to a request by Marshall and the planners by telephoning the President on the 3rd asking him to make no commitment to the project. Stimson Diary (MS.), 3 January 1942; and diary entries for January 2 and 3 in Stilwell, *Papers*, pp. 21–22.

49. Stimson Diary (MS.), 4 January 1942. War Department and Arnold notes on the conference in *Foreign Relations, Conferences 1941–1942*, pp. 162–170.

50. Messages of this nature were often forwarded to the White House. Although there is no evidence that it was done in this case, it is most likely that Hull passed the information on to the President. Kirk to State, 1 January 1942, 740.0011EW39/18131, State Dept. records, N.A. For other warnings of the same nature see Bullitt to FDR, 2 January 1942, *Foreign Relations, Conferences 1941–1942*, p. 252; and Memo, Donovan for President, 5 January 1942, ibid., p. 255.

51. Winston S. Churchill, *The Second World War*, vol. 4, *The Hinge of Fate*, pp. 21–22.

52. Memo, SW to General MacArthur, 31 December 1941, OPD, exec. 8, book 1, W.W. II Records. Although the defense of the Philippines was believed to be hopeless, a sense of duty and considerations of prestige and morale led Roosevelt to decide that the effort would have to be made. The American and Filipino forces held out against the Japanese until May 1942.

53. Entry for 11 January 1942 in Eisenhower Diary, in Alfred D. Chandler, Jr. (ed.), *The Papers of Dwight David Eisenhower*, vol. 1, *The War Years*, p. 46.

54. The foregoing account of the situation in the Pacific is based on Louis Morton, *The War in the Pacific, Strategy and Command: The First Two Years*, pp. 151–164.

55. The Soviets, who had concluded a nonaggression pact with Japan in 1941, did not declare war on Japan until the very last days of the war.

56. The minutes of this meeting are reproduced in Robert E. Sherwood, *Roosevelt and Hopkins*, pp. 460–466.

57. Memo on Conference at the White House, 14 January 1942, OPD, exec. 8, book 3, tab "Misc.", W.W. II Records. Printed in *Foreign Relations, Conferences 1941–1942*, pp. 203–208. The date for the attack was set at 25 May and the final decision on the operation was embodied in Combined Chiefs of Staff 5 (CCS 5), 20 January 1942, Records of the Combined Chiefs of Staff, CCS 381 (1–20–42). N.A.

58. Letter, President to Weygand, 27 December 1941, in *Foreign Relations 1941*, 2:502; Langer, *Vichy Gamble*, p. 209.

59. Letter, President to Leahy, cabled 20 January 1942, in *Foreign Relations, 1942*, 2:124.

60. General Maxime Weygand, *Recalled to Service*, pp. 390–393; William D. Leahy, *I Was There*, p. 75.

61. Weygand in his memoirs suggests that the approach would have been better directed to his successors in North Africa, Generals Juin and de Lattre. Weygand, *Recalled to Service*, p. 393.

62. Leahy to FDR, 25 January 1942, PSF "France, 1941" [closed], FDRL.

63. Leahy to President, 27 January 1942, *Foreign Relations, 1942*, 2:124–125.

64. Churchill, *Hinge of Fate*, chap. 2.

65. See Minutes of the British War Cabinet, Confidential Annex to 8th Meeting (17 January 1942), Minute 1, Public Records Office, London.

66. ABC-4/CS-1, "Washington War Conference, American-British Strategy, Memorandum by the U.S. and British Chiefs of Staff" (31 December 1941). Marked "Approved 10 Jan 42." CCS 381 (2–2–42) (1) in Records of the CCS. Richard M. Leighton has pointed out the American acceptance of the peripheral strategy at ARCADIA in his excellent article "Overlord Revisited: An Interpretation of American Strategy in the European War, 1942–1944," in the *American Historical Review*, 68, no. 4 (July 1963): 919–937.

67. A similar issue arose shortly after the Conference had begun, when Stimson and the Army leaders were shocked and angered to learn that Roosevelt had agreed to discuss with Churchill the possibility of diverting for British use American forces intended for the reinforcement of the Philippines. Stimson threatened to resign if any such diversion was made and the matter was dropped. The impression of Presidential irresponsibility, however, remained. Hopkins and Hull were also unhappy about Churchill's influence on the President. See Pogue, *Marshall*, 2:255–256, 270, and Breckinridge Long, *The War Diary of Breckinridge Long*, edited by Fred L. Israel, entry for 13 January 1942, p. 242; Morton, *Strategy and Command*, p. 165. Marshall also successfully insisted that the Permanent Combined Chiefs of Staff organization be located in Washington rather than in London, causing some unhappiness among the British. See Moran, *Churchill*, pp. 21–24. Pogue suggests that Marshall's opposition during ARCADIA to the creation of a combined civilian war material board was also based at least

in part on his fear that a civilian director might be overly sympathetic to British views. Pogue, *Marshall*, 2:286.

68. Stilwell, *Papers*, pp. 15–16. Stilwell also complained about excessive Navy influence with the President. Ibid., pp. 15–18.

69. Diary entry for 1 January 1942 in Dwight D. Eisenhower, *Crusade in Europe*, p. 22. See also Eisenhower diary entry for 4 January. On the 17th Eisenhower repeated this idea, going so far as to recommend (at least to his diary) that the replacement of British troops in Iceland be halted and the British advised to pull back their forces in Libya. Chandler, *Eisenhower Papers*, 1:39, 61–62.

70. General Headquarters was eliminated by the Army reorganization at the end of January. Ray S. Cline, *Washington Command Post*, pp. 11, 91.

71. Stilwell, *Papers*, p. 25.

72. McNair's substitute proposal was rejected as impracticable that same day by the Deputy Chief of Staff, General Gerow. Memo, McNair to C.G. Field Forces, "Future Operations," 15 January 1942, OPD, exec. 8, book 2, tab "Misc.", W.W. II Records.

73. Eisenhower diary entry for 22 January 1942, Chandler, *Eisenhower Papers*, 1:66.

74. Entry for 27 January 1942, ibid., p. 75.

75. Letter, Wyman to Eisenhower, 29 January 1942, OPD, exec. 10, item 27, W.W. II Records.

Chapter Four

1. The following summary of developments in the Pacific is based on the account in Louis Morton, *The War in the Pacific, Strategy and Command: The First Two Years*, pp. 157–224.

2. These were the areas to be held, not a line of fortified positions as one might assume. See J. M. A. Gwyer and J. R. M. Butler, *Grand Strategy*, 3:380.

3. See Robert E. Sherwood, *Roosevelt and Hopkins*, p. 458; and Henry L. Stimson and McGeorge Bundy, *On Active Service in Peace and War*, pp. 429–430.

4. The President could keep track of this development in a series of reports called "Editorial Opinion on the War" provided him by the Director of OFF. See reports for January 9, 16, and particularly January 30, in PSF "Treasury-Morgenthau," FDRL.

5. *New York Times*, 15 January 1942, p. 6:4.

6. *Time*, "Washington Wonders," 26 January 1942, pp. 12–13.

7. "Weekly Media Digest No. 2" (12 February 1942), box 232, OGR records, N.A.

8. OFF, "Editorial Opinion on the War," 30 January 1942, PSF "Treasury-Morgenthau"; and "Survey of Intelligence Materials, no. 8" (2 February 1942), PSF "OFF"; both in FDRL.

9. The question asked was which nation was it most important to concentrate on "right now." "Survey of Intelligence Materials, no. 21" (29 April 1942), PSF "OWI," in FDRL.

10. "Survey of Intelligence Materials, no. 7," (24 January 1942), ibid.

11. OFF, "Editorial Opinion on the War," 20 February 1942, PSF "Treasury-Morgenthau," FDRL.

12. Ibid., 6 March 1942.

13. "Survey of Intelligence Materials, no. 18" (8 April 1942), PSF "OWI," FDRL.

14. See OFF "Editorial Opinion on the War" (13 February 1942), PSF "Treasury-Morgenthau"; and "Survey of Intelligence Materials, no. 11" (23 February 1942), PSF "OWI"; both in FDRL.

15. *Time*, 16 February 1942, p. 11.

16. Arthur Krock, "Public is Slow to Grasp Spirit of War Urgency," *New York Times*, 8 February 1942, sec. 4, p. 3:1. Other contemporary comments on negative public attitudes in Joseph W. Stilwell, *The Stilwell Papers*, p. 39; William D. Leahy, *I Was There*, p. 86; Sherwood, *Roosevelt and Hopkins*, p. 491; Lewis Brereton, *The Brereton Diaries*, p. 91; Fred I. Israel (ed.), *The War Diary of Breckinridge Long*, entry for 15 February 1942, p. 251: David E. Lilienthal, *The Journals of David E. Lilienthal*, vol. 1, *The TVA Years, 1939–1945*, entry for 28 February 1942, p. 449.

17. Letter, Roper to MacLeish, 26 February 1942, folder "001," box 3, OWI records, N.A.

18. Presidential Press Conferences, 10 February 1942, FDRL.

19. *Time,* 23 February 1942, p. 13.

20. Samuel I. Rosenman, (ed.), *The Public Papers and Addresses of Franklin D. Roosevelt, 1942,* pp. 105–116.

21. OFF, "Editorial Opinion on the War" (27 February 1942), PSF "Treasury-Morgenthau," FDRL.

22. *New York Times,* 27 February 1942, p. 10:2.

23. Ibid., 3 March 1942, p. 1:2.

24. C. Brooks Peters, "Admiral King Promises Offensive," *New York Times,* 12 March 1942, p. 1:2.

25. "Weekly Media Report No. 6" (14 March 1942), OGR records, N.A.; OFF, "Editorial Opinion on the War," 6 and 13 March 1942, PSF "Treasury-Morgenthau," FDRL.

26. *New York Times,* editorial, 12 March 1942, p. 18:2. The editorial referred specifically to a message by the President accompanying a report to Congress on the "First Year of Lend-Lease" in which he declared that the war could be won only by "contact with the enemies, and by attack upon them." Rosenman, *Public Papers 1942,* pp. 155–156.

27. 34% wanted them kept at home; 10% offered no opinion. Hadley Cantril, the director of the Institute of Public Opinion Analysis, analyzed the public's attitude toward the war in the following way. Offensive-mindedness stemmed from a realization that maximum self-interest required an Axis defeat. Defensive-mindedness seemed to come from (1) a failure to regard the Axis threat as real, (2) the identification of self-interest with a narrow psychological world in which the daily struggle and pursuits of life were all-important, or (3) the feeling of some persons that they were none too well off now and that there was little for them to gain by taking any risks. Cantril found that the desire to keep American troops at home was almost twice as frequent among the poor and uneducated. Hadley Cantril, "Opinion Concerning Offensive and Defensive Strategy," 10 April 1942, box 256, OGR records, N.A.

28. The letter to Leffingwell, 16 March 1942, is printed in Elliott Roosevelt (ed.), *F.D.R.: His Personal Letters 1928–1945*, 2:1298–1299.

29. "I believe it is time for us to wave the flag." Conference 17 March 1942, in Presidential Press Conferences, FDRL. During the first two weeks of March, the President considered a proposal to "Increase Production Effectiveness through Intensification of the Victory Attitude," originally suggested by Vice President Wallace. On the 14th, Roosevelt approved such a plan and on the 30th Sidney Hillman, a Director of the War Production Board, Labor Division, informed the President that the plan was being put into effect. There are several memoranda in OF 407 and 788 dealing with the matter. The most significant is the note dated 14 March 1942 from FDR to Hillman, OF 407 "Labor," FDRL.

30. Memo, Alan Barth, "Peace Offensive, Divisionists, War Aims," 18 April 1942, box 256, OGR records, N.A.

31. "Survey of Intelligence Materials, no. 19" (15 April 1942), PSF "OWI," FDRL.

32. See *New York Times*, "The Mood of the Nation: A Survey of Our Present Sentiment," 22 March 1942, sec. 4, p. 7:1; *Time*, "Administration—The Miserable Truth," 12 January 1942, p. 12.

33. OFF, "Editorial Opinion on the War," 27 March 1942, PSF "Treasury-Morgenthau," FDRL.

34. Actually reorganization was underway in the War Department. It was completed in March, but did not involve the relationship between the Chief of Staff and the President.

35. Letter, Cochran to FDR, 28 January 1942, and the President's reply, 30 January 1942, in OF 4675, box 65. Senator Lister Hill of Alabama wrote Roosevelt in mid-March suggesting changes in the command structure. Hill to FDR, 14 March 1942, PPF 3927. Both in FDRL.

36. *Time*, "Bring Home MacArthur," 23 February 1942, p. 14. It need only be mentioned that MacArthur's return would have greatly increased his availability as a Republican presidential candidate in 1944; he was probably the only individual with a chance of success against Roosevelt should the latter choose to run again.

37. Winston S. Churchill, *The Second World War*, vol. 4, *The Hinge of Fate*, p. 200.

38. Stimson Diary (MS.), 25 February 1942. Marshall obviously could not suggest himself for the post. Leahy was intended as a neutral choice. He also had a reputation of getting along well with the Army. Apparently Marshall felt that the new setup would at least eliminate British influence from American strategy making.

39. The First Sea Lord in commenting on his meetings with the American Chiefs of Staff noted that the British were obliged to provide the secretarial arrangements for the Combined Chiefs meetings at ARCADIA, the Americans having not as yet established a secretariat for their military command. Minutes of the British War Cabinet, Confidential Annex to 8th War Cabinet Meeting (17 January 1942), Minute 1.

40. See for examples, Memo, FDR for Early, 2 May 1942, OF 4422, FDRL; and Stimson's account of an August Cabinet meeting in his Diary, 10 August 1942.

41. See Leahy, *I Was There*, p. 97.

42. Generalissimo Chiang Kai-Shek's attitude was, of course, an important consideration too. But satisfying Chiang was largely incompatible with pleasing Stalin and Churchill. Forced to choose, Roosevelt, true to the Europe-first formula, gradually abandoned serious efforts to meet Chinese demands.

43. The President's prewar thoughts of a limited involvement were never expressed once the war began.

44. See Minutes of the British War Cabinet, Confidential Annex to 90th Meeting (5 September 1941), Minute 1.

45. Eden to Foreign Office, 18 December 1941, attached to Minutes of the British War Cabinet, Confidential Annex to 131st Meeting (18 December 1941), Minute 2.

46. See telegram, Foreign Office to Moscow, 19 December 1941, in ibid., Confidential Annex to the 133rd Meeting (22 December 1942), Minute 8.

47. Ibid., Confidential Annex to 17th Meeting (6 February 1942), Minute 5.

48. Anthony Eden, *The Memoirs of Anthony Eden: The Reckoning,* p. 369.

49. Harold Macmillan, *The Blast of War, 1939–1945,* pp. 113–114; and Gwyer and Butler, *Grand Strategy,* 3:421.

50. Sumner Welles, *Seven Decisions That Shaped History,* pp. 126–128; *Foreign Relations 1941,* 1:192–194; Eden, *Reckoning,* pp. 326–352. The British had been informed of Roosevelt's attitude toward wartime arrangements as early as July 1941, a month after the German attack on Russia, and more than four months before the United States became involved in the war.

51. On 5 December 1941, Bullitt wrote the President urging him not to let Churchill "get you into any more specific engagements than those in the Atlantic Charter. Try to keep him from engaging himself vis-à-vis Russia. The treaties, if made, will be as difficult for you to handle as the secret treaties were for Wilson." Bullitt to FDR, 5 December 1941, PPF 1124 "Bullitt," FDRL.

52. Presidential Press Conferences, 24 February 1942, FDRL.

53. *Foreign Relations, 1942,* 3:505—512.

54. See Minutes of the British War Cabinet, Confidential Annex to 24th Meeting (26 February 1942), Minute 2; and telegram, Foreign Office to Halifax, 26 March 1942, attached to ibid, Confidential Annex to 37th Meeting (25 March 1942). See also *Foreign Relations, 1942,* 3:512–526.

55. Donovan Reports, 22 February 1942, FDRL.

56. According to the Order "the Red Army's aim is to drive out the German occupants from our country and liberate Soviet soil from the German fascist invaders." Joseph Stalin, *The Great Patriotic War of the Soviet Union,* pp. 39–46. Llewellyn Woodward, *British Foreign Policy in the Second World War,* pp. 192–193. During the first week in March, information reached Washington from "reliable sources" that a move was also underway in Germany to conclude an immediate separate peace with the Soviet Union. Telegram, Stockholm to State, 4 March 1942, 740.0011EW1939/19926, State Dept. records, N.A.

57. Churchill, *Hinge of Fate,* 4:189–194. This conclusion was confirmed in a message from the U.S. Chargé in London, Matthews to State, 5 March 1942, in *Foreign Relations, 1942,* 3:527–528.

58. Stimson Diary (MS.), 5 March 1942.

Chapter Five

1. Maurice Matloff and Edwin M. Snell, *Strategic Planning for Coalition Warfare, 1941–1942*, pp. 154–155.

2. Eisenhower diary entry for 17 February 1942 in Alfred D. Chandler, Jr. (ed.), *The Papers of Dwight David Eisenhower*, vol. 1, *The War Years*, p. 112.

3. Eisenhower diary entry for 22 February 1942, ibid., p. 126.

4. Stimson Diary (MS.), 24 February 1942.

5. Memo WPD [Eisenhower] for CofS, 28 February 1942, "Strategic Conceptions and Their Application to Southwest Pacific," in Chandler, *Eisenhower Papers*, 1:149–155.

6. Arnold had already (3 March) given Marshall his rather definite views on stopping the dispersion of Allied resources by seizing the initiative from the enemy. Arnold recommended concentrating offensive air strength in Britain for "direct action" against critical objectives. This would, he said, divert German air units from Russia and support an invasion of the Continent which he believed was "necessary at the earliest possible moment." Memo, Arnold to CofS, 3 March 1942, sub: "Employment of Army Air Forces," Special Office file 1941–45, box 39, Arnold Papers, L.C.

7. Hopkins also supported the scheme. Stimson Diary (MS.), 5 March 1942.

8. J. M. A. Gwyer and J. R. M. Butler, *Grand Strategy*, 3:566–567.

9. Memo, CNO for President, 5 March 1942, OPD, exec. 8, book 4, W.W. II Records.

10. Stimson Diary (MS.), 6 March 1942.

11. Harriman to FDR, 7 March 1942, PSF "Great Britain: Churchill" [closed], FDRL.

12. Message dated 7 March 1942, in Winston S. Churchill, *The Second World War*, vol. 4, *The Hinge of Fate*, pp. 195–196.

13. Ibid.

14. A major portion of Roosevelt's cable dealt with a proposal for the division of areas of strategic responsibility between Britain and the United States. The United States was to assume the decision making function for the whole Pacific area. The middle zone extending from Singapore to Libya and the Mediterranean would be under British direction and control. The North and South Atlantic and western Europe were to form a third area of joint responsibility. Ibid., pp. 197–199; Robert E. Sherwood, *Roosevelt and Hopkins*, p. 510.

15. Roosevelt's remarks to General Marshall, 8 March 1942, reported by Marshall in JCS 5th meeting (9 March 1942), in CCS 334 JCS (2-9-42), Records of the Combined Chiefs of Staff. The pressure for offensive action was also the subject of formal consideration by the military. A paper prepared by the Joint Psychological Warfare Committee of the JCS warned the Joint Chiefs that "the wave of popular enthusiasm for an offensive in the near future might assume such proportions as to become embarrassing to the actual conduct of the war." The JPWC suggested a counter propaganda campaign. See "Growing Popular Demand of United Nations Offensive," in JPWC 7 (21 March 1942) in CCS 385 (3-21-42), CCS records.

16. It is interesting to note in this connection that on the 19th Donovan reported to the President that what the dispirited British public wanted was "an offensive attitude on the part of the fighting forces instead of continual retreat and defense . . . some clear cut goal to strive for in the future." Donovan Reports, 10 March 1942, FDRL.

17. On the 14th, Hopkins wrote the President urging him to pursue "Arnold's plan in England: There is nothing to lose, the bridgehead does not need to be established unless air superiority is complete. I doubt if any single thing is as important as getting some sort of a front this summer against Germany. This will have to be worked out very carefully between you and Marshall, in the first instance, and you and Churchill in the second. I don't think there is any time to be lost because if we are to do it plans need to be made at once." Sherwood, *Roosevelt and Hopkins*, pp. 518–519.

18. There is no first hand record of this meeting. See Anthony Eden, *The Memoirs of Anthony Eden: The Reckoning*, p. 376.

19. The letter, dated 18 March, is reprinted in Churchill, *Hinge of Fate*, p. 200. The circumstances of its dispatch including the date are

derived from Roosevelt's correspondence with Harriman in PSF "Great Britain: Churchill" [closed], FDRL.

20. Telegram, Moscow to State, 26 March 1942, in *Foreign Relations, 1942*, 3:536.

21. He did not receive it until 1 April. Churchill, *Hinge of Fate*, p. 201.

22. Llewellyn Woodward, *British Foreign Policy in The Second World War*, p. 193; and Eden, *Reckoning*, p. 376.

23. Telegram, Eden to Halifax, which the Ambassador read to Welles. Memo of conversation, by Welles, 30 March 1942, in *Foreign Relations, 1942*, 3:536–538. Welles indicates his intention of informing the President of Eden's remarks immediately.

24. Stimson Diary (MS.), 8 March 1942.

25. Samuel Eliot Morison seems to suggest this in his *History of United States Naval Operations in World War II*, vol. 4, *Coral Sea, Midway and Submarine Actions*, p. 248.

26. Matloff and Snell, *Strategic Planning*, p. 161.

27. On 20 March Eisenhower reminded Marshall that a firm agreement on "the theater in which the first principal combat of the war must be fought" still had to be reached with King. "Memo of Subjects Suitable to Take up with Admiral King," Chandler, *Eisenhower Papers*, 1:197–198.

28. Matloff and Snell, *Strategic Planning*, p. 179.

29. Stimson Diary (MS.), 20 March 1942.

30. Ibid., 24 March 1942.

31. Memo, Eisenhower for CofS, "Critical Points in Development of Coordinated Viewpoint as to Major Tasks of the War," 25 March 1942, in Chandler, *Eisenhower Papers*, 1:205–207.

32. Stimson Diary (MS.), 25 March 1942.

33. Henry L. Stimson and McGeorge Bundy, *On Active Service in Peace and War*, pp. 417–418.

34. Matloff and Snell, *Strategic Planning*, p. 211.

35. The plan had already undergone several revisions.

36. Text of one of the several versions drafted is printed in full in Gwyer and Butler, *Grand Strategy*, 3:674–681. General Arnold has provided a worthwhile summary of the 1942 portion of the proposal:

"The proposition presented to the President provides for air units leaving as soon as possible and starting operations against the northwest coast of France, building to a maximum by April 1943; [at the same time ground units would be dispatched] so as to have a force which, tied in with the British and Canadians, would enable us to take advantage of any breaks which might come our way. We would be looking primarily for an opportunity when Germany had committed herself to such an extent in the . . . East that she had no reserves in the West; or that she was getting the worst of it in the East, or that a sacrifice force might be sent over there just to distract her from the East."

Conference at White House, 1 April 1943, in Notes on Conferences, box 180, Arnold Papers, L.C.

37. General Arnold, "Memo for Record," White House Meeting 1 April 1942, in Notes on Conferences, box 180, Arnold Papers, L.C. Discussed in Henry H. Arnold, *Global Mission*, pp. 304–305.

38. Five years later, in totally different circumstances, Marshall was faced with a similar problem and responded in much the same way. In April 1947 Marshall, now Secretary of State, recognizing the need for immediate American action to prevent the economic collapse of Europe, called in George F. Kennan to devise the American response. Kennan described Marshall's reasoning as follows: "Something would have to be done. If he did not take the initiative, others would. Others, particularly people in Congress would start coming up with ideas of their own about what ought to be done for Europe. He would then be forced on to the defensive. He was determined to avoid this if he possibly could." So with the injunction to "avoid trivia" Marshall set Kennan to the task of drawing up what was to become the Marshall Plan. George F. Kennan, *Memoirs, 1929–1950*, pp. 325–326. In interviews in 1956 Marshall noted his preoccupation in the spring of 1942 with countering the influence of Churchill and the Navy on the President. Quoted in Forrest C. Pogue. *George C. Marshall*, vol. 2, *Ordeal and Hope, 1939–1942*, pp. 329–330.

39. The President indicated that he would like to send a cable to the Soviet leader asking that "Molotov and one of their best generals" come to the United States to discuss the Army plan. At first Roosevelt suggested that this might be done before securing Churchill's approval of the scheme, and without informing the Prime Minister. However, after "considerable discussion," it was decided to wait until after Churchill had accepted the proposal. Arnold, Memo, White House Meeting 1 April 1942, in box 180, Arnold Papers, L.C.

Chapter Six

1. Messages dated 2 and 3 April printed in Winston S. Churchill, *The Second World War*, vol. 4, *The Hinge of Fate*, pp. 313–314. Interestingly, the day before the Marshall mission left for England, the Combined Planners after lengthy deliberation concluded that an invasion of the Continent in 1942 would not be possible. Combined Planners Report, 3 April 1942, summarized in Maurice Matloff and Edwin M. Snell, *Strategic Planning for Coalition Warfare, 1941–1942*, p. 180.

2. J. M. A. Gwyer and J. R. M. Butler, *Grand Strategy*, 3:566–572.

3. Meeting of 9 April.

4. Account based on Hopkins' own record reproduced in Robert E. Sherwood, *Roosevelt and Hopkins*, pp. 522–542.

5. Minutes of the 112th meeting (Minute 5) of the Chiefs of Staff (9 April 1942), "Meeting with General Marshall," in CCS 381 (3-23-42), part 3, Records of the Combined Chiefs of Staff.

6. Combined Planning Staff Estimate 26/1 (3 April 1942), CCS 381 (3-23-42), part 2, CCS records. Findings summarized in Matloff and Snell, *Strategic Planning*, p. 180.

7. Arthur Bryant, *The Turn of the Tide*, pp. 288–289. Brooke may have reached this conclusion on the basis of Marshall's remarks pointing up the dangers emanating from the Pacific-first agitation.

8. Telegram, Marshall to McNarney, 14 April 1942, OPD, exec. 1, item 5, W.W. II Records.

9. For the views of the British Chiefs and Churchill on the extent of their commitment see: Bryant, *Turn of the Tide*, p. 287; Gwyer and Butler, *Grand Strategy*, 3:576–579; Churchill, *Hinge of Fate*, p. 322; Lord

Moran (Sir Charles Wilson), *Churchill: The Struggle for Survival, 1940–1965, Taken from the Diaries of Lord Moran,* p. 38.

10. Telegram, Marshall to Milid, 13 April 1942, OPD, exec. 1, item 5, W.W. II Records. Col. A.C. Wedemeyer, Marshall's planning assistant on the mission, shared these doubts. See Albert C. Wedemeyer, *Wedemeyer Reports!,* pp. 113, 119.

11. Eisenhower diary entry for 20 April 1942 in Alfred D. Chandler, Jr. (ed.), *The Papers of Dwight David Eisenhower,* vol. 1, *The War Years,* p. 260.

12. Anthony Eden, *The Memoirs of Anthony Eden: The Reckoning,* p. 376.

13. Joseph Stalin, *Stalin's Correspondence with Churchill, Roosevelt and Truman, 1941–1945,* pp. 22–23.

14. Ibid., p. 23.

15. Ibid., p. 44.

16. On the following day the State Department received from Ambassador Standley in Moscow the latest in a number of reports indicating that a German peace offer to the Russians was imminent. Moscow to State, 5 May 1942, 740.00119EW39/1056, State Dept. records, N.A.

17. Winant to President, 4 May 1942, in *Foreign Relations, 1942,* 3:552–553.

18. *Time,* 20 April 1942, p. 22.

19. Made while visiting American troops in Northern Ireland, ibid., "U.S. Offensive," 27 April 1942, p. 22.

20. In a speech delivered in New York, *New York Times* editorial, 24 April 1942, p. 16:1.

21. "Weekly Media Report no. 12" (25 April 1942), OGR records, N.A.

22. Comments on the new and growing optimism may be found in: Sherwood, *Roosevelt and Hopkins,* p. 542; *New York Times,* 10 May 1942, p. 3:1; ibid, 24 May 1942, sec. 4, p. 8:1 (edit.) "Are We Too Hopeful?"; Arthur Krock, "Wave of War Optimism Disturbs Many Leaders," ibid., p. 3:1; "Weekly Media Report no. 19" (13 June 1942), OGR records,

N.A.; *Time,* "The Power and the Grief," 15 June 1942, p. 9; "Weekly Media Report no. 26" (1 August 1942), OGR records, N.A. OFF's information policy may have contributed to the growing enthusiasm. Since the information agency was not privy to strategic planning, Mac-Leish and his subordinates were guided largely by their own hopes concerning the course of the war, unadulterated by "inside" information as to military realities.

23. "Weekly Media Report no. 12" (25 April 1942). A meeting of the Committee on War Information took up the problem on the 27th—with no result. Agenda of Meeting of CWI, 27 April 1942, box 13. Both in OGR records, N.A. The Psychological Warfare Committee of the Joint Chiefs of Staff had already issued a similar warning: "Popular enthusiasm for an offensive [might] . . . become embarrassing to the actual conduct of the war." See Report, "Growing Popular Demand for Offensive," JPWC 7 (21 March 1942), in CCS 385 (3-21-42), CCS records, N.A.

24. *New York Times,* 21 April 1942, p. 13:2.

25. Memo, CofS for President, "Transport Airplanes for Russia," 27 April 1942, WDCSA 400.3295 "Russia," in W.W. II Records, N.A. See Matloff and Snell, *Strategic Planning,* pp. 206–209.

26. *New York Times,* 21 March 1942, "MacArthur Ordered to Take Offensive," p. 1:8.

27. It is doubtful that MacArthur's interpretation of Roosevelt's instructions was shared by the President or America's military chiefs. It is certain, however, that the Australian Government welcomed MacArthur as an ally in its efforts to obtain greater support for efforts to remove the Japanese menace from its doorstep.

28. *Time,* 23 March 1942, p. 17.

29. Ibid., 30 March 1942, pp. 17–18.

30. "Weekly Media Report no. 8" (27 March 1942), OGR records, N.A.

31. *Time,* "Battle of Australia—doubt," 20 April 1942, p. 25.

32. Matloff and Snell, *Strategic Planning,* pp. 212–213.

33. Ibid., p. 217.

34. CofS for President, 3 May 1942, OPD, exec. 10, item 53, W.W. II Records.

35. Memo, King for CofS, 4 May 1942, in PSF "Geo. C. Marshall" (Safe), FDRL. See Matloff and Snell, *Strategic Planning*, p. 212.

36. On April 18, the Navy Chief in giving Admiral Ghormley command of Naval forces in the South Pacific indicated "in time, possibly this fall, we hope to start an offensive from the South Pacific." Samuel Eliot Morison, *History of United States Naval Operations in World War II*, vol. 4, *Coral Sea, Midway and Submarine Actions*, p. 251.

37. Eisenhower diary entry for 5 May 1942, in Chandler, *Eisenhower Papers*, 1:282.

38. Memo, CofS for President, 6 May 1942, "The Pacific Theater versus 'Bolero'," OPD 381 (General), case 62, W.W. II Records. See Matloff and Snell, *Strategic Planning*, pp. 218–219.

39. See Robert W. Coakley, "The Persian Corridor as a Route for Aid to the USSR," in *Command Decisions*, ed. by Kent Roberts Greenfield, pp. 225–253.

40. Churchill, *Hinge of Fate*, pp. 257–260.

41. A previous draft of this message, drawn up by Hopkins on the 25th, while including references to the difficulties experienced by the convoys, made no mention of the Molotov trip. It is not unlikely that the President suggested the inclusion of this reference, and that he attached some significance to coupling this reminder with the hint of bad news which the message primarily intended to convey. The draft and final version (4 May 1942) are in Safe file "Russia," FDRL.

42. Notes written by General Marshall attached to President's memo to Marshall of 6 May 1942, in PSF "Gen. G. C. Marshall, 1942" [closed], FDRL.

43. It should be noted that *both* alternatives also indicated that aid to Russia would have to be confined to the Persian Corridor route: "Keep up aid to Russia, but via Basra." This confirms that Roosevelt's acceptance of a curtailment of shipments to Russia was not actually based on the need to provide munitions and shipping for SLEDGEHAMMER, as he intended to tell Molotov. According to the President's outline, shipments over the hazardous northern route would be cut back in either event, ie., whether SLEDGEHAMMER was on or not.

44. Matloff and Snell, *Strategic Planning,* p. 219.

45. Memo, FDR. for SW, CofS, etc., 6 May 1942, in PSF "Gen. Geo. C. Marshall, 1942" [Closed], FDRL.

46. See King's comments at 14th meeting of the JCS (11 May 1942), in CCS 334 JCS (4–20–42), CCS records.

47. "Minutes of Conf. at White House on Landing Craft for BOLERO, . . . 5 May 42," in CCS 381 (3–23–42) part 3, CCS records; and Memo, Somervell and Vice Admiral F. J. Horne for President, "Landing Craft for BOLERO Operations," 14 May 1942, PSF "War Department" (Safe), FDRL.

48. Llewellyn Woodward, *British Foreign Policy in the Second World War,* pp. 193–194.

49. Ibid., pp. 194–195; and Eden, *Reckoning,* p. 380.

50. Churchill, *Hinge of Fate,* p. 333.

51. See Eden's account to the War Cabinet, 25 May 1942, in Minutes of the British War Cabinet, Confidential Annex to 66th Meeting.

52. Letter, Winant to FDR, 3 June 1942, in PSF "Winant" [closed], FDRL.

53. Memo, "Molotov Conversations, May 29, 7:40 PM" [by S. Cross, who acted as interpreter], box 306, folder "Molotov Visit," Hopkins Papers, FDRL.

54. Notes on meeting of 30 May printed in Sherwood, *Roosevelt and Hopkins,* pp. 561–568.

55. Ibid., pp. 574–575.

56. The text of the conversation of 1 June is printed in ibid., pp. 571–575.

57. Ibid., p. 577.

58. Roosevelt originally intended to specify August as the month for beginning operations but was dissuaded from doing so by Marshall and Hopkins.

59. FDR to Churchill, 31 May 1942, box 320, folder 7, Hopkins Papers, FDRL.

Chapter Seven

1. See "Weekly Media Report no. 22" (3 July 1942) and no. 24 (25 July 1942), OWI records, N.A. Also, "Survey of Intelligence Materials no. 30" (1 July 1942) in PSF "OWI," FDRL.

2. For a firsthand account of the Russian reaction see Alexander Werth, *Russia at War 1941–1945,* pp. 381–386.

3. The Office of War Information (OWI) was established on 13 June 1942 to direct and coordinate all government information programs at home and abroad. Under the new arrangement both Lowell Mellett's Office of Government Reports, which had conducted and reportedon extensive samplings of news media, and Archibald MacLeish's Office of Facts and Figures, which had conducted and analyzed public opinion surveys, were incorporated into the new OWI headed by radio commentator Elmer Davis. The Bureau of Intelligence originally in OFF continued under OWI, providing reports on American public opinion to interested government agencies and the White House, based on analyses of public opinion polls and media surveys.

4. "Intelligence Report no. 34" (29 July 1942), in PSF "OWI," FDRL. See also Report, G.S. Pettee to O.E. Benson, 2 October 1942, Sources Division Reports, box 254, OWI records, N.A.

5. Telegram dated 22 June 1942 in *Foreign Relations, 1942,* 3: 598. See also William H. Standley and A.A. Ageton, *Admiral Ambassador to Russia,* pp. 203–205. Standley reported that his prediction concerning the reaction of the Russian people was subsequently borne out. Ibid., p. 204.

6. The Chiefs, however, did agree that a large-scale raid (two to four divisions) which would remain on the Continent from one to four weeks, *might* be substituted for the sacrifice operation with the object of provoking air battles which hopefully would draw German air forces from the Russian front. J. M. A. Gwyer and J. R. M. Butler, *Grand Strategy,* 3:619.

7. On 11 June the War Cabinet accepted this decision. Ibid., p. 597.

8. Vice-Admiral Lord Louis Mountbatten, Chief of Combined Operations Headquarters (the office charged with advising the services on planning, preparation, and launching amphibious operations). Mount-

batten had stayed at the White House briefly in October 1941. General Eisenhower, who had gone to England on the 23rd with Arnold to see what was delaying planning for BOLERO, brought with him an invitation from Marshall for Mountbatten to come to the United States for a visit. Eisenhower diary entry for 21 May 1942, and "Notes to Take to Great Britain," by Eisenhower, 22 May 1942; both in Alfred D. Chandler, Jr. (ed.), *The Papers of Dwight David Eisenhower*, vol. 1, *The War Years*, pp. 315, 316–317.

9. Winston S. Churchill, *The Second World War*, vol. 4, *The Hinge of Fate*, p. 340.

10. Gwyer and Butler, *Grand Strategy*, 3:621.

11. Terence Robertson, *Dieppe: The Shame and the Glory*, pp. 1–72, 385–418.

12. Arthur Bryant, *The Turn of the Tide*, p. 301.

13. Churchill, *Hinge of Fate*, p. 246. See also Gwyer and Butler, *Grand Strategy*, 3:598–599, 617.

14. *Aide-memoire* handed to Molotov 10 June 1942. Attached to Confidential Annex of the 73rd Meeting (11 June 1942), Minutes of the British War Cabinet.

15. Ibid., Confidential Annex to 73rd Meeting.

16. Churchill had never made any such commitment, although in view of the confused and misleading discussions concerning SLEDGE-HAMMER it is easy to understand how the President thought that he had.

17. Mountbatten's summary of the conversation is reproduced in part in Robert E. Sherwood, *Roosevelt and Hopkins*, pp. 582–583. Mountbatten's misgivings concerning SLEDGEHAMMER came on the heels of reports that all was not well with plans and preparations for the cross-Channel attack. On June 3rd, for example, Ambassador Winant had written Roosevelt that "there has been a dropping off of sustained interest by ranking people, so far as 1942 is concerned. . . . I believe a great deal more could be done than is now being done, but only with your personal intervention and vigorous support. . . . You undoubtedly know that [RAF Chief Sir Charles] Portal is the only Chief of Staff officer whom we can count on for the present to support an early '42 attack." Winant to FDR, 3 June 1942, in PSF "Winant"

[closed], FDRL. On the 6th Harry Hopkins wrote Churchill of his anxiety over the indefiniteness of Allied plans for helping Russia, noting also that he was "discouraged about our getting into the war in a manner that I think our military strength deserves." Sherwood, *Roosevelt and Hopkins*, pp. 580–581.

18. The Midway victory also produced a reemergence of the "beat Japan first" theme and a temporary decline in interest in the "Second Front" in the nation's news media. "Weekly Media Report no. 19" (12 June 1942), OWI records, N.A.

19. Currently available information concerning the North African situation did not bear this out. A June 5th message from the Counselor of the American Embassy in Vichy noted that General Weygand believed that the adminstrative and military structure he had built in North Africa had deteriorated since his retirement and that the attitude of the French in Africa was such that an American landing could not expect French assistance and might even be opposed. Weygand suggested that a landing in France would be preferable. Message, Tuck to State, 5 June 1942, sent by General Marshall to Harry Hopkins 13 June 1942, quoted in Sherwood, *Roosevelt and Hopkins*, p. 550. A letter from the American Consul General in Casablanca to the State Department, 15 May 1942, generally supported the pessimistic outlook for American operations in North Africa, noting that the French Navy would follow any Government orders to resist an American invasion force. Russell to State, 740.0011EW39/21951, received by State June 3rd, forwarded to War Department June 10th, State Dept. records, N.A.

20. At least one and probably several of these messages had reached the President by the 17th. Telegrams, Kirk to State, 28 May 1942, 740.0011EW39/21810 (forwarded to the President by Welles, 29 May 1942); 16 June 1942, 740.0011EW39/22268; 17 June 1942, 740.0011EW39/2310, State Dept. records, N.A. A letter written by the President on the 17th mirrored the anxiety over the deterioration of British fortunes in the desert. Writing to Ambassador John Winant, he declared that "the situation in Libya is by no means rosy" and observed that he "would be satisfied with a draw battle at this time." Letter, FDR to Winant, 17 June 1942, PSF "Winant" [closed], FDRL.

21. "King wobbled around in a way that made me rather sick with him. He is firm and brave outside the White House but as soon as he gets in the presence of the President he crumbles up." Stimson's diary

quoted in Elting E. Morison, *Turmoil and Tradition,* note on p. 584.

22. Account of meeting based on notes taken by General Henry H. Arnold, box 180, Arnold Papers, L.C. See also Henry L. Stimson and McGeorge Bundy, *On Active Service in Peace and War,* p. 419.

23. Letter printed in full in Stimson and Bundy, *On Active Service,* pp. 420–423.

24. Memo, Marshall and King to FDR, Sub: "Gymnast Operations," no date [19 June 1942], PSF "Geo. C. Marshall" (Safe), box 6, FDRL. Copy of this document dated the 19th found in records of the Office of the CofS, WDCSA 381 "GYMNAST," W.W. II Records. It appears that this joint memorandum is based on the memo drafted for Marshall by OPD on the 16th and used by him at the meeting of the 17th.

25. Minutes of meeting of 19th in *Foreign Relations of the United States, The Conferences at Washington 1941–1942,* pp. 422–428.

26. Ibid., pp. 429–431.

27. Churchill, *Hinge of Fate,* pp. 381–382.

28. Sherwood, *Roosevelt and Hopkins,* pp. 586–588.

29. This quotation, which appeared in an early draft, was deleted from the final version of this memo. Memo, T. Handy (OPD), to CofS, 20 June 1942, Sub: "Offensive Action Prior to Sept. 15, 1942 to Compel the Germans to Withdraw Forces from the Russian Front," OPD, exec. 1, item 10a, tab 5; and draft memo, CofS to President, N.D., Sub: "Offensive Action Prior . . . [etc.]," OPD, exec. 10, item 32, W. W. I. Records, See also Albert C. Wedemeyer, *Wedemeyer Reports!,* pp. 155–156.

30. Stimson attributed this opposition and indeed the whole mission to Washington to Roosevelt's unfortunate reference to the 1942 cross-Channel attack as a "sacrifice" landing during Mountbatten's visit at the beginning of June.

31. Hastings Ismay, *The Memoirs of General Lord Ismay,* pp. 254–255.

32. The original version of the Anglo-American agreement drafted by General Ismay referred to GYMNAST as the "best alternative in 1942" provided that political conditions were favorable. Marshall, however, succeeded in eliminating the preferential status for GYMNAST in the

final agreement. Maurice Matloff and Edwin M. Snell, *Strategic Planning for Coalition Warfare 1941–1942*, p. 244. The account of the meeting of the 21st is based on: Stimson and Bundy, *On Active Service*, pp. 423–424; Bryant, *Turn of the Tide*, pp. 328–329; Matloff and Snell, *Strategic Planning*, pp. 249–250; Churchill, *Hinge of Fate*, pp. 383–384.

33. Stimson Diary (MS.), 22 June 1942.

34. Draft Memo, CofS to President, no date [22 June 1942], no sub., records of the CofS, exec. 10, item 53, W.W. II Records.

35. Memo, CofS for President, 23 June 1942, in *Foreign Relations, Conferences*, pp. 473–475.

36. Stimson Diary (MS.).

37. Marshall's remarks to a group of senior War Department officials, 22 June 1942, in Notes on War Council, WDCSA, SW Conferences, vol. 2, W.W. II Records. It is likely that many members of the War Department felt that the British were themselves largely responsible for their current difficulties in the Middle East. Stimson found that a perusal of Feller's dispatches revealed "how ineptly the British have walked into this last defeat," and made it clear that there was no use trying to redeem the disaster flowing from inherent British shortcomings. Stimson Diary (MS.), 20 June 1942.

38. War Council Notes, 29 June 1942, SW Conferences, vol. 2, W.W. II Records.

39. This fact had been acknowledged by General Marshall at a CCS meeting on 2 July 1942. Minutes of the 30th meeting (2 July 1942), CCS 334 (5–26–42), CCS records, N.A.

40. Minutes of the British War Cabinet, Confidential Annexes to 85th Meeting (3 July 1942), Minute 4; and 87th Meeting (7 July 1942), including Minute by the Prime Minister dated 5 July 1942, and Chiefs of Staff reply thereto dated 7 July 1942 attached as appendices. See also Gwyer and Butler, *Grand Strategy*, 3:630.

41. Churchill, *Hinge of Fate*, p. 424.

42. Minutes of the 24th meeting of the JCS (10 July 1942) in CCS 334 JCS (6–23–42), CCS records, N.A.

43. Stimson Diary (MS.), 10 July 1942.

44. Memo quoted in Matloff and Snell, *Strategic Planning*, pp. 268–269.

45. Ibid., p. 269.

46. There is no indication whether this proposed message was sent to the White House. Even if it was, it was certainly never used by the President. Memorandum in OPD, exec. 1, item 4, no date [11 July 1942], sub: BOLERO (a similar version marked "last draft 7/14/42 may be found in exec. 5, item 9, tab 9/16.) W.W. II Records. However, the substance of the threat was conveyed to Churchill by Dill on the 8th, Stimson Diary (MS.), 12 July 1942.

47. Forrest C. Pogue, *George C. Marshall*, vol. 2, *Ordeal and Hope, 1939–1942*, pp. 431–432. Stimson, after the war at least, agreed that both he and Marshall supported the alternative as a bluff. This interpretation appears in his account of his public service, published in 1947. Stimson and Bundy, *Active Service*, p. 425.

48. This course of action, it will be recalled, had been suggested to Marshall by General Eisenhower when the BOLERO scheme was first drawn up.

49. Ernest J. King and Walter M. Whitehill, *Fleet Admiral King*, pp. 386–388; Samuel Eliot Morison, *History of United States Naval Operations in World War II*, vol. 4, *Coral Sea, Midway and Submarine Actions*, pp. 259–263. Minutes of the 24th meeting of the JCS (10 July 1942), CCS 334 JCS (6–23–42), CCS records.

50. Stimson Diary (MS.), 12 July 1942.

51. Matloff and Snell, *Strategic Planning*, p. 270.

52. Both Admiral King and General Arnold signed the note which was sent off to the President at Hyde Park on the 12th. Ibid., pp. 270–271.

53. Ibid., p. 272.

54. Wedemeyer, *Reports*, p. 160. Arnold was so distressed by the renewed British challenge to the BOLERO concept, and the fact that at this late date the Allies were still "discussing which continent should be given our major attention," that he suggested to Hopkins the need for a drastic reorganization of the Allied command structure: "The United Nations dispersion, indecision and vacillation are inevitable

results of multiple military command with staff action and advice by committees in various guises. The remedy is as simple as it is urgent. The disunited, dispersed and to date, impotent forces of the democracies can defeat the efficient Axis military machine only if an American is appointed Supreme Commander of the Armed Forces of the United Nations." Memo, Arnold for Hopkins, 15 July 1942, in box 113, Arnold Papers, L.C.

55. These remarks by the President are recorded in a memo, CofS to Admiral King, 15 July 1942, WDCSA 381, W.W. II Records. Marshall indicates that King and he were to discuss the President's suggestion. Here again there is no suggestion that Marshall considered the Pacific alternative a bluff. Instead he attempts to defend the suggestion against the charge that it amounted to abandonment of the British by indicating that the United States would still maintain the ground forces that had been sent to Northern Ireland (MAGNET) and a considerable air contingent in the British Isles.

56. Stimson Diary (MS.), 15 July 1942, quoted in part in Stimson and Bundy, *Active Service*, p. 425; Hopkins' notes of conversation with Roosevelt on the evening of the 15th printed in Sherwood, *Roosevelt and Hopkins*, pp. 602–603.

57. The final version of the instructions is reprinted in Sherwood, *Roosevelt and Hopkins*, pp. 603–605. The final draft of these instructions with hand-written emendations by Roosevelt, as well as the original Hopkins version of the instructions dated 15 July, are found in folder labeled "Bk IV, HLH Returns to London," box 304, Hopkins Papers, FDRL.

58. Hopkins' original version makes no mention of these catastrophic possibilities. It simply lists operations in North Africa and the Middle East as two prime alternatives to SLEDGEHAMMER.

59. Necessary preliminaries to the campaign were accomplished at the end of May with the rout of the Russians at Kharkov and the elimination of Soviet forces in the Kerch peninsula. This latter action cleared the way for a full-scale operation to eliminate the Russian bastion at Sevastapol, under seige since the preceding October. The effort which began the first week in June ended on 4 July with the capture of the fortress. Meanwhile, at the end of June the Germans had begun their drive on the Volga (which was to climax with the battle for Stalingrad) as a first step toward a movement south into the Caucasus.

Based on Walter Gorlitz, "The Battle for Stalingrad 1942–3," in *Decisive Battles of World War II: The German View*, ed. by H.A. Jacobsen and J. Rohwer, pp. 219–253; and Werth, *Russia at War*, pp. 387–409.

60. A personal memorandum written by Roosevelt for South African Prime Minister Jan C. Smuts, 3 August 1942, also indicates the primacy of the Middle East in Roosevelt's thinking at this time. Memo in PSF "Union of South Africa," FDRL.

61. The Prime Minister was for the second time during the war experiencing serious political difficulties as a result of recent defeats. See Lord Moran (Sir Charles Wilson), *Churchill: The Struggle for Survival, 1940–1965, Taken from the Diaries of Lord Moran*, p. 46; Sherwood, *Roosevelt and Hopkins*, pp. 601–602; Harold Nicholson, *Diaries and Letters*, vol. 2, *The War Years 1939–1945*, pp. 235–236.

62. This was especially important since the Arctic convoy scheduled for the end of July had to be cancelled. It will be recalled that the convoys which began in September 1941 had from the end of February 1942 on suffered increasing losses. This led to talk by the British of suspending the operation, which in turn influenced Roosevelt's handling of discussions with Molotov at the end of May. Nevertheless, a convoy (P.Q. 16) was dispatched on 21 May with the resultant loss of nearly a quarter of its cargo. British shipping was diverted to the urgent resupply of Malta during June, but at the end of the month P.Q. 17 set out from Iceland. Only eleven of the original 39 ships in the convoy reached their destination on July 10th. As a result, the convoys were suspended with the President's concurrence. Chuchill informed the Russians of the suspension on the 17th. See Gwyer and Butler, *Grand Strategy*, 3:506, 588–589.

Chapter Eight

1. Draft telegram, CofS to Eisenhower, 16 July 1942, WDCSA, Codes—SLEDGEHAMMER, W.W. II Records.

2. The limited construction of the President's purposes indicated in this message was earlier apparent in a draft set of instructions which the General prepared for Roosevelt on the 15th. This document would have directed the mission to investigate the possibility of executing SLEDGEHAMMER. If the operation proved feasible, even though it involved maximum effort and the acceptance of grave risks, the mission was to urge that efforts toward its execution be vigorously pursued. On

the other hand, should SLEDGEHAMMER prove impossible, that was to be reported to the President, who, according to Marshall, would then feel that the Allies should "continue our present plans and preparations for ROUNDUP, while carrying out *planned* activities and *present* commitments in other areas," i.e., in the Pacific. [Emphasis in original.] Almost incredibly, in view of the President's actual views, this document omits any mention of alternatives to SLEDGEHAMMER in 1942; totally ignores GYMNAST; and only mentions a front in the Middle East as a possible course of action in case of Russian collapse. Document reproduced in full in appendix to Maurice Matloff and Edwin M. Snell, *Strategic Planning for Coalition Warfare 1941–1942*, pp. 384–385.

3. From the 16 July 1942 entry in the diary of Capt. Harry C. Butcher, Naval Aide to General Eisenhower, printed in Harry C. Butcher, *My Three Years With Eisenhower*, p. 23.

4. "Conclusions as to Practicability of SLEDGEHAMMER," prepared by Eisenhower, et. al., for General Marshall, 17 July 1942, in Alfred D. Chandler, Jr. (ed.), *The Papers of Dwight David Eisenhower*, vol. 1, *The War Years*, pp. 388–391. Quoted in part in Gordon A. Harrison, *Cross-Channel Attack*, p. 29. Chapter one of Harrison's book provides a useful summary of BOLERO planning for 1942.

5. British studies based on an analysis of Channel weather over the past ten years had recently concluded that the weather broke between the second and third weeks of September and the second week in October. During October there were usually about two periods of four consecutive days suitable for landing operations, as compared to double that number in September. Also, westerly gales were three times more likely to occur in October as in September. Report by the Chief of the Naval Staff in Minutes of the British War Cabinet, Confidential Annex to 94th Meeting (22 July 1942).

6. Memo, Eisenhower for Marshall and King, 19 July 1942, in Chandler, *Eisenhower Papers*, 1:393–395.

7. See Butcher Diary (MS.), 19 July 1942, Eisenhower project; and Robert E. Sherwood, *Roosevelt and Hopkins*, p. 608.

8. Arthur Bryant, *The Turn of the Tide*, p. 341.

9. J. M. A. Gwyer and J. R. M. Butler, *Grand Strategy*, 3:633.

10. Bryant, *Turn of the Tide*, p. 342.

11. "Notes for Commander Butcher," 20 July 1942, Chandler, *Eisenhower Papers*, 1:400–401. Paraphrased in Butcher, *My Three Years*, pp. 25–26. In his book Butcher uses the word "favorable" in place of the original "desirable." Bryant, *Turn of the Tide*, p. 342.

12. Bryant, *Turn of the Tide*, p. 342; Butcher, *My Three Years*, p. 27–28.

13. Memo, Eisenhower for CofS, 21 July 1942, in Chandler, *Eisenhower Papers*, 1:402–405.

14. Bryant, *Turn of the Tide*, (diary entry for 21st), pp. 342–343.

15. Memo to Butcher, 22 July 1942, in Chandler, *Eisenhower Papers*, 1:405–406.

16. Minutes of the British War Cabinet, Confidential Annex to 94th Meeting (22 July 1942). See also Gwyer and Butler, *Grand Strategy*, 3:634; and Bryant, *Turn of the Tide* (diary entry for 22nd), p. 343. Marshall's views were shared by General Eisenhower who had informed Marshall that his only "real reason for favoring it [SLEDGEHAMMER] was the fear of becoming so deeply involved elsewhere that the major cross-Channel attack would be indefinitely postponed, possibly even cancelled." Dwight D. Eisenhower, *Crusade in Europe*, p. 70.

17. Following the capture of Tobruk, Rommel, eschewing a pause in operations, pressed the British to the full extent of his Army's diminished capacity. German attempts during the first five days of July to break through British fortified positions at El Alamein, however, were repulsed. Repeated British efforts at counterattack (10 through 26 July) ended indecisively. Now exhausted, both sides remained relatively inactive preparing for a final effort. At the beginning of September the British began an offensive which, together with TORCH (Anglo-American landings in French Africa 8 November) was to clear the enemy from Africa. I.S.O. Playfair, *The Mediterranean and Middle East*, 3:331–36off.

18. Message, FDR to Hopkins, Marshall and King, [23 July 1942], in folder "book IV, HLH Returns to London," box 304, Hopkins Papers, FDRL. The message from Berne, which is not attached to the above, was located in State Department records, Berne to State, 21 July 1942, 740.0011EW39/22994, N.A.

19. Stimson Diary (MS.), entry for 23 July 1942. This entry includes a copy of Stimson's letter to the President.

20. Butcher, *My Three Years* (entry for July 23), p. 29.

21. Should the Russians appear at that time able to survive the current German offensive, he recommended that operations in 1942 be confined to the reinforcement of the Middle East, which he felt would not seriously hurt the preparations for the cross-Channel attack. On the other hand, should it appear that the Soviets were not going to be actively fighting in 1943, then ROUNDUP was definitely out, and GYMNAST and a generally defensive policy in the West became the best course of action. Memo, Eisenhower to CofS, 23 July 1942, "Survey of Strategic Situation," in Chandler, *Eisenhower Papers*, 1:407–413.

22. Robert E. Sherwood, *Roosevelt and Hopkins*, p. 611.

23. FDR to Hopkins, Marshall, and King, 24 July 1942, folder, "Book IV, HLH Returns to London," in box 304, Hopkins Papers, FDRL.

24. Minutes of the 32nd Meeting of the CCS (24 July 1942), and Memorandum from U.S. Chiefs of Staff to British Chiefs of Staff (24 July 1942) in CCS 334 (5–26–42) and CCS 381 (3–23–42), part 3, sec. 2. Records of the Combined Chiefs. See also Telegram, Marshall and King to President (tel. no. 625), 24 July 1942, exec. 5, item 2a, tab 1, W.W. II Records. Discussed in Matloff and Snell, *Strategic Planning*, pp. 280–281.

25. Minutes of the British War Cabinet, Confidential Annex to 95th Meeting (24 July 1942), Minute 3.

26. Hopkins to FDR, 25 July 1942, "folder VII footnotes," box 320, Hopkins Papers, FDRL.

27. Stimson also revived the idea of a Pacific alternative. Stimson Diary (MS.), 25 July 1942; and Memo, Sec. War for President, 25 July 1942, sub: "My Views as to the Proposals in Message 625," Office of the Secretary of War, "White House File," W.W. II Records.

28. "Memo to go with Memorandum from Sec. of War, dated July 25, 1942, in relation to proposals in message no. 625 from Marshall and King in London," 29 July 1942, signed F.D.R. in folder "VII footnotes," box 321, Hopkins Papers, FDRL. Stimson's continued support of SLEDGEHAMMER indicates that he was not yet aware that Marshall had abandoned this ploy in favor of a strategy of delay.

29. As paraphrased by Sherwood, *Roosevelt and Hopkins*, pp. 611–612.

30. Stimson Diary (MS.), 27 July 1942. Stimson (rightly) felt that Marshall had deliberately left open the possibility that SLEDGEHAMMER would be revived: "I think he feels that the British leaders' hands may be forced by the pressure of public opinion. . . . If it should ever get out that the Americans had urged going forward with SLEDGEHAMMER, and that a second front this autumn was stopped solely by the British, there would be a tremendous outcry in Great Britain and, needless to say, in Russia." Stimson also thought the President was hoping for the same thing. Stimson Diary (MS.), 28 July 1942.

31. The appointment was in response to pressures being exerted on the President from two sources. The first from General Marshall was for closer contact between the White House and the Joint Chiefs, both so that the military deliberations could be readily made known to the President, and more importantly, so that the Chiefs would be current on Presidential thought and actions on military issues. The second pressure came from the press, which had rather consistently, but especially in bad times, insisted that a military man be appointed Commander-in-Chief of all the armed services. Leahy was not to fill this function at all, however he may have given the appearance of doing so, and from the President's point of view that was the same thing.

32. Minutes of the 34th Meeting of the Combined Chiefs of Staff (30 July 1942), CCS 334 (5–26–42), in CCS records. See also Matloff and Snell, *Strategic Planning*, pp. 282–283.

33. Memorandum on the White House meeting prepared by General Smith for the Joint Chiefs, quoted in Matloff and Snell, *Strategic Planning*, p. 283.

34. The date of the attack was left for Eisenhower to determine. In mid-September he settled on November 8th. The details of the preliminaries to the invasion may be found in George F. Howe, *Northwest Africa: Seizing the Initiative in the West*, chaps. 1–3.

Index

235

Index

Index

Index